CONTENTS

AREA MAP OF SHROPSHIRE AIRFIELDS

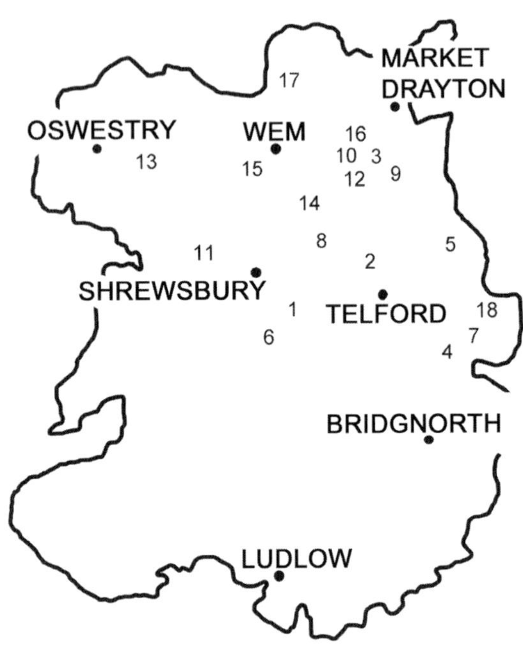

KEY TO AIRFIELDS

1. Atcham
2. Bratton
3. Bridleway Gate
4. Brockton
5. Chetwynd
6. Condover
7. Cosford
8. High Ercall
9. Hinstock
10. Hodnet
11. Montford Bridge
12. Peplow
13. Rednal
14. Shawbury
15. Sleap
16. Tern Hill
17. Tilstock
18. Weston Park

SHROPSHIRE AIRFIELDS IN THE SECOND WORLD WAR

Robin J. Brooks

COUNTRYSIDE BOOKS
NEWBURY BERKSHIRE

First published 2008
© Robin J. Brooks, 2008

All rights reserved. No reproduction
permitted without the prior permission
of the publisher:

COUNTRYSIDE BOOKS
3 Catherine Road
Newbury, Berkshire

To view our complete range of books,
please visit us at
www.countrysidebooks.co.uk

ISBN 978 1 84674 105 0

The cover picture shows Spitfires of 61 OTU, Rednal
and is from an original painting by
Colin Doggett

Produced through MRM Associates Ltd., Reading
Typeset by CJWT Solutions, St Helens
Printed by Information Press, Oxford

*All material for the manufacture of this book
was sourced from sustainable forests*

INTRODUCTION

When, as a twenty-year-old National Serviceman, I arrived at RAF Bridgnorth in 1961 to commence my eight weeks of 'square-bashing', little did I think that in years to come I would be writing about the nineteen wartime airfields of Shropshire. Just that brief period brought about a love affair with the county that I have renewed over the past two years of research.

There are still many wartime buildings and pieces of tarmac to remind the intrepid historian, and anyone else who is interested, of the part played by, and the importance afforded to, these airfields. Many of the photographs in the book were taken by personnel equipped with that most basic of cameras, the Box Brownie. Their reproduction is at times rather blurred and for this I apologise. They are, however, reminiscent of the period.

As with every war, the civilians had to endure shortages of food and material items, with injury and death never far away. Yet this seemed to encourage a type of camaraderie that is not apparent today. For the military, day after day, night after night, aircraft flew from the Shropshire airfields for the purpose of training young men to operate a killing machine. Here too there was danger, yet, like a factory, production of such men never stopped.

Today it is the helicopter that is most often seen in the skies of Shropshire carrying on the tradition of training men, and now women, to go to war, but the memories of those dark days between 1939 and 1945 are still evident in the eyes of those who lived through that time. I dedicate these pages to the men and women who made the ultimate sacrifice, and to those left behind.

Robin J. Brooks

I
SETTING THE SCENE

On the western borders of Shropshire it is impossible to tell without the aid of a map where England ends and Wales begins. In days gone by the ancient earthwork known as Offa's Dyke divided the two countries with its twelve foot high defensive mounds, and woe betide anyone who crossed the boundary! War, however, knows no such restrictions and this entire area – the county of Shropshire and into Wales – became a huge military training ground in the 20th century. Of great prominence was the RAF, which based its training and maintenance airfields far from the battle front in the south of the country. Here young men learned how to fly and maintain aircraft, and how to become a member of a crew whose lives depended on each other. It was a dangerous business and with the proximity of the high peak known as the Wrekin and the Welsh mountains not too distant, death and injury were never far away. Although Shropshire did not suffer the blitz, nor attract the attention of the Luftwaffe as much as nearby industrial cities and towns such as Birmingham and Wolverhampton, it did experience the horrors of war first hand, both in the air and on the ground.

Prior to the First World War, any large field could be used for experimenting with balloons and home-made aircraft. It is claimed that in 1904, several years before the Wright brothers' achievements, a local Shropshire man, Ernest Maund, had successfully built a monoplane in his garage and flown it. Sadly, this is unsubstantiated and we must therefore assume that powered flight came to the county as it did with the country as a whole, via the Wright brothers.

The First World War left Shropshire virtually unscathed despite the fact that three large fields in the county were already in use for pilot training. Known as Training Depot Stations, these were Shawbury, Monkmoor and Tern Hill, the latter having links with ballooning going back to 1906. All three closed at the end of the First World War, Tern Hill's demise being hastened by a huge fire which engulfed most of the station. Not until the mid-1930s would interest be shown in re-establishing them and planning be undertaken for new airfields.

As with most counties, the end of the war saw military aviation decline rapidly in Shropshire. It was a fact that having suffered aerial bombardment and dismissed the aeroplane as a weapon only of war, the general public were simply not 'airminded'. It was left to people like Sir Alan Cobham to rekindle public interest and this he did in a magnificent way.

In May 1919, Cobham, together with his partner Jack Holmes, formed the Berkshire Aviation Company with one airworthy Avro 504K and over the following years the company visited towns throughout the country and gave many people their first flight in an aeroplane. In the summer of 1919 he came to Shrewsbury and landed in a large field on the outskirts of the town. The public arrived in their thousands to watch a display and to take a flight over Shrewsbury. Sir Alan returned on 8th June 1933 and this time he brought several aircraft under the banner of the National Aviation Day Tours. Visiting Shrewsbury and Bridgnorth, it was a way for him to bring aviation to the people. It is almost certain that the airfield used for his displays was Monkmoor. The National Aviation Day Tour came back to Shropshire in 1935 but it appears that very little use was otherwise made of Monkmoor airfield.

In the meantime the question of Britain's own defence had come to the fore. It was fine to have all this joyriding with civilian aircraft but what about defence if another war occurred? A Metropolitan Air Force had been agreed between the government and the Air Ministry as far back as 1922. This was to consist of fourteen bomber and nine fighter squadrons. However, when the time came to implement this suggestion, the government, ever cautious of expenditure and the fact that Germany was barred by the Treaty of Versailles from making warplanes, back-pedalled on the agreement. It was only the determination of Lord Trenchard, the then Chief of the Air Staff, in calling for a coherent policy for the future defence of the country, that enabled the military, especially the RAF, to begin a programme of expansion.

In Shropshire, Tern Hill and Shawbury were the first to be reinvestigated as future airfields. They were to be twice as large as the former First World War sites and at the same time six other training

Alan Cobham – pioneer aviator who brought flying to Shropshire. (Flight Refuelling)

Airspeed Horsa gliders at a Shropshire MU. (Imperial War Museum)

stations were planned. In this quiet corner of England it was felt that the lack of any enemy interruption would allow training to take on an accelerated pace. With this thought, it was also intended to build large Aircraft Storage Units and Maintenance Units in the county. At Cosford, a large training establishment would train groundcrew in engineering trades such as radio, engine, airframe and armoury. Work had begun by 1935 on all these major sites but strangely, in a repeat of a past tragedy, fire broke out at Tern Hill on Wednesday, 9th October 1936, destroying almost all the domestic accommodation as well as hangars.

The expansion of the RAF from 1935 to 1939 provided the Air Ministry Works Directorate with an opportunity to design and construct permanent buildings of character on all the new airfields. Using a standard design for all buildings would also save time and more importantly, money. Britain was still recovering from the enormous expense incurred by the First World War and governments worldwide were looking to economise. However, the one thing the airfields had in common was that they were all built with classic expansion period architecture in mind and as such, were subject to approval by the Royal Fine Arts Commission and the Society for the Preservation of Rural England. A definite 'Georgian' influence can be seen in those still standing, buildings that have stood the test of time.

For Shropshire, only Shawbury, Tern Hill and Cosford were built or re-established by the time war broke out on 3rd September 1939. They

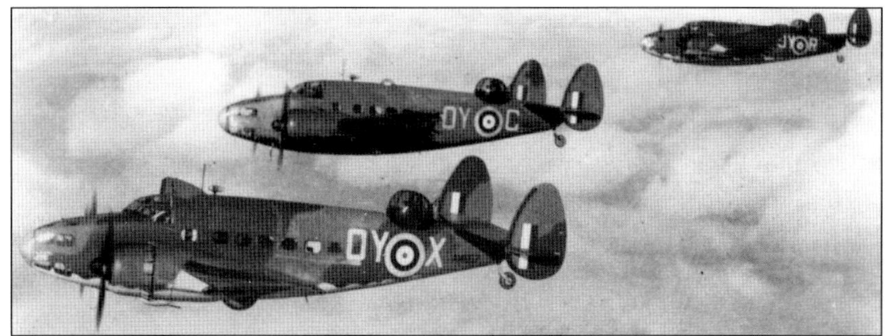

Lockheed Hudsons of No 48 Squadron. Many were despatched by Shropshire MUs. (MAP)

were to be mainly used for training, storage and maintenance though at least one, Tern Hill, was to see resident squadrons based there during the wartime period. Other major training airfields were to be established once the war had begun.

Many of the airfields remained grass throughout their usage. Bratton was one that was used very little. It was a Relief Landing Ground (RLG) for Shawbury and was also used by the Fleet Air Arm during 1944, finally closing in 1945. Bridleway Gate was another RLG, again mainly used by aircraft from Shawbury. Brockton was to become a Satellite Landing Ground (SLG) with limited use. Chetwynd on the other hand, although small, still survives today as a satellite for the Defence Helicopter Flying School at Shawbury. Condover, although a three-runway airfield, was never used to its full potential though it did become Shawbury's most important RLG, only being sold by the Ministry of Defence in 1961. Of the remaining small airfields in the

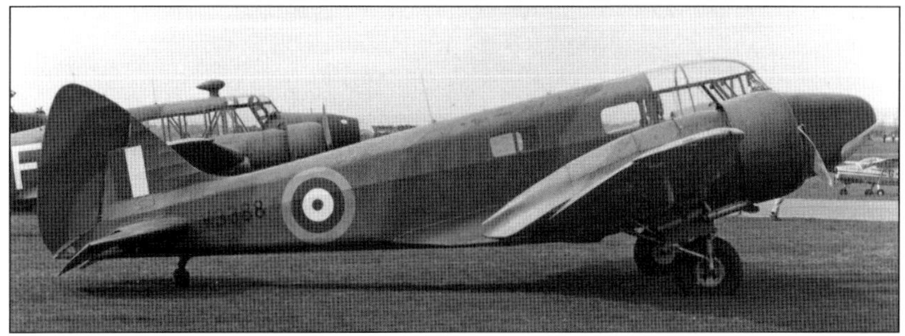

Airspeed Oxford and Avro Anson – many flew from the Shropshire OTUs. (MAP)

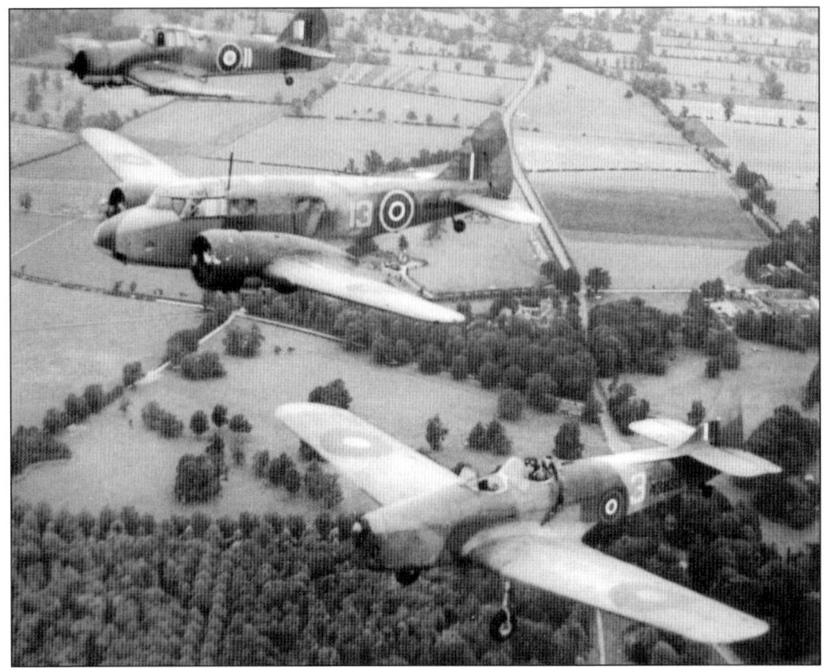

Three of the main RAF training aircraft seen in Shropshire skies. From top: Miles Master, Airspeed Oxford, Miles Magister. (P. Tilley via T. Hughes)

county, Montford Bridge was a satellite to Rednal, whereas Hodnet and Weston Park were SLGs that saw moderate use. All have reverted to their former use although Montford Bridge is still used for parachute dropping.

The major airfields in Shropshire were heavily used. Atcham was initially a fighter station with a satellite at Condover. At the same time, 9 Group Sector Operations Room transferred from Tern Hill to new buildings just one mile away. Several fighter squadrons were to be based at Atcham before it was transferred to the infant Eighth Air Force of the USAAF. They used it mainly for working up fighter groups prior to sending them down south and closer to the action. It was a Combat Crew Replacement Center for two years before becoming a Republic P-47 Thunderbolt training station. Returned to the RAF in March 1945, it was rarely used and went back to agriculture in 1946.

High Ercall was a major maintenance depot, a Turbinlite squadron station, and also an important base for the USAAF; No 29 Maintenance Unit (MU) was civilian-manned and did not close until 1962 having handled thousands of different aircraft during and after the war. Hinstock, sometimes known as Ollerton, was a major naval training airfield. It only closed when nearby Peplow, vacated by the RAF in 1947, became a more suitable base for the peacetime Royal Navy. Peplow, also known as Childs Ercall, was intended to become a major bomber base and had a concrete runway. However, a change in direction saw it become a major bomber Operational Training Unit (OTU) carrying out intensive 'Nickel' operations (leaflet drops over enemy territory). It was also the home of a Heavy Glider Conversion Unit (HGCU) in late 1944, and finally closed in 1949.

Rednal was a major fighter OTU and it was here that Pierre Clostermann, author of *The Big Show* (Chatto & Windus, 1951) commenced his flying training on Spitfires. George 'Screwball' Beurling, a Canadian pilot, also did his pilot training at Rednal and later became one of the top-scoring aces on the island of Malta.

Intended as a satellite for Tilstock, Sleap became far more than that – No 81 OTU's Whitleys used it when Tilstock became overcrowded and it was a major base to train crews for glider towing. It remains a flying field today and is the home of the Shropshire Aero Club.

The last airfield to mention in this chapter is Tilstock, sometimes known as Whitchurch Heath. This was the parent station for No 81 OTU

The captain maps out the day's flying training at one of the Shropshire OTUs. (Crown)

At 21.35 hrs on 22nd October 1941 a Junkers Ju 88 was shot down near Woore in Shropshire. The crew were buried with full military honours by a party from No 5 FTS at Tern Hill. (The National Archives)

for most of the war. After Arnhem it also became the home of No 1665 HGCU, and finally closed in 1946. Today it is a popular parachuting centre.

Whilst setting the scene for this book we must not forget the plight of the civilian population. Though the blitz suffered by London and other cities was not repeated in Shropshire, civilians did see and feel the effects of enemy bombing, in addition to enduring social and economic hardship. The trauma of losing a loved one was all too common. Many child evacuees arrived in the county, from the industrial suburbs of the Midlands as well as London. Many had never seen or experienced country life and therefore found it difficult to adjust so far from home and their parents.

One potential target in Shropshire was Donnington, near Telford. It was to here that much of the Woolwich Arsenal moved in anticipation of the outbreak of war. Between 1941 and 1943, 844 houses were built to accommodate the influx of workers at the 'Ordnance'. It is still open today and is run by the MOD (it holds the bronze from enemy guns captured during the Crimean War and used in the making of each Victoria Cross). There were other ordnance depots at Harlescott, Ditton Priors and Kinnerley. Ammunition dumps and storage depots for armaments were also numerous throughout the county.

Shropshire had its own Army regiment, the King's Shropshire Light Infantry, which fought valiantly in Europe and North Africa. Consisting mainly of local men, it had a glorious history, having been formed in 1881 by the amalgamation of the 53rd Regiment and the 85th (King's) Light Infantry. Two VCs were awarded to men of the regiment, Sgt George Eardley and Private James Stokes, one of them posthumously.

And so Shropshire prepared for its role in the Second World War. In the following pages we will learn of the part the airfields, together with the long-suffering civilians, played in the path to final victory.

The Building of the Airfields

The building of Britain's airfields during the period 1935 to 1939 was the largest civil engineering work undertaken since the coming of the railways. It was more commonly known as the 'expansion miracle', given that in 1924 there were just 27 RAF and seventeen civil airfields established and by 1942 it was estimated that there would be a need for 700 military airfields alone! Most of the First World War airfields had been of a temporary nature and unless upgraded, were not suitable for the aircraft of the expanding Royal Air Force.

Early in the 1930s the Air Ministry Works Department (AMWD) was formed with the responsibility of planning and organising new airfields together with improving the First World War airfields still available. The government of the day had suddenly realised that Hitler's seizure of power in 1933 and the withdrawal of Nazi Germany from the League of Nations in October meant that Europe was no longer stable and that perhaps another war with Germany was inevitable. The Commander-in-Chief of the Air Defence of Great Britain, Air Chief Marshal Sir Robert Brooke-Popham was worried by the apparent restlessness in Germany. He set about writing a paper entitled 'Re-Orientation Scheme' which laid out a series of coded schemes by which the RAF could be built up into a coherent fighting force. Under these schemes the ADGB was scrapped in July 1936 and replaced by four Commands – Fighter, Bomber, Coastal and Training.

This change of direction allowed the AMWD to form the Air Ministry Aerodromes Board in May 1934. It was obvious that in order to create new airfields vast expanses of good agricultural land would have to be

Heavy machinery for the task of preparing airfields. (John Laing plc)

built upon. The Board therefore worked closely with the Air Ministry Lands Branch, whose officers had the unenviable task of telling landowners that their land was being compulsorily requisitioned under the Defence Regulations of the Emergency Powers (Defence) Act of 1939. Many farmers objected strongly to this action, but requisitioning went ahead. All the landowner got was a legal document stating that at the end of the war the land would be offered back to them plus a measly rent payment for each year the Air Ministry used it.

It was judged by the Board that potential sites should be at least three miles apart, although this eventually became five miles. Likely sites were usually chosen using the one-inch Ordnance Survey map and were areas free from obstructions. Once a site had been chosen, consideration had to be given to drainage, which was most important given the British weather.

Most of the First World War airfields were grass and with the belief still prevalent that grass was best for a runway, it fell to the seed company of James Hunter to carry out experiments in this field. They laid many of the minor airfields that were to remain grass for the

Building one of the Shropshire airfields. (John Laing plc)

duration of the war, but it soon became obvious that as aircraft got heavier, concrete runways would have to be laid. The bad winter of 1936/37 accentuated this fact, yet due to the cost of laying such runways, the Air Ministry were already making excuses not to do so. These prevarications rumbled on until the very eve of war. Only in April 1939 did an Air Ministry conference decide that hard runways should be laid at certain airfields, dependent upon their system of priorities. It was only just in time for with the unpredictable weather, many a critical airfield in 1940 would have been inoperable.

The early hard runways were tarmac, usually about two to five inches thick and laid on a brick or stone hardcore. On top of this was added a coat of asphalt with ditches alongside the runway for drainage. Fighter airfields were to take priority, with most bomber airfields having at least one hard runway by 1941.

One of the largest companies awarded contracts to build the airfields was Wimpey. In 1936 they got a contract to build one station at a cost of £500,000. Two years later they were asked to tender for thirteen more but in the event got seven contracts because other large building companies such as John Laing plc and McAlpines were also successful in winning contracts. Indeed, some of the larger Shropshire airfields were built by the latter. To judge how quickly the work was done we only have to look at the fact that a target of 75 additional airfields to be ready by August 1940 was superseded by the completion of 104 by the same date. This was due in part to an enormous influx of Irish labour.

Two years into the war the building programme employed a peak force of 60,000 men. With the expected arrival of the USAAF in Britain, Ernest Bevin, then Minister of Labour and National Service, decided that 28,000 men due to be called up for military service would remain in the building trade until October 1942. In addition to the civilian contractors, the RAF Airfield Construction Service, which had been formed in March 1941 specifically to carry out the emergency repair of bombed airfields, was given the task of constructing airfields, though these were mainly grass. In August 1942 the first of the American construction units arrived in the country to help build the new American bases that were springing up in East Anglia. All of these construction companies, both civilian and military, played a vital part in realising the fact that between 1939 and 1945, no less than 444 airfields were built. It was indeed an 'expansion miracle'.

Hangars

Some of the largest buildings on airfields are the aircraft hangars. Even during the Great War the aircraft on small grass airfields needed some type of protection which usually took the form of a canvas hangar, used mainly in the field, or a large wooden shed. Next to be designed for the period were the timber-framed Bessonneaux, many of which survived to be used in the second conflict. The 1916 General Service Shed became the standard hangar in the latter years of the Royal Flying Corps and was in turn superseded by the Belfast wooden truss hangar.

Between the wars it was generally felt that steel would give aircraft and the groundcrews working on them better protection, and thus the design of hangars took a giant step forward. First to be designed and constructed was the 'F' Type shed which had side-opening doors. The Hinaidi hangar was very prevalent in the neighbouring county of Hereford but none seem to have been erected in Shropshire. The first new design to appear during the expansion period was the 'C' Type, several examples of which can still be seen today on the county's remaining airfields.

The year 1936 saw the start of the construction of Aircraft Storage Units. These included the 'E' Type hangar made of concrete and sometimes covered in grass or earth for camouflage. Many fine examples can be seen at Cosford and Shawbury, the latter sadly having been reclad whilst Cosford's are still covered with grass, making excellent camouflage.

Construction of hangars begins at Cosford in 1938. (Alfred McAlpine)

Shropshire had an abundance of hangar designs, many of which remain today though used for various purposes. There are 'K' Types at High Ercall, Callender-Hamiltons at Atcham, 'D' Types at Tern Hill; the list goes on. Despite this vast range of hangar architecture that is still visible, surely one of the most distinctive designs is the smallest hangar of all: the Blister. Designed and produced by Messrs C. Miskins and Sons in 1939, over 3,000 were eventually built. They came in three sizes. The standard Blister clad with corrugated iron had a width of 45 ft and was the most common. A larger version called the 'Over Blister' was 65 ft in width and the 'Extra Over Blister' was 69 ft wide. They were low to the ground and consequently very draughty for men carrying out maintenance on aircraft housed inside. Some protection was afforded by hanging a curtain at one end but even this did not please the poor groundcrews. In the end it became more beneficial to brick up one of the hangar entrances. Not many are in use on airfields today; most of the survivors are used by farmers whose land was returned to them after wartime use.

As the war progressed it was found necessary in some cases to expand the airfields. This required extra hangars to be erected quickly and for this purpose the Transportable Hangar was designed. There were two main designs: the Callender-Hamilton and the Bellman. The latter was an all-welded shed 95 ft by 180 ft with a door height of 25 ft, made of corrugated steel sheeting; around 400 were sited on various airfields. As aircraft grew in size there came a need for even larger hangars. The Teeside Bridge and Engineering Works developed the standard 'T' hangar, a design that suited most wartime and peacetime airfields. By 1945 some 900 had been erected and those that are still standing on old airfields have been put to a variety of uses by local farmers.

The last type of hangar to be found in Shropshire still survives on Hinstock airfield. Being a naval shore station, Hinstock got a hangar known as a Pentad. Designed in 1943, it was similar to the 'T' Type with the exception of having sloping side walls.

Shropshire was to have most types of hangarage to suit its needs. Some are plainly visible today and some are hidden amongst woods. Those operational airfields still in the county also have an abundance of designs to suit all their current needs.

Watch Office/Control Tower

If hangars are the largest buildings to be seen on airfields then the watch office, or to use the American expression, control tower, has to be the most nostalgic. Many still stand like sentinels guarding long-forgotten airfields.

Prior to 1939, control of aircraft movements was non-existent. Pilots landed when they wanted, where they wanted and almost parked where they wanted. The one onus on the pilot was to report to the duty officer sitting in his little hut. With the coming of another war it became obvious that strict airfield control, in the air and on the ground, was essential. It was therefore decided that a brick building, as opposed to wooden, would best withstand the test of time. Initially a two-storey building consisting of the duty pilots' room on the ground floor and a watch office on the upper floor, various designs were adapted to suit the needs of a particular airfield. This is very apparent in Shropshire where, although the airfields were mainly used in the training role, there is a good selection of different types of control towers still standing. Most, sadly, are in a state of disrepair.

Many fighter stations and their OTUs had the standard-pattern 518/40 type tower. The example at Rednal had a meteorological office added. Still standing, the tower looks very sad as it is now being used for paintballing. Condover on the other hand has survived two towers. The original was a 17658/40 type, parts of which can still be seen today. This was replaced by a much larger watch office (for a bomber satellite station) known as a 13726/41 type. Again the latter is still standing but is subject to the ravages of time. Tilstock suffers a similar fate with its wartime watch office intended for all commands designated a 12779/41 type with medium front windows to 343/43.

Of the many satellite airfields in the county the most interesting is the upgraded tower at Montford Bridge. This was designated a watch office for fighter satellite stations 17658/40, which was later updated with a two-storey side extension with observation room 7332/42. Again, though still standing, it is in poor condition and is usually surrounded by cows or sheep!

Of the RAF stations still operational in the county, Shawbury has a wartime 1938 Chief Flying Instructors Block 5740/36 type. This was extended for peacetime operations and is now classed as a 1958 Post-war Control Tower Vertical Split Control Type 2548c/55. It is not now in use for its intended purpose, as a new control tower has been built on the opposite side of the runway. Tern Hill, still operational for the use of helicopters from Shawbury, had the same type of tower, which has been heavily modified to include a visual control room.

One tower that is exclusive to Cosford is the early 'Fort Type' watch office built to pattern 1959/34. Consisting of a ground floor with extended windows and a single tower with all-round observation built on top, it is still in use today. Another very interesting tower from this period, though not now in use for its intended purpose, is the standard naval four-storey at Hinstock. This has not gone the way of most of the others due to the fact that it has been converted into a private house and is thus very much preserved.

There is no doubt that of the many counties I have written about, Shropshire has the greatest abundance of control towers still standing – and nearly every one of them, according to local folk, has a ghost!

Domestic and Technical Sites

The domestic and technical sites of the wartime airfields had a good selection of various buildings. The expansion period saw a standard pattern emerging for all new airfields but prior to this, buildings varied in design and size. The earlier hangars such as the 'C' Type had technical buildings incorporated alongside and attached to the main hangar length. The realisation that hangars would be a prime target for enemy attack led to the building of individual technical blocks. These often took the form of huts, many of which survive today and are used for various civilian occupations.

In 1935 two forms of hutting were devised. The first was to have a life expectancy of five years and was known as the 'B' Type. A second design was to have a life expectancy of ten to fifteen years and was called the 'A' Type. Both were of wooden construction, a commodity that at that time was plentiful. However, with the advent of war, timber was at a premium and so other methods of construction came about. Designs were put forward that used less or no timber at all. These included the Ministry of Supply Timber Hut; the Laing Hut, which was light timber, plasterboard and felt; and the one most often seen today on the old airfields, the Maycrete Concrete Hut. A further prefabricated building was the Romney Hut which was quick and easy to construct. Other designs were the Orlit Hut, Handcraft Hut (a fine example can be seen at

Sleap) and the Marston Hut. Perhaps the most recognisable of the period, with many still standing today, is the Nissen Hut. Designed by Colonel P. Nissen for use during the First World War, it was revived in 1939 and built in very large numbers to three widths of 16 ft, 24 ft and 30 ft.

Each airfield had different buildings suited to its role. In the case of training airfields, buildings not seen on operational airfields were constructed. These included, as in the case of Sleap, a turret trainer for the training of air gunners, a Link Trainer room for trainee pilots, dummy operations rooms, navigation rooms and so on. For accommodation there were numerous huts but from 1942 onwards they were brick-built, and from 1944 for those wartime airfields that would be required in peacetime, the standard 'H' blocks were built for airmen ranks. Other buildings were provided for fire engines, parachutes, armouries, photography and a number of other duties. All of these were the result of the Director of Works telling the Air Member for Supply and Organisation that guidance was needed if the airfields and personnel were to be as safe as possible from bomb damage.

In the case of the nerve-centre of the airfield, the operations room, it was realised that this should be semi-sunk into the ground and protected by natural earth banking all around as well as a solid reinforced concrete roof. Should this building have been put out of action by enemy attacks, control of the airfield defences would then have been undertaken from a sunken Battle Headquarters, a fine example of which remains at Montford Bridge. Again protected by a reinforced concrete roof, it was buried entirely in the ground with just the square concrete viewing cupola protruding above the grass line. Known as an RAF Type 11008/41 Battle Headquarters, it consisted of five underground rooms accessed via a flight of concrete steps. No other such Battle Headquarters have been found at any of the other airfields in the county and it is both unusual and interesting that Montford Bridge, a fighter satellite station and thus quite small, should have one.

The guidance given to the Director of Works also stated that air raid shelters would be needed for personnel in order to protect them from bomb attacks. Many were built at all of the Shropshire airfields, but most are now either bricked off for safety reasons or have been removed entirely.

All of this building work was arduous yet necessary if the airfields were to survive an enemy attack or at the worst, invasion.

Decoys and Camouflage

The historical interest of the decoy programme was its immensity, whether military or civil. Decoys were provided for a number of institutions ranging from the RAF, Army and the Navy through to towns, cities, industrial targets, oil installations etc. By the end of the construction programme, there were 797 sites consisting of 1,100 decoys of various types. After the war it was estimated that the weight of bombs dropped on these sites must have saved around 2,500 people from death by bombing. The programme provided an opportunity for military and civilian organisations to work together, something that is more prevalent in today's military forces than it was then.

Four months before the Munich crisis, Gp Cpt F.J. Winnell, the Air Ministry Deputy Director of War Operations, suggested the idea of decoys to the government. Nothing was done about discussing the subject further until September 1938, one year before war began. Even then it did not relate to specific sites but only to the building of dummy aircraft for an unspecified purpose. Given a budget, the Air Ministry went about tendering for the building of these aircraft and found that the cost was both expensive and varied. The cheapest quotes were for a dummy Whitley bomber costing £377, to a Hurricane fighter costing £105. Even the latter cost more than the Air Ministry could afford to pay!

Having flown over Shropshire and got hopelessly lost, this Heinkel He 111 finally crashed in Cheshire. (ATB)

Airmen from a Shropshire airfield sift through the wreckage of a downed Junkers Ju 88. (Crown)

It was time for a rethink and but for the intervention of Gp Cpt D.P. Stevenson at the Ministry, this might have lingered on for longer than it actually did. He came up with the idea of involving film companies, experts in the field of make-believe, to tender for the manufacture of dummy aircraft. This was in June 1939 but again, there was little sense of urgency. In fact it was not until September 1939, when war broke out, that the decoy programme was put on a firm footing.

It fell to a retired Royal Engineers officer, Colonel John Fisher Turner, to make the programme a reality. Having taken up the post of Director of Works and Buildings at the Air Ministry, a civil service appointment, in 1931 he had in-house knowledge of the entire expansion period, making him an obvious choice to head the decoy programme. With the war already started, and despite the fact that this was the 'phoney' period, there was much to do.

The film studios at Denham had become involved in making dummy aircraft and buildings at a far lower cost than independent companies had been quoting. 'Colonel Turner's Department', a title that deliberately gave no indications as to what its work involved, now put his ideas into reality.

Day decoys were to be of two kinds – one to imitate an all-grass airfield and the other a defined airfield with specific runways. Night decoys would have paraffin flarepaths with a set of yellow lights indicating the T-shaped wind direction indicator. Further red lights would represent obstruction lights indicating high buildings, and a single recognition light would be lit if a friendly aircraft attempted to land. The entire set-up would be controlled by airmen in a sunken control room.

The film companies involved in the discussions and tendering to build dummy aircraft were Warner Brothers, Alexander Korda's London Film Company and Gaumont British. However, by far the best quotation for a Wellington bomber came from Sound City Films at Shepperton at a reasonable cost of £225 (since the early days the Air Ministry had been forced to rethink the cost of such dummies). Colonel Turner on several occasions visited the studios to see the Sound City technicians at work. Impressed with what he saw, Colonel Turner's thoughts now turned to what sites and types of decoys were to be provided.

The task of finding sites did not prove easy with landowners objecting to having to give up their land. Many had already been forced to give up some for the building of the new airfields and to be asked to give even more for a dummy site to be built close by was rubbing salt in the wound. Deciding on the types of decoys proved easier and the Air Ministry under Colonel Turner's guidance issued instructions that work should begin immediately. For day use, a 'K' site would be built with dummy aircraft and buildings. For night, a 'Q' site simulating the lighting of an airfield and sometimes operating alongside a 'K' site would also be built.

With the war already started, both sites first became operational in January 1940. By 1st August, 36 'K' and 56 'Q' sites were in operation with 406 dummy aircraft built to place upon them. There appear to have been five types of mock aircraft – Hurricanes, Wellingtons, Battles, Bostons and Tiger Moths. These were mainly wooden-framed models but later ones were made of a metal tube frame covered with a rubber canvas material. There were also a few cardboard models installed.

By mid-1940 the 'Q' site night decoys were fully operational. Where they were placed next to a day site, the decoy became a 'KQ' site. The earlier paraffin gooseneck flares had been found to be unreliable and were now replaced by Glim electric lights. As far as the records show, only five airfields in Shropshire had decoys:

> Tern Hill – Chipnall (Type Q)
> Shawbury – Withington (Type Q/QF)
> High Ercall – Kinnersley (Type Q)
> Atcham – Cressage (Type Q)
> Cosford – Boningale (Type QF)

A dummy Hurricane on a decoy airfield. (Imperial War Museum)

Where the type shows 'QF', this indicates a night decoy with small fires to imitate bomb explosions or crashed aircraft.

Fire was used to a much greater degree for the civil decoys. Once the airfield programme was under way, other targets such as aircraft factories, munitions factories, cities and large towns with barracks were considered worthy of a decoy site. Known initially as 'special fires', they became better known as Starfish.

Some targets had only one Starfish while larger targets had a ring of Starfish sites. They consisted of very clever pyrotechnic tricks made with a fire basket soaked in creosote. Further braziers could be added, loaded with firewood which when set alight created an enormous fire when seen from the air. Later ones used various types of oil which were fed to the burn sites to give continuous fire. There were different combinations of fire types arranged in groups and controlled from a sunken control room nearby manned by either RAF or Army personnel. Though Shropshire had no major industrial centres, the nearby West Midlands did. Listed below are the Starfish sites closest to the county:

Birmingham: Ballsal, Holt End, Maxstroke, Fairfield, Bickenhill,
    Peopleton, Halford, Silvington
Wolverhampton: Shipley, Blakes Hall
Newport: Llanwern, Duffryn, St Brides Wentloog

At the end of 1941 with the heavy attacks dwindling, there were only three 'K' sites left in operation but there were still 112 'Q' sites backed up by 90 'QFs' (small fires) and 170 'QLs' (large fires), together with 164 Starfish. In May 1943 all dummy aircraft were taken over by the Army and in October 1943, Starfish and 'Q' sites began to close down as the war was carried back to the enemy. The decoy programme cost millions of pounds but the saving in lives and *matériel* was incalculable.

Developed in parallel with the decoys was the camouflaging of airfields and their buildings. As early as 1935 the Director of Works had pointed out to the Air Staff the need for a national camouflage scheme. As with the decoys, it fell on deaf ears. That was until 1939 when, with a real threat appearing to come from Germany, the Air Staff appointed an artist, Norman Wilkinson, to design and draw suitable camouflage schemes. He was given the honorary rank of Air Commodore and told to form a camouflage division. This he did and was given one officer with which to take on an enormous task.

Natural camouflage was the first to be looked at, with the strategic planting of trees and hedges to allow aircraft to be dispersed amongst foliage. The disguising of buildings and hangars by painting roofs and sides to merge in with natural surroundings was done to good effect. Paths that had previously had white kerbstones were suddenly darkened by paint in order not to be so obvious from the air. Runways, perimeter tracks and taxiways were prone to shine in all weathers and were dulled by laying a 'tennis court' finish on the top. Another experiment on these large areas was to lay stone chippings over the surface but this led to tyre damage. The best method was found to be to lay a rubber solution on the concrete but when this commodity became scarce, it fell to wood chips to do the job. This method did actually become the standard solution to shiny concrete.

By 1942 over 330 people were employed in designing colour schemes for the purpose of disguise. Over 1,000 personnel carried out the work using 22 million gallons of paint. These requirements were, however, reduced in 1943 as the level of enemy aircraft attacks over Britain dwindled. The decoy and camouflage ideas of Colonel Turner's Department had played their part in full and saved many lives and much destruction of airfields and war installations.

Airfield Defences

The most apparent defence structure on or near any airfield is the surface pillbox. The construction followed a basic pattern designed by Branch FW3 (Fortress Works Department 3) of the War Office's Directorate of Fortifications and Works and roughly the same as the series of pillboxes erected in France and Belgium by the British Expeditionary Force. Known as 'Types', the numbers ran from 22 to 28. Just as with the construction of airfields, the building of pillboxes was a tremendous project and was carried out mainly by the Royal Engineers helped by civilian labour. So great was the task that in 1940, 150,000 civilians, many of them Irish, were employed on pillbox construction.

The most common pillbox design to be seen was the Type 22. Built to bulletproof standard, its main feature was its hexagonal shape. With an entrance in the rear wall, each side had a slit through which the gunners inside could fire. This was a pillbox for hand-held weapons and not for anti-aircraft guns. The second-most common was the Type 27, a fine example of which is still intact at Shawbury. Larger in size than the Type 22, it was octagonal in shape with far larger firing slits. It was usual for this type of pillbox to have a machine gun fitted in a recessed well on the top of the structure, usually a .303 Lewis or a .303 Bren gun. The walls were generally up to three feet thick with the inside of the pillbox holding around ten men.

One of the more unusual pillboxes was the Pickett/Hamilton 'Pop Up' Gun Fort, a gun turret sunk into the ground with an inner sleeve that was able to rise above ground level. This was achieved by either pumping a hydraulic ram which pushed this sleeve upwards or by means of a compressed-air bottle. Capable of holding at least three men, they were situated alongside runways. In the event of an enemy attack, the inner part would rise to allow the men inside to fire their guns. At the end of any action, this part would then sink back into the ground. Many hundreds were constructed and installed but whilst in theory it was a good idea, it proved to be impractical in use due to constant flooding and the fact that the airmen inside would have been subjected to very cramped conditions while waiting for the enemy to arrive.

Apart from mobile, lightly armed defence wagons such as the Armadillo, equipped with a 1½-pounder gun and machine guns, and the Beaverette armed with machine guns, it was left to individual stations to improvise on airfield defence. Some very ingenious person

Pillbox attached to the side of a hangar still remains at High Ercall. (Author)

at Shawbury converted a Morris lorry into a machine gun carrier by mounting two dustbins on the back capable of holding an armed airman in each one. Such was the necessity of wartime inventions!

The final type of airfield defence to mention is the Pipe Mine System. There were two main types, these being the Canadian Pipe Mine System and the Mole Plough. The former consisted of a series of steel pipes filled with explosive and buried alongside runways. In the event of an enemy invasion, these pipes could then be detonated, denying the enemy the use of the runways. The second was explosive covered in a thin skin of flexible rubber. This again would be buried underground by trailing it behind a standard farmer's plough of that period. Though less effective in terms of damage caused by the detonation, it was far easier and quicker to conceal.

All of these precautions were necessary as the threat of invasion grew in 1940. The threat was still there in 1942 and designs for further defence measures were ongoing. Many of them are still to be found today, most deeply buried in undergrowth but nonetheless of great interest to the historian.

2
ATCHAM

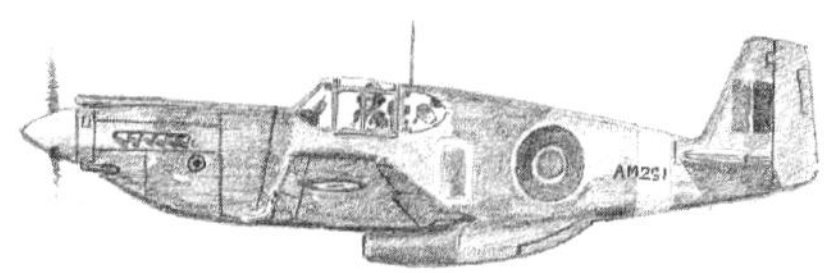

On 22nd December 1941, two weeks after the United States had been forced into the war by Japanese aggression, Prime Minister Churchill arrived in Washington to take part in a series of meetings with President Roosevelt. They agreed that the war against Germany was to take priority over the fight against Japan and that the United States was to establish as soon as feasible an Army Air Force (AAF) in Britain which would mount a strategic offensive against industrial targets in Germany and occupied Europe. The Eighth Air Force, as this arm of the USAAF was to become known, was scheduled to include bombardment (heavy) and fighter groups. This force was activated on 22nd February 1942 and soon many villages and towns in the country were to see the first American uniforms on British soil. Though most of the American bases were concentrated in East Anglia and the East Midlands, Shropshire was also a witness to this remarkable explosion of strangers in their lives when the USAAF came to Atcham.

One of the closest airfields to the medieval town of Shrewsbury, Atcham lay four miles south-east of the town on the B4394 road. Known to the Americans as Station 342 or Atcham Field, it began life as an RAF station and was planned originally to be a sector station. Intended to house two fighter squadrons with a satellite airfield at Condover, it was later felt that perhaps Atcham would be too far inland to be of use as a fighter station. It was downgraded to become a fighter training base and although used by the RAF for certain periods of the war, it was the intensive use by the USAAF that is its claim to glory.

Built during the expansion period, Atcham, like several other Shropshire airfields, became part of No 9 Group Fighter Command. It came under the umbrella of No 12 Group operational control which had its headquarters at Watnall in Nottinghamshire. Deemed a sector station when 9 Group Sector Operations Room transferred from Tern Hill to a new building a mile from the airfield, the first squadron to use

The superb control tower at Atcham in 1943.

Atcham was No 131 (County of Kent), commanded by Sqd Ldr J.M. Thompson, DFC.

The squadron had re-formed at Ouston on 30th June 1941 before moving to Atcham on 27th September. They had successively converted from the Spitfire I to the IIa and were in the process of further converting to the Mk Vb on their arrival. Tasked with carrying out air defence duties, No 131 was unique for two reasons. The first was that it was the only squadron to have been entirely financed by donations from the people of Kent and the second was that it had a high proportion of Belgian pilots. This presented some language difficulties but with classes in the English language, by the time the squadron arrived at Atcham the problems were few. Shortly after their arrival, however, the CO and twelve Belgian pilots left to form the nucleus of No 350 Squadron. The new CO, Sqd Ldr M.G.F. Pedley, DFC, had the task of declaring the squadron non-operational whilst the new pilots drafted in to replace the Belgians began a work-up period to bring them to operational standards. This was achieved by December 1941, allowing regular patrols to be carried out in defence of the Midlands.

As well as being a 'gift of war' squadron in respect of donations, No 131 was also the first squadron to have the name of a Kent city or

Airmen at Atcham pose for the camera.

town emblazoned on its Spitfire fuselages. This set a pattern for other cities and towns to follow, as well as countries from around the Commonwealth.

The first Christmas at Atcham passed quietly. No 131, although now operational, had no success in finding the enemy. Not until 12th March 1942, when Flt Lt Harries put a Junkers Ju 88 into the sea off Anglesey did their scoring open. However, by then the squadron had moved over to Llanbedr in Wales leaving Atcham devoid of aircraft.

The new year at last saw the bulk of the construction work at Atcham finished by the main contractor, and sub-contractors were then free to commence building accommodation blocks, paths and roads etc. This was to take some time; so much so that the officers of No 131 Squadron, tired of walking through mud to get to their mess, took it upon themselves to lay their own cinder track. This was accomplished in very quick time, much to the anguish of the contractors. Work continued on three Callender-Hamilton hangars together with eight Blister hangars. The control tower was of a 518/40 design, the standard for fighter airfields and the largest of the wartime towers. It had an all-timber first floor and balcony together with a meteorological office on the lower floor.

It fell to No 74 (Trinidad) Squadron to bring Atcham back to operational status. A First World War squadron, their badge was a tiger's head with the motto: 'I fear no man'. Known as the 'Tiger Squadron' and commanded by Sqd Ldr P.C.H. Mathews, No 74 and their Spitfire IIas stayed little more than a month before being posted overseas. With their departure, No 232 Squadron under the command of Sqd Ldr A. McDowell, DFM, reformed at Atcham having been stood down on 25th February 1942. Again the Spitfire Vbs remained barely one month before moving on to Llanbedr and Ayr. Their time at Atcham, however, had not been wasted, with daily practice interceptions of friendly aircraft.

Enemy activity over this part of middle England was rare but there were occasions when the Luftwaffe was seen in the skies of Shropshire. January 1942 started with enemy air activity though on a much smaller scale compared to the blitz. A return to night operations by the Luftwaffe resulted in sporadic attacks by lone aircraft, one of which happened on the night of 10th/11th January. The sound of enemy aircraft was heard in the area of Atcham at around 12.30 hrs. The aircraft was a Dorner Do 217E-2 (1191) crewed by Oberfw P. Wolf, Uffz W. Weiland, Obergefr H. Vacano and Oberfw H. Leppin. On patrol that night was a Beaufighter IIf of No 456 Squadron equipped with a new version of airborne radar. Flown by Sqd Ldr Hamilton and PO Norris-Smith, the aircraft was 30 minutes into its patrol when their radar picked up the enemy aircraft that had been heard over Atcham. Coming up behind the unsuspecting German, the Beaufighter's pilot fired his guns and seconds later had the satisfaction of seeing fire take hold. Watching their victim enter an uncontrollable dive, the crew of the Beaufighter saw it crash at Lawn Farm, Arbury at 01.55 hrs. Four parachutes were seen leaving the Do 217 before it crashed and with only one injury on landing, the crew were taken prisoner.

With no squadrons, Atcham entered a quiet phase before it began a new era. For some time it had been rumoured that it was to become an American base; now these rumours were about to come true. Although the German blitz was on the ebb and the danger of an invasion had abated, the war was entering different but equally dangerous times. Since the entry of the United States into the war on 7th December 1941, a body known as Air Support Command had been constituted, with the formation of the Eighth Air Force. Five fighter groups were initially selected for assignment to the Eighth, flying such aircraft as the Lockheed P-38 Lightning and Bell P-39 Airacobra. It was also to incorporate three regular RAF squadrons that were manned by American personnel. Known as the 'Eagle' squadrons, they were Nos 71, 121 and 133. Already flying Spitfires, they were to transfer to the USAAF

The Americans await the scramble at Atcham. Lt Warren R. Lobdell is pictured on the right. (G. Hackenberg)

where they became the 334th, 335th and 336th Fighter Squadrons (FS) of the 4th Fighter Group (FG).

One of the problems immediately encountered by the USAAF was just how to get the American aircraft to Britain. With the constant mauling of vessels by U-boats in the Atlantic, shipping the aircraft could prove very costly. It was therefore decided to fly them across the water. In this respect, Lockheed themselves came to the rescue when they developed a drop tank capable of carrying 165 US gallons (625 litres) of extra fuel. With these fitted the P-38 Lightning had a range with reserves of 1,700 miles (2,735 km), allowing the 1st and 14th Fighter Groups to ferry their aircraft from America to Britain.

Tracing its ancestry back to the original 1st Pursuit Group, which had been organised in France on 5th May 1918 as part of the Air Service of the American Expeditionary Force, the 1st Fighter Group flew its P-38Fs across the Atlantic, with the first aircraft leaving America on 23rd June 1942. Known as Operation 'Bolero', the aircraft arrived in Scotland in July after the 2,965 mile (4,770 km) route from Presque Isle, Maine to Prestwick via Goose Bay, Bluie West and Reykjavik. The P-39, however, was found to be unsuitable for operations in the European Theater of Operations, leaving the personnel of the 31st and 52nd Fighter Groups

A Spitfire of the 308th Fighter Squadron of the 31st Fighter Group. This unit arrived at Atcham in June 1942. (308th Fighter Group)

to sail to England without their aircraft. Upon arrival the 31st and 52nd Fighter Groups were equipped with 200 Spitfire Vbs supplied by Britain under the reverse Lend/Lease Act.

At Atcham arrangements were ongoing for the arrival of the 31st Fighter Group comprising the 307th, 308th and 309th Fighter Squadrons, with just the 309th finally being based at Atcham. Officially handed over to the USAAF on 15th June 1942, five days later 35 Spitfires were ferried in for the unit to begin training. Over the next few weeks the skies around Atcham reverberated with the sound of Rolls-Royce Merlin engines as the Americans got to know their new aircraft. After flying several sorties with other Spitfire squadrons of the RAF, the first squadron-strength mission was carried out on 5th August. The unit became fully operational two weeks later when 2nd Lt Sam Junkins shot down an FW 190A whilst the 31st Fighter Group was flying in support of the Dieppe landings.

With the arrival of the squadron at Atcham, many top American brass chose to visit, including Generals Eaker and Spaatz, the latter being the Commander of the USAAF in Britain. By 1st August the three squadrons were deemed operational and moved closer to the action, with the 307th moving to Biggin Hill in Kent, the 308th to Kenley in Surrey and the 309th to Westhampnett in West Sussex.

They were replaced by the 14th Fighter Group on 18th August, who flew their P-38 Lightnings in from Hamilton Air Force Base in California, following the same route as the 31st Fighter Group. It

Republic P-47 Thunderbolt. Many were used for pilot training at Atcham.

comprised the 48th and 49th Fighter Squadrons. Immediately upon their arrival at Atcham it was found that the radios that were installed were not compatible with those used by the RAF. Crews immediately got to work on changing these to the new VHF sets. Other minor technical problems also occurred when the training of pilots began, which again delayed the Group seeing any action. It was in fact not until October that the 14th were ready for action. Again, they moved down south for a limited period before the fighter groups of the Eighth Air Force were notified that they were to be transferred to the newly formed Twelfth Air Force. Shortly after, the 14th FG left Atcham for North Africa.

Once again the base became strangely quiet. Still used by the Americans, in November a Combat Crew Replacement Center had been established there. Part of the 6th Fighter Wing (FW), it had Spitfires and Airacobras on strength but around Christmas 1942 a signal was received notifying the Wing that it was to be re-equipped with the mighty P-47 Thunderbolt. It was this fighter that was to bring more complaints from local people regarding noise than any other aircraft that had used Atcham. Born of the American predilection to 'think big', the Thunderbolt remains one of the classic warplanes of the Second World War with its combination of high power and clean lines. Its armament of eight 0.5 in fixed forward-firing machine guns in the leading-edges of the wings, plus an external bomb and rocket load of 2,500 lb (1,134 kg) made it one of the most formidable aircraft of the entire conflict.

The duty of the unit was once again to train pilots for operations over Europe. From the time of arrival in November 1942 and whenever the weather permitted, the Thunderbolts flew from dawn to dusk. It was dangerous flying in an area scattered with hills and even the odd mountain. One of the closest hazards to Atcham was the large hill known as the Wrekin. One of Shropshire's best-loved landmarks, it rises 1,335 ft above sea level and is a danger even in the best of weather. On a good day it was plainly visible from the airfield but in bad visibility, it disappeared completely. Although it did have a warning light on the top, this clearly presented a difficulty for aircraft taking off in the direction of the Wrekin and after several near misses, it became obvious that something more had to be done about it.

Cliff Marsh was working for a civilian contractor at Atcham and recalls going up the Wrekin to construct a more powerful beacon: 'The commanding officer asked us to take a trip up the Wrekin to see what else could be done about making it more visible in bad weather. A Jeep arrived to take us up to the summit, and what a ride that was! At the top the Colonel pointed out the spot where he wanted the new beacon to go. For the next two or three days a lorry went to and fro carrying up cement and other items needed to secure the beacon. Once it was in position and switched on it was a case of going up to see it every so often to maintain it.'

A WAAF plotter who worked in the operations room at Atcham recalls her duty of operating the beacon: 'We were billeted at Attingham Hall, a lovely ancestral house about a mile and a half from the airfield. One of my jobs was to plot aircraft in the vicinity and also to control the light on top of the Wrekin. There was a large sign on the wall of the operations room which read "WREKIN BEACON-ON – WREKIN BEACON-OFF". Obviously this was of great importance when flying was in progress. The light was always switched off when hostile aircraft were in the sector. On one occasion when enemy aircraft were in the area the WAAF sergeant switched off the beacon and the controller ordered that the air raid sirens were to be sounded in Shrewsbury. The enemy then flew directly over the airfield but did not drop bombs or anything. For us it was just a bit of excitement.'

The beacon was lit for the duration of the war, and was upgraded in 1947 when Atcham closed. Responsibility for its operation then passed to High Ercall and when that closed to Shawbury, from where it is controlled to this day.

For the rest of 1942 and well into 1943 the Thunderbolts continued their training role. In October the 6th FW was renamed the 2906th Observation Training Group, later to become the 495th Fighter Training Group (FTG). This consisted of two units, the 551st and 552nd

Relaxing at dispersal. Pilots of the 495th Fighter Training Group, Atcham 1943/44. (G. Hackenberg)

Fighter Training Squadrons. The new year also saw the 1st Provisional Gunnery Flight change its name on 24th February to the 2025th Gunnery Flight. Flying Westland Lysanders and Miles Masters, it was formed as an American unit but flew British aircraft in the target-towing role.

One of the American pilots posted to Atcham was Major Ervin 'Dusty' Miller. He became the chief flying instructor in August 1943 and was later the station commander. He recalled that when he arrived at Atcham there was not much there, just a few Thunderbolts, some Harvards, a couple of Spitfires and a P-38 or two. He further recalled how the Wrekin was a good weather chart: if you could see it you could fly, if not you stayed on the ground. Major Miller had his own distinctive silver Thunderbolt which was easily recognisable over the county. It was not only the colour that was distinctive but the fact that it was a lengthened P-47 with several modifications. In his words, 'It was a hot aircraft. The trainee pilots couldn't catch me. Good thing, as they were young and eager and I was the elder.'

The training schedule at Atcham was dangerous, with 167 accidents and 35 fatalities. Teaching instrument flying, formation flying and low-level flying all took their toll. There were also take-off and landing accidents together with pilots becoming lost when the weather closed in. Despite warnings, the Welsh hills, very tempting for low flying down in the valleys, also claimed many victims.

One of the young men who trained at Atcham and sadly lost his life later in the war was Warren R. 'Russell' Lobdell. Hailing from Baton Rouge, Louisiana, he arrived in England to join the 495th Fighter Training Group at Atcham. He was young, keen and energetic and was to become a fine fighter pilot. In his letters home he told his family of what life was like in a foreign country and in particular in Shropshire. He wrote of how the local people 'opened their homes to the Americans' and that he found the English people 'very nice but of

Lt Warren R. 'Russell' Lobdell of the 495th Fighter Training Group, Atcham 1942. (G. Hackenberg)

Lt Warren R. 'Russell' Lobdell and 'The Flying Ute', Atcham 1944.

course they have other things on their minds'. Shortly after getting his 'wings' at Atcham, Lobdell was posted to High Halden, an Advanced Landing Ground in Kent, from where, sadly, he lost his life flying over France. He was just 23 years old.

The unconditional surrender of Italy on 8th September 1943 and the crossing of the River Dnieper by the Soviet Red Army one month later took the Germans by surprise. It soon became apparent to all that it was the beginning of the end of the Third Reich. With the RAF promising to bomb Berlin to nothing by night and the Americans bombing the German cities by day, a feeling of distant victory became a reality.

With the increase in American bombing came the necessity for fighter protection for the B-17s and B-24s that were carrying the war back to Germany. The training routine at Atcham continued as more pilots were needed to carry out the escort duties. Once trained, they would move to fighter groups stationed in Britain. Having learned the fighter tactics required to escort large formations of bombers at Atcham, it was now time to put them into practice. Taking advantage of their better performance at high altitudes, the Thunderbolts of the

P-47 Thunderbolts over the Wrekin, Atcham 1944. (G. Hackenberg)

Eighth Air Force usually flew above the heavy bomber formations. These 'little friends' as they became known were to save many a bomber from attack and destruction by enemy fighters.

The 495th Fighter Training Group stayed until February 1945 before moving to Cheddington. With their departure Atcham was returned to the RAF on 14th March 1945. It became a satellite to Tern Hill and was used by No 5 (Pilot) Advanced Flying Unit and No 6 Service Flying Training School. A detachment of No 577 Squadron arrived for the purpose of target towing equipped with Spitfires and Vengeances. They remained until summer 1946 and Atcham was finally abandoned on 22nd October 1946.

There was no place for such a large training airfield in the peacetime RAF and it was finally disposed of on 20th January 1958. Much of the land was returned to its owners and the runways were broken up to provide hardcore for various building projects. Sadly the control tower was demolished, but the three T2 hangars remained together with many of the administrative buildings. Today the airfield is Atcham Industrial Estate, but it is fondly remembered by many of the Americans who served there. Some come back to visit but are dismayed to find very little left of what used to be their home.

3
BRIDGNORTH

It was an RAF station without runways. It was also an RAF station the name of which struck dread into many National Servicemen due to its establishment as one of the main recruit centres during peacetime. That meant drill, drill and more drill. However, during wartime Bridgnorth fulfilled the very necessary duty of training young men to be airmen.

Bridgnorth was intended from the beginning to be a training station. Built during the expansion period, it was ready for occupation by 6th November 1939. Although nearer to the village of Stanmore, it was decided to name the camp Bridgnorth due to the fact that there was already an RAF establishment named Stanmore close to London. Most of the construction was of wooden huts and therefore the building and occupation of the station did not take long. There was no levelling or laying of runways to be done, although two T2 hangars were constructed for the storage of aircraft to be used for instructional purposes. Some brick buildings were evident, these mainly being the equipment store and radio sheds.

Passing out parade at Bridgnorth (date unknown).

An advance party arrived from Padgate, the previous recruit training depot, in January 1940 but found that the station was not finished, and so were accommodated at various hotels around town. Officially known as No 4 Recruit Centre, Bridgnorth now became the main training centre for new airmen, both in aircrew and ground trades.

Fully completed by the time of the Dunkirk evacuation, it was used temporarily to accommodate returning men of the British Expeditionary Force. Also included were men from the French, Belgian, Dutch and Czech forces who found Bridgnorth a refuge before moving on to other stations. By the end of June 1940 most of them had left and the station began a rigorous training programme.

While the Battle of Britain raged in the south-east of the country, very little happened to interrupt the initial training of recruits. It was a strict regime with orders to march everywhere. The wooden huts had proved to be very cold over the winter of 1939/40, which turned out to be one of the coldest with heavy falls of snow all over the county.

No 4 Recruit Centre left Bridgnorth on 4th June 1941 when the station was designated a WAAF training centre. The Women's Auxiliary Air Force had been formed on 28th June 1939, a few days before the Great National Defence Rally in Hyde Park, when the military women marched before the King who commented favourably on their appearance. Like the men, at Bridgnorth they were expected to march everywhere and from dawn to dusk the basic training consisted of drill, RAF law, RAF history and physical training. The issue of uniforms began, consisting of beret, badge, armband, raincoat, overall, two shirts, four collars, two vests and underwear. Tunics and skirts were to come later. The wooden huts vacated by the airmen suddenly began to take on a more feminine appearance. While at Bridgnorth the women performed many civic duties within the town, but a change of policy dictated that the station was once again to become a male training camp and accordingly the women left at the end of September 1942.

Bridgnorth now became No 1 Elementary Air Navigation School (EANS). It was established to teach aircrew navigators the basic elements of air navigation before moving on to flying training schools. At the same time a number of airframes arrived at the station, transported by Queen Mary low-loaders. This was not so much to do with the training but to enable Bridgnorth to look like an RAF station. They were to become gate guardians and several Hurricanes and Spitfires, retired aircraft, duly graced the gate and alongside the parade ground.

By 1942 the station was playing a very active training role, for in addition to navigator training it also undertook battle training in

A sight that greeted every raw recruit. The entrance to Bridgnorth Training Camp. (C. F. Gwilt)

ground combat together with training in flying control. A boost for No 1 EANS came in June 1943 when the Empire Air Navigation School moved in. It was joined by Nos 14 and 18 Initial Training Wings (ITW) shortly thereafter. With so many aircrew needed at this period of the war, Bridgnorth was to play a major part in providing the squadrons with trained navigators.

Nothing happened to interrupt the training although raiders did pass

Same place (as above) but several years later. This was the entrance in 1960 when the author arrived at Bridgnorth. (C.F. Gwilt)

Hurricane gate guardian at Bridgnorth. (C.F. Gwilt)

overhead on their way to and from the Midlands. Further training units arrived when Nos 80 and 81 ITW were instigated to train air gunners, No 50 ITW for training navigators and bomb-aimers and No 70 ITW for wireless operators. All of these units were subjected to the rigours of square-bashing, firearms drill, PT and lectures. Haircuts and kitchen duties became part of everyday life for all recruits, while recreation came in the form of the Astra cinema on camp or travelling further abroad to the pubs and clubs of Wolverhampton. Come the passing out parade and the station would be full of proud parents to watch their sons march with flags flying and bands playing. (How well the writer remembers this occasion when in 1962, he himself passed out from Bridgnorth.)

A wartime recruit recalled his initial training: 'I arrived on 16th December 1942 with a small suitcase in which my civilian clothes were to be sent home when I was kitted out. We were issued with our Service numbers, Airman's Service and Pay Book (Form 64), uniforms and other kit and we sat an intelligence test. The drilling was a particular worry for me as I have always had difficulty with my right and my left, perhaps a consequence of being born left-handed and forced to change to being right-handed. On parade I constantly reminded myself of which was my right hand and fortunately I never made a mistake. We had lectures ranging from VD to aircraft recognition – we were shown aircraft silhouettes against a painted cyclorama which could be lit to represent day or night. Although the square-bashing was set for eight weeks, a group of us were called to the office after six weeks and told that we were to start our one-year course of training as wireless mechanics.'

The basic aircrew training continued until October 1945 when with victory, the station reverted back to training group personnel only. It was renamed No 7 School of Recruit Training with the station crest graciously approved by His Majesty The King on 23rd March 1945. This incorporated a torch in front of a portcullis with the translation of the Latin motto being, 'This is the gate, the walls are the men'. Bearing the King's Crown, the surrounding words were 'Royal Air Force School of Recruit Training'. Jet aircraft such as the Meteor and Vampire were later

RAF Bridgnorth station crest. Inscription 'This is the gate, the walls are the men'. (C.F. Gwilt)

A Gloster Meteor gate guardian at Bridgnorth. (C.F. Gwilt)

National Servicemen all! The inside of one of the recruits' billets at Bridgnorth.
(C.F. Gwilt)

placed as gate guardians, giving the station a very modern air force look.

The general consensus was that Bridgnorth's new training role satisfied all the requirements of a peacetime air force. Thousands of recruits were trained here when Hednesford, the original recruit training station for National Servicemen, closed. No 7 School of Recruit Training was joined by Nos 30 and 34 Reception and Reclassification Wings and Personnel Selection WAAF Training School at the end of October 1945. With both men and women again being trained at Bridgnorth, a stronger civic tie with the local community was forged, culminating in October 1947 when the station was adopted by the Borough of Bridgnorth.

For many recruits it was their first taste of life away from home, and some suffered from homesickness. The good people of Bridgnorth took them under their wing and in return for such kindness, the RAF invited local people to attend demonstrations of the training routine on many occasions. The bond between RAF Bridgnorth and the locals was further cemented when the station became the first RAF base to be awarded the Freedom of the Borough. The charter awarded allowed the station 'to enter the town on all ceremonial occasions and march through the street with bayonets fixed, drums beating and colours

A row of airmen's billets, RAF Bridgnorth. (C.F. Gwilt)

flying'. The official scroll, encased in a casket made from Shropshire oak, was presented to the CO, Grp Cpt G.J. Read, by the Mayor in a ceremony attended by many high-ranking RAF officers.

In 1955 it was announced that National Service would end in early 1960, for two reasons. One was in order to save money and the other was that the RAF no longer had difficulty in recruiting regular servicemen. A message from the Air Ministry stated, 'it was no longer economical to keep the camp open in view of the reduction in the RAF's establishments'. The last annual inspection was carried out on 20th July 1962, the last Remembrance Parade was held on 11th November 1962 and the last intake of recruits was accepted on 11th December 1962. On Thursday, 7th February 1963, the RAF Ensign was lowered for the last time at a 'Beat the Retreat' ceremony.

Since 1939 over a million men and women had received their basic training at Bridgnorth but by 1st May 1963, it was all over. The land was put up for disposal and some of it was auctioned in 1964. Most of the station went the usual way of disused airfields, becoming an industrial site. A memorial plaque was unveiled on 28th May 1994 when a Spitfire overflew the site and a new area of the airfield was designated as the Severn Valley Country Park.

I was one of the last National Servicemen to leave Bridgnorth in 1962. On reflection I never felt fitter or more proud of my country than when I had my first leave and presented myself to my parents in RAF blue. Though Bridgnorth never had heroes like those of the fighter and bomber airfields, it changed the attitudes of certain individuals with the fear of eight weeks' hard 'slog'. Bridgnorth thus earned its place in Shropshire airfield history.

4
COSFORD

With expansion of the airfields came a need for Aircraft Storage Units (ASU) and extra training facilities. The latter had already been established at Halton, Cranwell and Uxbridge but it soon became obvious that more would be needed. The Air Ministry felt that an airfield housing an ASU could also easily accommodate a training school.

It was originally thought that the site at nearby Shifnal would be an appropriate place to build the new airfield but in the end, a new site between the A41 and A464, one mile north-west of Albrighton, was chosen. Originally to be called RAF Donnington after the nearby village, it was feared that it would be confused with a nearby Army camp of the same name. Instead it was decided to name the airfield after Cosford Grange, a large Victorian house.

Contracts for its construction were tendered, with the major contract going to Robert McAlpine Ltd. Preparation of the site began in August 1937 and building began in February 1938. As with most of the airfield construction programme, gangs of workers were brought in from all over the county. As the rumblings from Germany became louder, the civilian labourers worked tirelessly; so much so that it was deemed by the Air Ministry that, although not complete, the airfield would be ready for occupation by July 1938. This was not achieved without problems. The site chosen for Cosford was good, fertile land and local landowners naturally did not want their precious land taken from them. An attempt was even made to move the site of the planned airfield, but in the end these proposals failed and compulsory purchase orders were handed to the farmers and landowners.

It fell to Sqd Ldr A.L. Franks, AFC, to officially declare RAF Cosford open. Arriving with a small advance party on 15th July 1938, he found an airfield far from completion. Most of the buildings such as the instructional workshops and lecture rooms were ready, allowing No 2 School of Technical Training (SoTT) to become established, but the

One of the large 'C' Type hangars at Cosford. (Alfred McAlpine)

School was intended to work up to a strength of 4,000 personnel and Sqd Ldr Franks found accommodation for barely 1,000. Subsequently a fast building programme of hutted accommodation began in order to allow the airfield to begin its training itinerary.

Although Lord Trenchard could never have envisaged, when he reorganised the RAF in 1919, that a second world war would happen, his inspiration brought about a highly efficient technical element in support of the flying arm of the RAF. In this regard No 2 SoTT was to provide technical training to aircraft engineering tradesmen of various trades and experience. The trades to be conducted at Cosford were Fitter II (Engine), Fitter II (Airframe) and Fitter Armourer. In addition, a number of Flight Mechanics and Flight Riggers were also to train at the airfield.

By 1938 the School was already functioning well. With the obvious signs of an approaching war, courses were reduced from three years to two and a half years. This would be reduced further to two years at the outbreak of war, so desperate was the need for skilled groundcrew.

Anyone entering No 2 SoTT was immediately classified as an apprentice. Unlike a civilian apprentice, the RAF had to apply special conditions. Men were expected to sign on for a number of years but at the same time they would be assured of timely promotion to NCO. They would also receive encouragement and further training with a view to becoming an officer in the engineering branch. There is no doubt that without training such as this, the RAF in 1939 would have been ill-equipped to go to war.

On 1st September 1939, Germany invaded Poland. The King and Queen broke off their holiday at Balmoral and returned to London. Winston Churchill was appointed First Lord of the Admiralty and at

A Lamella hangar under construction at Cosford. (Alfred McAlpine)

Cosford, the station tannoys relayed the announcement by Prime Minister Neville Chamberlain. The expected war had finally come and the demands placed upon No 2 SoTT would become even greater.

By this time most of the airfield was finished. The massive 'C' Type hangars that had been constructed for the purpose of storage and maintenance of aircraft were taken over by No 9 Maintenance Unit (MU) on 15th March 1939. Various smaller hangars had also been constructed consisting of 'D' Types, Bellmans, and large Blisters covered in grass and known as Lamellas or 'E' Types. Two Bellman hangars were erected at the northern end of the airfield to be used by Vickers Supermarine as a small Spitfire production unit. With the close proximity of the government-financed factory at Castle Bromwich near Birmingham for building Spitfires, Cosford became the closest airfield to be used for flight-test purposes. Managed and equipped by Morris Motors Ltd, the factory and the test unit at Cosford were to play an important part in the Spitfire story.

No 9 MU occupied the 'A' site of the airfield, closest to the large hangars. It also incorporated No 76 MU whose primary job was to pack aircraft for overseas despatch. Like most MUs, No 9 was civilian-manned but under military control. Its motto and badge were perhaps the most appropriate of all such. With the badge consisting of a phoenix bird on a globe, the motto was *Reddimus Tamquam Nova*, the translation of which is 'We Restore as New'.

Cosford in 1939/40 was a grass airfield; but with the MU accepting heavier aircraft as well as fighters, it became imperative that a hard runway was laid. This took place on 23rd July 1941 when runway

06/24 was laid with asphalt. Its dimensions were 1,146 yds long and 46 yds wide. The first aircraft to land on it did so because of a forced-landing. A Spitfire V (X4485) was carrying out a test flight when engine problems forced the pilot to return to Cosford. Though newly laid, the runway surface held up well and far heavier aircraft were to use it throughout the war.

With such a large maintenance unit, good defence of the site was imperative. In May 1940 the Air Ministry formed a Directorate of Ground Defence, which made hasty arrangements with station commanders as to what level of defence was required and who should provide it. It was felt by the air commanders that if defence were to be provided by the Army, they might attempt to interfere with the air operations. However, when war broke out the RAF had so few ground weapons in the way of large guns that the Army had to be called upon to defend airfields. It was only later that the RAF Regiment was formed to carry out such duties.

The recommendation for Cosford stated that a large force of infantry including the MU's own Home Guard unit, should be attached for defence purposes. Further recommendations stated that the airfield should be defended by a heavy anti-aircraft battery, 22 Lewis guns, eight Vickers guns, 42 Hispano cannon and four armoured vehicles. Camouflage of the landing area was to be undertaken by painting thick green lines across the grass to represent hedges and ditches from the air. Natural cover for aircraft would be provided by the woods around the airfield and buildings were to be painted to blend in with the ground. Although Cosford was far from the main battle front, it was felt that such precautions were necessary in case an enemy aircraft should see and bomb what was fast becoming a very important airfield.

Although no permanent squadrons were ever based at Cosford, there were incidents which brought the war home to the personnel. One of the first was shortly after the outbreak of war. No 9 MU was by January 1940 receiving many different types of aircraft for onward delivery and also for storage. On 10th January PO J. Nicholson of No 2 Ferry Pilots School brought Spitfire K9789 to Cosford. It was a day of bad visibility yet somehow the pilot found the airfield. Coming in on the approach, he overshot the landing area and whilst braking heavily to stop, the Spitfire tipped on its nose, damaging the propeller.

Five days later a Blackburn Skua suffered engine failure whilst on a test flight from Cosford. Again, in a hasty landing the pilot overran the landing area, finally colliding with a mobile building and causing severe damage to the aircraft. The only other incident in 1940 occurred on

12th October and involved Hawker Audax K3684. Tasked to deliver the aircraft from No 9 Unit to RAF Desford, Sgt W.E. Elvidge took off at 12.15 hrs only to suffer engine failure which forced him to crash-land at Atherstone. Unfortunately the aircraft hit some stone obstacles and tipped on its nose, causing Sgt Elvidge to suffer mouth and face injuries.

The winter of 1939/40 was harsh in the extreme. Cosford, not yet with its hard runway, suffered from mud and slush. For the trainees at No 2 SoTT, life became unbearable. Marching to their classrooms, marching to lunch, marching back again to the classrooms and then marching to their wooden billets involved crossing grass that was sodden to the core. Life was not much better for the civilian workers at No 9 MU. With heavier aircraft such as Wellingtons, Ansons, Battles etc arriving day by day, the landing area resembled a mud field. It would be late 1941, however, before the hard runway was built.

The winter lull in activity by the Luftwaffe due to bad weather came to an abrupt end in March 1941. The previous autumn had seen the end of the Battle of Britain, after which the might of the Luftwaffe was turned against the civilian population. The blitz on the Midlands, the heart of wartime heavy manufacturing, now began in earnest.

Shropshire was spared much of this with Cosford receiving just one attack, in daylight on 11th March 1941, which was a cloudy day with minimal visibility. Despite this the enemy mounted a large raid on Birmingham. Not all of the bombers found the city and one, possibly a Heinkel He 111, saw Cosford below and released its bombs. The drone of the engines had sent people rushing to the shelters, with the exception of the airfield defence forces. As they blazed away at the enemy, incendiary bombs fell on the landing area and HE bombs fell on 'B' site. That it was an unco-ordinated attack was proved when only slight damage was caused by the incendiaries; the large bombs that landed by one of the Lamella hangars damaged only two Lysander aircraft. No loss of life was incurred but to the disgust of the Army gunners, the enemy aircraft disappeared into cloud. No other major attack was ever carried out on Cosford.

As the year went on it was found that No 9 MU would require more space. Accordingly, No 30 Satellite Landing Ground (SLG) was opened at Brockton on 30th June. Two grass landing strips were prepared for aircraft such as Blenheims, Whitleys, Wellingtons, Beaufighters and Spitfires to land. Although relatively small when compared to Cosford, it served its purpose well. A year on from the opening of Brockton, yet another SLG, No 33 at Weston Park, had to be constructed.

With the majority of Service pilots on active duty, other means had to be found of ferrying aircraft to and from airfields, factories and maintenance units. The Air Transport Auxiliary (ATA) had been formed for this very task and employed more women than men. No 12 Ferry Pilots Pool (FPP) under the command of Mr G.A. Stedall was formed at Cosford in late 1941 from a nucleus of pilots from No 6 FPP. With the Spitfire test unit located at Cosford, it was obvious that most ferrying would be done on that type. However, when delivering a Spitfire to an operational airfield, invariably there was another aircraft to be bought back to the MU, be it a fighter or bomber. It was arduous work and involved many hours away from home. It was also not without its dangers, as one incident in January 1941 was to prove.

Amy Mollinson, more commonly known by her maiden name of Amy Johnson, was born in 1904. One of the pioneer female aviators, she was the first woman to make a solo flight from England to Australia, in May 1930. This was followed by record solo flights to Tokyo (1931) and Cape Town and back (1932). With the outbreak of war she joined the ATA, and flew many different types of aircraft. Her appearances at Cosford were always welcomed but sadly she was to lose her life eighteen months after the declaration of war. Ferrying an Airspeed Oxford from Blackpool to Kidlington in Oxfordshire, bad weather forced her to change her planned route. That took her too far south, forcing her to enter an area known as the London Gun Barrage. Reports indicate that her aircraft was heard over the Thames Estuary in the area of Herne Bay and that a parachute was seen floating down at the same time. The captain of a patrolling destroyer, HMS *Hazlemere*, saw the parachute hit the water and steamed as fast as possible to the spot. No trace was found of the parachute or the pilot.

Several theories have been put forward as to what happened. It is known that low cloud and poor visibility caused her to stray from her planned flightpath and fly below the cloud. The anti-aircraft guns in the Thames Estuary were on full alert on hearing aircraft engines and it may have been a case of 'friendly fire'. Another possibility is that with the detour in routing, she may well have just run out of fuel, abandoned her aircraft and sadly drowned in the ice-cold water. Amy's body was never found and the incident became one of the many unsolved wartime mysteries.

At Cosford, news of her loss was received with great sadness. Another ATA pilot who flew from Cosford (and was sadly killed in February 1944) wrote of Amy: 'She was a popular girl at Cosford, especially with the control tower guys. Whenever she flew in there was always a packet of cigarettes left for them. She was easily recognised due to the fact she always carried a large cushion with "Amy" written on it. Most of us needed cushions to sit on due to the fact we could often not reach the rudder pedals without one.'

One of the lesser-known units at Cosford was the 'Czechoslovak' Depot. Its task was the training and classification of Czech Air Force personnel who had flown to Britain when their country was overrun by the Nazis. Wishing to continue serving their cause, they were based at Cosford to sit certain trade tests before being posted to Czech squadrons already doing battle as part of the RAF. From Cosford the Depot moved to RAF Wilmslow before returning to Cosford in 1944. Whilst the uniform was the standard RAF issue, the word 'Czechoslovakia' was emblazoned on the upper left sleeve. Like the Polish airmen, the Czechs fought hard and made a definite contribution to the final victory.

Another important unit at Cosford was Princess Mary's Royal Air Force Hospital. Beginning as large sick-quarters at the outbreak of war, it grew to a considerable size and served the RAF and the local community until 1977 when it finally closed. Consisting entirely of wooden huts joined by covered corridors, it housed an operating theatre, X-ray department and laboratory and dentistry facilities. Such was the usage of the hospital that an extra site had to be constructed, this becoming the regional hospital. When both sites were up and running it had a total of 503 beds. In 1941 a burns unit was established to cope with the ever-increasing number of aircrew who had suffered severe burning in combat. An example of just how much the hospital was used is the fact that from January to March 1943, it housed 2,688 inpatients and 5,057 outpatients, undertook 792 operations, 3,147 X-rays and 6,019 laboratory tests, and plastered 393 limbs. It was also to play a large part in the repatriation of POWs at the end of the war, most of them suffering from malnutrition. It was a sad day when the hospital finally closed as part of the reorganisation of military hospitals.

Being near to the Welsh mountains, low cloud and mist were often a problem at Cosford. It was these conditions that caused a fatal accident on 14th May 1941. Spitfire P8151 was on flight-test after repair at Cosford, flown by Sgt C.E. Bell. He was seen to make a perfect take-off and leave the area. Thirty minutes later a telephone call to Cosford infomed the duty ATC officer that Bell had crashed after striking a ridge in conditions of low mist. Sadly he did not survive.

Serious injury was also caused to Flt Lt C.W. Francis on 10th September 1941 when the de Havilland Dragonfly (X9390) that he was testing suffered an engine failure at just 50 ft. It plummeted to the

Preparing for D-Day – Horsa gliders awaiting a tow. (Imperial War Museum)

ground, striking trees and crashing near Cosford Waterworks. The crewman, Flt Lt Holdsworth, suffered slight injuries.

The years 1943 and 1944 became known as 'the path to victory'. In July 1943 the Allies landed in Sicily and later the same month, Mussolini was overthrown. January 1944 saw the Allied landing at Anzio, Italy and preparations were at an advanced stage for Operation 'Overlord', the Allied invasion of France. Preparations for this massive operation had also been going on within No 9 MU at Cosford since July 1942, when several Airspeed Horsa gliders had arrived to be tested.

Following the early successes of the German airborne forces in Europe, the British Government decided to start training our own parachutists. The Central Landing School began this work in July 1940 and in 1942 No 1 Glider Training School (GTS) opened at RAF Croughton. The first British airborne operations with gliders took place in November 1942 over Norway and, with the arrival of the gliders at Cosford, a special tug and glider flight was formed.

At the same time as the Allied invasion of Europe was under way, a new and sinister type of warfare was unfolding. The advent of the V1 'Doodlebug' flying bomb brought death and destruction to the capital on a large scale and it was one of the attacks on London that ensured the quick relocation of an essential part of the training programme.

No 7 Radio School had been established in South Kensington to provide more technicians to cope with the ever changing needs and fast pace of radar technology. A separate training school to any at Cosford, it had been decided by the Air Ministry in early 1944 that it should become part of No 2 SoTT, but no definite date had been given for the move until the issue was forced by an incident which had become commonplace to people living in the south. The peak of the V1 attacks was reached during the week ending 8th July when over 800 V1s were launched. It was one of these that fell in Kensington Road where No 7 Radio School was installed. Luckily there was no loss of life and its one saving grace was that it prompted the quick relocation of the School to Cosford. In a very short time all officers, men and retrievable equipment arrived to form No 15 Radio School.

The last years of the war saw little change at Cosford. The ATA Ferry Pool had become the first to be manned completely by women, whilst No 9 MU and all its satellites carried on their sterling work.

In July 1945 the MU had 382 aircraft on charge including several of the new Gloster Meteor fighter jets. No 2 SoTT continued in its training role, though on a somewhat reduced scale. By this time the School had trained over 70,000 airmen and airwomen in various trades.

However, the end of hostilities did not mark the end of Cosford's war as thousands of Allied POWs now returned to Britain. It was obvious that many of them would need medical treatment and supervision and so, in March 1944, it was decided that all repatriated POWs would be processed through Cosford. For this role, No 106 Personnel Reception Centre (PRC) was formed on 7th March 1945 and worked in conjunction with Princess Mary's RAF Nursing Service. The initial return of 1,000 POWs from Germany brought the realisation that larger and extra units would be needed to cope with prisoners needing long-term care. No 108 PRC was therefore formed on 16th April, to later become No 4 Medical Rehabilitation Unit (MRU).

With Cosford only having a relatively small landing area and an even smaller hard runway, returning POWs were flown to either RAF Wing or Westcott, both situated in the Thames Valley region. They were then bussed to Cosford. Many were in a poor state of health, with diarrhoea and malnutrition very prevalent. The staff at Cosford worked hard to gently get the men back to health. When the POWs from Japan began to arrive, many of the Cosford personnel, despite having seen how bad the POWs from German camps looked, were shocked and angry at the effects of Japanese treatment of Allied prisoners, for they were in a far worse condition. By the time No 106 PRC closed on 23rd August 1948, over 13,000 POWs had been

The arrival of the WAAFs at Cosford was welcomed by all male personnel. (Crown)

processed. There were many others who had to remain at No 4 MRU for long-term treatment.

With the end of hostilities, hundreds of aircraft arrived at Cosford for scrapping by No 9 MU, with Spitfires being the most numerous. The last task of the MU was to carry out further scrapping of Lancasters, Mosquitos, Beaufighters and Horsa gliders. The MU continued its fine work until 22nd June 1956 when it was stood down.

Today, Cosford is a place for aviation enthusiasts, with its fine aerospace museum and the recently opened Cold War Museum. It is still a military airfield, training airmen and airwomen in various trades. The Defence Training Review in 2001 saw the whole of the MOD's Phase 2 training placed within one of six training streams. In the case of Cosford, it became the headquarters of the Defence College of Aeronautical Engineering, which entailed renaming the airfield as DCAE Cosford. No 1 Radio School and the Defence School of Photography remain there, together with the RAF School of Physical Training. In addition, it is home to the University of Birmingham Air Squadron and No 8 Air Experience Flight, both of which fly the Grob 115E Tutor and are supported by No 633 Volunteer Gliding School which flies the Grob Vigilant T1 powered glider. Cosford's contribution to the war effort in the training role was unsurpassed, and that role continues as an essential part of today's RAF.

5
HIGH ERCALL

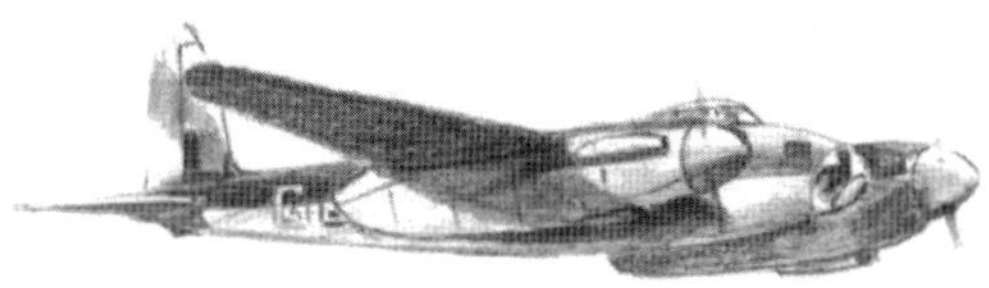

During the long winter of 1940/41, England was subjected to almost constant bombing by the Luftwaffe. Night-time defence by RAF aircraft was virtually ineffectual. This brought about a period of experiment in the detection of the enemy at night by airborne radar, equipment that was very much still in its infancy. Many ideas were forthcoming and High Ercall was associated with one such experiment, known as the Turbinlite.

The idea came from Wg Cdr W. Helmore, then attached to the Ministry of Aircraft Production. His suggestion of an enormous searchlight fitted in the nose of an aircraft was greeted with enthusiasm at the Air Ministry. A fighter aircraft would accompany this airborne searchlight, the idea being that when illumination of an enemy aircraft took place, the fighter could then shoot it down.

The technical aspect of production of the searchlight was given to the General Electric Company at Wembley. For the light to be of any use an output of 50 megacandles was needed. After much research, the first Turbinlite, as the lamp was known, was produced, consuming 140 kilowatts of power and with a horizontal spread of 30 degrees. All that was needed was an aircraft to carry this enormous weight.

The choice made was the American Douglas Havoc II, which was a product of the Lend/Lease agreement with America and was just entering service with the RAF. The conversion unit at Burtonwood adapted the aircraft to incorporate the searchlight and in June 1942, No 1456 Flight arrived at High Ercall. A period of flying experiments for the station had begun.

Constructed by G. Walker and Slater Ltd as one of the post-expansion airfields, High Ercall was one of the few to have three tarmac runways from the beginning. In order for the site to be completed on time, and bearing in mind that war had already started, construction gangs were bussed to High Ercall from all over the Midlands. In a reversal of the

Spitfire maintenance at No 29 MU, outside '3' shed. (J. Harris)

normal sequence of building, the hangars were erected first in order to house cement and various other construction materials.

The official opening came on 1st October 1940, with the installation of No 29 Maintenance Unit (MU), a civilian organisation that repaired and test-flew previously damaged aircraft. Part of its duty was to assemble and test-fly American aircraft delivered under the Lend/Lease agreement. Despite the arrival of a few Curtiss Mohawks on 22nd November, however, very few American aircraft materialised.

Upon completion, High Ercall was a very large airfield. In addition to several 'J' Type hangars used for the storage of aircraft, many smaller 'L' Types were built to accommodate large numbers of aircraft. These were supplemented by T2 and Blister hangars and even the enlarged Over Blister hangar. The runways were the usual bomber configuration consisting of Runway 11/20 which was 4,740 ft long, 05/23 (4,130 ft) and 35/17 (3,750 ft).

Despite the increased workforce brought in, even by early 1941 the airfield was far from complete. The arrival of several RAF officers was an indication that the military were to make use of High Ercall, although No 29 MU remained the sole occupants until well into 1941.

Since the First World War, servicing procedures had changed very little, the exception being the employment of civilians instead of military personnel. The added pressures of maintenance and storage during the war years required several changes to the system. Aircraft damaged in action were placed into five categories. Light damage became Categories 1 and 2, usually handled by civilians under military supervision. Category 3 required the services of a visiting repair and salvage unit, while Category 4 required a maintenance unit's service at a depot. Category 5 was deemed to be beyond repair and usually meant that the airframe was taken either for instructional purposes or for spares. All of these categories would be handled by No 29 MU at High Ercall as well as the station becoming a major storage base.

The first of the aircraft to be stored arrived shortly after Christmas Day 1940, but misfortune befell a North American Harvard when one of a group of three attempting to land suddenly plunged to the ground, causing severe injuries to the pilot. With the crash services soon on the scene, it was one of the first aircraft to be deemed 'Cat 5'.

Once Christmas was past the hopes were that High Ercall would be finished during the coming year. Although many workmen were still apparent on the site, it had been considered that No 306 (Torun) Squadron, a Polish unit stationed at nearby Tern Hill, might be offered the use of the base should theirs become untenable. In the event the Hurricanes did not appear and instead No 13 Squadron from Hooton Park brought their Westland Lysanders in for a brief period in February 1941, the first RAF aircraft to use the new facilities.

By November 1940 the Battle of Britain was over. It had petered out as the Luftwaffe withdrew from the daylight assault and winter set in. Earlier that month, Goering had issued new orders for attacks on Britain by night. Had this not been the case and had the assaults on the airfields in the south continued, a very different scenario would have developed. As it was, the destruction of Britain's towns and cities by night took precedence.

The new year saw the German bomber offensive hampered by bad weather. No bomber operations were possible for thirteen consecutive nights, but by the middle of January the blitz got into its stride and it was the major cities of the Midlands lying close to the Shropshire border, as well as the capital, that became the targets.

Records show that Friday, 7th March 1941 was a day of extensive cloud with generally poor visibility. It was similar on the Continent but despite this, the Luftwaffe prepared for a raid as dusk was approaching. Earlier that day, an attack on a ball-bearing factory at Newark had left 36 people dead but later raids were carried out by

Spitfires ready to be broken up at the end of the war by No 29 MU. (J. Harris)

single aircraft taking advantage of cloud cover. These raids were known in Germany as 'pirate attacks' but by the RAF as 'hit and runs'. One such attack was carried out by an enemy aircraft, thought to be a Ju 88, on High Ercall, which dropped four 500 lb HE bombs and four incendiary bombs during poor visibility and low cloud. It then turned and machine-gunned a large area of the airfield, but by then most personnel had taken to the shelters. Consequently no casualties were sustained although several buildings were damaged. Under heavy fire from the airfield defences, the raider took advantage of the cloud cover and got away. Although High Ercall was attacked by lone aircraft on several occasions, this was considered the worst raid.

Since the establishment of MUs in 1938, No 29 had operated within No 51 Wing with its headquarters at Broughton Hall in Flintshire. The expansion of No 29 MU during 1941 was such that despite storing aircraft around the perimeter on hard standings and even amongst the trees surrounding the airfield, a Satellite Landing Ground (SLG) had to be established at Teddesley Park. Opened on 1st June, it was officially called SLG 48. However, by 4th July SLG 21 had opened at Ollerton for the further storage of aircraft and SLG 46 was opened at Brinklow on

The CO and civilians, complete with mascot, of No 29 MU. (J. Harris)

20th July. Further SLGs were made available in the later years of the war, indicating the amount of work the MUs undertook.

With the nightly blitz on the Midlands increasing, it was deemed necessary to base a night-fighter squadron at High Ercall. No 68 Squadron had formed at Catterick on 7th January 1941 solely for the defence of the Midlands and it became fully operational with Bristol Blenheim night-fighters on 7th April, moving to High Ercall ten days later.

Known as 'Britain's First', the Blenheim was a military development of the Type 142 presented to the nation by Lord Rothermere. This was the first of the new monoplane bombers ordered under the expansion scheme and represented a huge technical advance on the biplane bombers previously in service. The Air Ministry ordered the aircraft direct from the drawing board with the first consignment of 150 Blenheims leaving the factory in November 1936. The Blenheim If, the night-fighter version, was a conversion of the Blenheim I undertaken from a kit supplied by the Southern Railways Ashford Factory, and had its forward armament augmented by four Browning machine guns in a gun pack beneath the fuselage. With the addition of an early form of airborne radar, the Mk If served through the blitz of 1940/41.

Beaufighters thought to be from No 68 Squadron at High Ercall. (Crown)

However, with rapid developments in aircraft manufacture, the Blenheims were exchanged for the more powerful Bristol Beaufighter a month after their arrival at High Ercall. Once again, the Beaufighter If added a new chapter to RAF history when it became the first night-fighter with the performance and radar capability to really make a difference when attacking enemy bombers. High Ercall now officially became a night-fighter station in the Tern Hill sector which had control of the Midlands region. With the more powerful Beaufighter it was not long before No 68 Squadron made their presence felt.

The night of 16th/17th June saw the Heinkel He 111s of Kampfgeschwader 100, a group encompassed within Luftflotte 2 and flying from Vannes in Belgium, roaming over the Midlands looking for targets of opportunity. At High Ercall the Beaufighters were on full stand-by until shortly before midnight when they were scrambled to intercept the raiders. One Beaufighter flown by Flt Lt D.S. Pain, DFC, and FO Davies got a firm contact on their airborne radar at around 01.30 hrs. Coming to within yards of the unsuspecting He 111 H-3 (5633) the guns of the Beaufighter blazed, with shots being registered as hitting the enemy aircraft. As it began its plunge to earth, Fw G. Deininger managed to bale out leaving Oberlt H. Pohner, Fw K. Ott, Fw O. Hertzberg and Fw K. Engels to die in the crash at Combe Hill, Bratton in Wiltshire at 01.50 hrs.

Back at High Ercall, with news of the success having preceded them, the crew were welcomed back and congratulated. With the night's operations over, all the aircrew were sent to get the usual breakfast of bacon and eggs before retiring to bed. Outside the diligent groundcrews inspected, refuelled and re-armed the aircraft, and made sure all was ready for the next night's operations.

The rest of the year saw No 68 Squadron flying night patrols whenever required. In October it flew 48 patrols and again found success for one of the crews. One of the more notorious units of the Luftwaffe was KG40. They were, again, a unit within Luftflotte 2, whose Generalfeldmarschall was Albert Kesselring. Based at Brest on the Brittany coast, one of their main functions was anti-shipping patrols. One such sortie over the Irish Sea was planned for the night of 12th/13th October 1941. Lifting off from Brest at around 22.00 hrs, He 111 H-6 (426) crewed by Hptmn P. Romisch, Lt W. Kreutzer, Uffz H. Leitner and Fw E. Uredat was the first to get airborne, followed by He 111 H-6 (4141) crewed by Obergefr J. Wettengel, Obergefr K. Buchgraber, Gefr D. Hankel and Gefr H. Mening. Both formated over the French coast and settled down to what they hoped would be a quiet night's operations.

Back at High Ercall, a briefing was taking place regarding the night's sorties. By 22.00 hrs several of No 68 Squadron's Beaufighters were airborne and under the control of a ground control intercepting (GCI). radar station. It was not long before the controller had a contact on his screen and was able to vector the Beaufighter flown by PO M.J. Mansfield to a position where his airborne radar could take over. The crew of the enemy bomber were unaware they were being stalked until bullets began to rake their aircraft. There was no time for them to take to their parachutes as, firing at three-second intervals, PO Mansfield had the satisfaction of seeing his quarry dive into the sea off Holyhead at 11.35 hrs. Five minutes later, Mansfield's navigator got another firm contact on his radar and gave directions to his pilot to come up from beneath the He 111 of Obergefr Wettenger. Once again the guns of the Beaufighter blazed, raking the enemy aircraft from nose to tail. Minutes later the Heinkel joined its fellow aircraft in the Irish Sea. Again, no parachutes were seen and the bodies of the crewmen were never found. It was a bad night for the Luftwaffe, but a good one for Mansfield and his navigator.

No 68 Squadron remained at High Ercall until 8th March 1942 when they moved to Coltishall after a very successful stay. Four days earlier the Beaufighter IIfs of No 255 Squadron had left Coltishall and arrived at High Ercall under the command of Wg Cdr D.P. Kelly. The squadron had a very apt badge containing a panther's face and the motto *Ad*

A Beaufighter and aircrew of No 248 Squadron. The Beaufighter was a common sight over Shropshire during the war. (Crown)

T4712

Painting depicting a Beaufighter from No 68 Squadron, High Ercall, shooting down a Heinkel He 111. (via Ian Miller)

Auroram, translated as 'To the break of dawn'. The panther is known for its power, speed and ability to kill at night, and No 255 certainly hoped that this would be the case whilst at High Ercall.

Flying the new production Beaufighter, the crews found it to be a vast improvement on the previous mark. Two Rolls-Royce Merlin XX engines had replaced the previous Bristol Hercules, giving increased power. In addition, vast improvements had been made in the airborne radar and instead of the protruding 'stick' aerials, which created drag and therefore slowed the aircraft, a scanner was now mounted in a new nose fairing.

By nightfall the aircrews and groundcrews had settled into the buildings left vacant by No 68 Squadron. Their arrival had not been without incident when one of the aircraft ran off the runway and got its wheels stuck firm in the grass. However, the squadron was able to carry out several sorties during the night, though without success.

No 29 MU had by this time got used to sharing the airfield with operational units. With the storage and repair of aircraft increasing, and a surplus of over 700 aircraft to disperse, further SLGs were required. SLG 33 was opened at Weston Park, thus making No 29 MU one of the largest units of its kind.

Halifax VI RG786 fitted with a belly-mounted radar scanner at No 29 MU. (J. Harris)

Disappointingly, No 255 had no success in finding enemy aircraft despite again converting, this time to the superior Beaufighter VIf. They moved over to Honiley on 6th June 1942 after suffering a high accident rate for no gain. This had reduced morale to an all-time low, although they were to find the enemy whilst flying from Honiley and later West Malling in Kent (see *Kent Airfields in the Second World War*, published by Countryside Books).

In exchange, No 257 (Burma) Squadron under the command of Sqd Ldr D.G. Wykeham-Barnes, DFC and Bar, brought their Hurricane IIbs in from Honiley. This was one of the squadrons often referred to as 'gifts of war', because it was purchased by donations from the people of Burma and called 'The Burma Fund'. No 257 was one of the first to be so named and the Air Ministry promised that as long as there was a No 257 Squadron in existence, the good and kind Burmese people would be kept informed about its actions.

The squadron did not arrive alone for during their stay at Honiley they had partnered a Turbinlite squadron. The Turbinlite unit that came to High Ercall was formed at Honiley on 2nd November 1941 and was known as No 1456 Flight. It received several Havoc Is that were to fly in conjunction with the Hurricanes of No 257 Squadron. Both aircraft were fitted with formation-keeping lights and the operational

High Ercall's hangars, now devoid of any aircraft or action. (Author)

procedure was for them to take off independently and form up over the airfield. A GCI station would then vector the Turbinlite-equipped Havoc to the area where the enemy aircraft had been plotted, where the Havoc's own airborne radar would bring it to within 3,000 ft. Once a contact was made the navigator of the Havoc would pass the codeword 'Hot' to the Hurricane pilot. When the target was firmly locked on, the codeword 'Boiling' was passed to the Hurricane, which would then drop 300 ft below the Havoc and open up to full power. When the mother aircraft was 900 ft from its target it would switch on its Turbinlite, in the glare of which the enemy aircraft would be caught and then shot down by the Hurricane, hopefully! In all a total of ten Turbinlite flights were formed (Nos 1451–1460) between May and December 1941.

From the outset, however, difficulties began to present themselves. First, the Turbinlite Flights were dependent on the operational requirements of the escorting fighters, i.e. the fighters might be needed for offensive operations. Second, if the enemy pilot realised that he was about to be attacked and took evasive action, it was difficult to keep track of him and any drastic changes in direction might cause a mid-air collision between the Turbinlite Havoc and the Hurricane. This was partly solved in September 1942 when the Flights were given Squadron status (Nos 530–539) and worked with a resident Flight of fighters.

The whole idea, however, did not live up to expectations and with the vast improvements in aircraft fitted with superior radar and more

Mosquito outside 'J' shed at No 29 MU. (J. Harris)

gun power, all ten Turbinlite squadrons were disbanded in January 1943. Although many contacts had been made, records show that only one enemy aircraft was destroyed, one probably destroyed and two damaged. The Turbinlite went into the history books as just another wartime invention that looked good in principle. No 1456 Flight was originally commanded by Sqd Ldr I.E. Chalmers-Watson, AFC, and in August 1942, when the Flight was given Squadron status, he handed the reins over to Sqd Ldr B.N. Moloney. At this point it became No 535 Squadron and it was he who oversaw its disbandment in January 1943.

By the summer of 1943 High Ercall was a very busy station indeed. In addition to the aforementioned Turbinlites, Hurricanes of No 257 were busy with bomber escorts over the Continent combined with normal sector patrols. No 29 MU was again looking for additional room to store aircraft and as if to exacerbate the problem, in May No 222 MU Aircraft Packing Depot had been established for the purpose of dismantling aircraft for passage by sea or air overseas. Then came the Americans!

The 31st Fighter Group (FG) was the first American unit to be equipped with the unique Bell P-39 Airacobra. The aircraft was a bold attempt to create an advanced fighter by locating the engine in the fuselage behind the cockpit. From here it drove the tractor propeller by means of a long extension shaft which ran between the pilot's legs. This configuration left the nose free for a battery of forward-firing guns. Despite serving with thirteen fighter groups, the US Army never deemed it a success, as the decision not to fly them to High Ercall illustrated.

The 31st FG was activated at Selfridge Field, Michigan on 1st February 1940 and had been scheduled to fly P-39Fs across the Atlantic to join the Eighth Air Force during the summer of 1942. However, as the P-39 was found to be unsuitable for operations in the European Theater of Operations, the personnel moved to England without aircraft and on arrival were equipped with Spitfires Vbs obtained under the reverse Lend/Lease Act. The arrival of the Americans, the 309th Fighter Squadron (FS), at High Ercall was something of a shock to the locals!

With the war now going the way of the Allies, intruder operations over the Continent were gathering pace. One of the newer aircraft used in this attack scenario was the de Havilland Mosquito, often called the 'Wooden Wonder'. Equally at home as a day- or night-fighter, as the latter it was fitted with a new, highly secret type of airborne radar. Such was the aircraft's performance and usage that whereas previous training for the type had been done at the OTUs, now more specialised training was required to produce even more Mosquito pilots. High Ercall was one of the bases chosen and in consequence, No 60 OTU formed there on 17th May 1942 with 24 Mosquitos, two Ansons and an Oxford.

Meanwhile the Americans were beginning to work up on their Spitfires. In order to help them get to know the way the RAF operated, a number of sorties were flown with RAF pilots, beginning on 26th July. The first Group-strength mission was flown on 29th August to establish the 31st FG as the first Eighth Air Force fighter group to commence combat operations. Their stay at High Ercall, however, was short as September saw them transferred to the Twelfth Air Force for operations in North Africa.

With good weather prevailing during July and August, the intruder missions over France increased. No 257 Squadron briefly exchanged their Hurricanes for Spitfire Vbs before reverting to Hurricanes prior to re-equipping with the new Hawker Typhoon. Not quite living up to expectations as an interceptor fighter, the Typhoon went on to achieve great success as the backbone of the 2nd Tactical Air Force in the ground attack role. Its devastating firepower and rocket attacks brought it fame as the scourge of enemy-held Europe.

Operation 'Jubilee', the ill-fated Dieppe landing, took place on the beaches of France on 6th August 1942. This was a combined assault although the majority of troops were Canadians. From the beginning it was a disaster as the enemy fought back, having been forewarned of the assault. Out of 6,000 brave men who went to Dieppe, only a few survived. They left behind more than two thirds of their original numbers, either dead or taken prisoner by the Germans. For days, the RAF had bombarded the French coastline and No 257 Squadron, with their rocket-firing Typhoons, played a part in this operation. From their cockpits the pilots could only look on in despair at what they saw going on down below. Feeling desperately sorry, they returned to High Ercall and gave graphic accounts of what they had seen to the Intelligence Officer. The impact of the failure of the operation permeated the entire station.

With high August came the return of the Americans. The Eighth Air Force, the UK-based component of the USAAF (as it became known in April 1942), was scheduled to include fighter groups as well as the heavy bombardment groups. Five fighter groups were initially selected for the Eighth including the 1st Fighter Group equipped with P-38F Lightnings. The 27th Fighter Squadron was one of the squadrons included and, eager to get to England, they were disappointed when a delay occurred after a signal was received assigning the squadron to the Iceland Base Command. The delay, however, was not long and on 21st August the P-38Fs flew into High Ercall.

The three weeks they were to spend at the station were used to fit the aircraft with VHF radio equipment compatible with that being used by the RAF. It was also an opportunity to train the pilots in operational conditions. However, with the arrival of the Americans the station strength increased dramatically to 2,183, made up of 1,286 airmen, 222 airmen on detachment to High Ercall, 255 WAAFs, 23 Army attached, 309 US personnel and 88 RAF officers. This together with the civilians employed in the MU saw High Ercall ready to burst at the seams. The situation was eased slightly when the Americans left High Ercall on 14th September and were transferred to the Twelfth Air Force for operations in support of Operation 'Torch', the Allied invasion of North Africa in November 1942.

Another 'named squadron' arrived on 21st September. Formed with a donation of £210,000, No 247 (China/British) flew their Hurricane IIcs in from Exeter. Commanded by Sqd Ldr J.C.J. Melvill, they had previously flown 'Roadsteads', attacks on enemy coastal shipping at night, but upon arrival at High Ercall and No 9 Group, they ceased operations in September in readiness for conversion to the Typhoon. A detachment from the squadron was sent to Valley as High Ercall now became a Typhoon base.

The last American aircraft to be based at the station came in the form of the aforementioned P-39 Airacobra, thirteen of which were flown in

Staff of No 29 MU circa 1942. (J. Harris)

from Burtonwood for the 92nd Fighter Squadron, whose personnel arrived several days later. Again it was a brief stay, as they left on 12th December, and like the other American squadrons, converted to Spitfires at their new home.

High Ercall could look back on a fairly successful year of operations. Though there had been tragedies, they were below the rate expected of such a high-usage airfield. One of the last duties of the year fell to the station fire section when they were called to assist in fighting a huge fire that had broken out at the village hall. Attending with the local National Fire Service vehicles, they tried to save the wooden hall from being completely destroyed, but it was burned to a cinder. This, together with a Hurricane crash in which Sgt H.E. Bailey of No 247 Squadron was killed, was not a good end to 1942.

It was also not a good beginning to 1943 when another pilot of No 247 Squadron, Canadian Flt Sgt Quentin MacPhail Shippee, just 22 years of age, crashed near Madeley. Observers said that his Typhoon went into a spin from which it never recovered, with the impact near Windmill Farm Aqueduct. The High Ercall Operations Record Book gives the date of his crash as 24th February whilst the Commonwealth

The King and Queen visit the Turbinlite squadron at High Ercall on 16th July 1942. (The National Archives)

War Graves Commission dates his death as 19th March. In any event, it was a sad end to No 247's stay at High Ercall as they left for Middle Wallop airfield on 28th February.

The equivalent of the RAF MUs in the Fleet Air Arm were known as Aircraft Maintenance Yards. These came into existence in late 1942 and early 1943 and were established exclusively for the storage and maintenance of naval aircraft. However, by late 1943 it had become obvious that they did not have the capacity to cope with such a large workload. Consequently much of the work was contracted out to the RAF MUs, including No 29. This extra work warranted a larger workforce which resulted in 69 naval ratings being stationed at High Ercall to swell the civilian workforce which now stood at over 700 employees.

One of the civilian charge-hands working in the MU was Alf 'Jim' Harris: 'We wondered just why naval officers and ratings were coming to the MU but it all became clear when No 2 site 'A' shed was taken over by HMS *Daedalus*, a shore-based unit from Plymouth. They were here on a secret and highly guarded project, fitting [ASV Mk XI] radar to Swordfish aircraft which we were producing on another site. These Swordfish had a scanner unit under the belly and when the radar and radio ratings had finished fitting and ground-testing the equipment it had to be tested in flight, which took several hours. I had a groundcrew of naval ratings to oversee the preparing of aircraft for the flight-test, then our No 29 MU test pilots flew the aircraft with naval radar experts in the back seat doing the testing and adjusting. These aircraft apparently did a great job in destroying German shipping. Just to show how secret this job was, an armed guard was on every entrance to this hangar; everyone requiring to enter for any reason had to have a special permit signed by the station adjutant. Security officers in plain clothes often turned up from the Air Ministry and attempted to get in with false passes on the pretext of checking the engines for certain modifications or some other reason.'

No 41 Squadron was a famous unit, having been formed during the First World War and seeing action. Disbanded after the Armistice, it was reformed during the second conflict and had seen action over Dunkirk as well as during the Battle of Britain. The squadron badge was adapted from the arms of St Omer, the squadron's second posting in October 1916, together with a double-armed cross and the motto 'Seek and Destroy'. The Spitfires led by Sqd Ldr T.F. Neil, DFC and Bar, carried out offensive patrols from High Ercall over the Irish Sea for three months in early 1943. From High Ercall they moved down south to Hawkinge and later to Biggin Hill. No 41 Squadron was to be the last permanent squadron to use High Ercall as the nightly blitz of the Midlands lessened in intensity. This left the Mosquitos of No 60 OTU and the MUs. Still a very busy station, High Ercall in 1943 saw many of the Mosquitos come to grief.

One such incident happened on 1st May 1943 when a Mosquito collided with a Spitfire from No 61 OTU at Rednal. The collision happened on the outkirts of Shrewsbury, some smaller pieces of debris falling very near the town. Four days after the crash, the Mosquito pilot, Flt Lt G.W. Mason, was buried with military honours in High Ercall churchyard. August and September saw further Mosquito crashes, all with the loss of airmen; a harrowing time for the station. Yet amidst the tragedy, preparations had already begun for the invasion of Europe and hopefully the beginning of the end of the war. In this respect, the men of No 29 MU were already aware of what was going to happen.

Charge-hand Jim Harris knew earlier than most:

De Havilland Mosquito. Many passed through the Maintenance Units of Shropshire. (MAP)

In my logbook the mention of 21st September 1942 brings back memories of the Horsa gliders made by Harris Lebus, the furniture makers who were installed in No 2 'A' hangar. When they had completed them they handed them over to us on the airfield for test flying before despatch to various units for the invasion of Europe and, of course, the landings at Arnhem. Our test pilots didn't fly the Horsas because when we had several ready for test, a Lancaster came and brought the towing cables and some Army glider pilots. We would tow the gliders out to the end of the runway, laying the tow rope out in a zig-zag pattern and as the Lancaster slowly moved away to 'take up the slack', we would give the rear gunner the OK just as the rope became tight and he told the pilot 'full throttle' and they were away. After the test flight they again appeared over the airfield, casting off the glider. The glider pilot did an almost vertical descent till almost back to our parking spaces with the speed he had. We parked them on the airfield until they were assigned to their various units. We all knew that something big was going to happen but did not know exactly what until the invasion actually happened.

Being such a large airfield, High Ercall was often a haven for returning bombers in distress. In the late afternoon of 29th September a B-17 Flying Fortress of the 384th Bombardment Group from Grafton Underwood saw High Ercall and proceeded to land. It had been part of a large force of B-17s that had attacked Nantes and Chateau-Bougon. On the homeward leg they had been attacked by enemy aircraft, and suffered several losses and damage to others. Having encountered a bad weather front, many aircraft became lost, including this one that spotted the large runway at High Ercall. With three crew members badly injured, the aircraft landed safely as the crash crews and ambulance rushed to assist. The injured were taken to the sick-quarters and hurried repairs were carried out on the B-17, which allowed it to leave the next day. Seeing High Ercall had saved an entire crew and was just one of many similar incidents. Sadly, 1943 was to end badly for No 60 OTU when three Mosquitos crashed during December, killing all three of the two-man crews.

December was again one of the coldest on record and for the poor men of the MU life could be very miserable, as Jim Harris again recalls:

When the weather was bad and flying could not be done, aircraft started to pile up at Receipt and Despatch either waiting for despatch or waiting to be air-tested. All these had to be inspected every day, ground-tested and the Form 700 signed ready for flight. One day was particularly horrible to say the least: freezing fog with visibility just a few yards.

Parked on some grass beside a road leading to a small site canteen was a very well-worn Lysander that was ready to go away for a complete refurbishing. The crew doing the inspection had arrived at the time in the servicing to ground-run the engine. With the starter truck containing heavy-duty batteries plugged in, the man on the truck shouted 'All clear' as the fitter in the cockpit pressed the starter button, pumping the primer at the same time. Now with a cold, wet engine, as soon as she fires up you must give a quick stab on the throttle to catch it before it dies on you. As this is happening, everyone else is cheering, stamping their feet and beating their arms to keep warm and shouting 'Keep it going', only to be rewarded with a big bang as the engine decides not to start but to 'blow back' down the carburettor air intake.

Then the procedure starts again, but by now petrol is dripping down from the carb intake; but not to worry because

The rusting remains of an air raid siren on a 'D' Type hangar. (Author)

Superbly presented 'K' Type hanger at High Ercall. (Author)

Station guardroom pictured in 2007. (Author)

on the lid of the starter truck is a small Pyrene pump-type fire extinguisher. The next attempt, the engine does the same but this time as it blows back, flames come down the air intake setting light to all the spare petrol, even on the floor. Not to worry; we are used to this and a few pumps on the extinguisher and it's all over apart from being gassed from the fumes given off by using the extinguisher. Everything is ready for another try! This time the same thing happens but the extinguisher is now empty before the fire is out so things start to burn.

Now I must tell you at this stage that our mornings began at 7.30 and at 10.30 we were allowed a tea break, and on these sort of mornings when the tea arrived at the crew room a cry went out into the fog, 'Tea up'. The labourer on tea duty, having confirmed how many wanted tea, would go to the site canteen, collect a bucket of tea and take it back to the crew room with a shout of again 'Tea up'. On this particular morning he had to walk past the Lysander and as he did so, in desperation, one of the groundcrew on the Lysander grabbed the bucket of tea and threw it over the burning engine, putting out the fire. This caused fury as the decision in the crew room was that the plane should have burned as that was the last of the rations for the morning! The lad that threw the tea was worthy of death but, ironically, we did get the engine going after a while and finished the inspection.

No 60 OTU merged with No 13 OTU in March 1945 and moved to Finmere. High Ercall lost its OTU status and reverted back to 41 Group Maintenance Command for the storage and scrapping of literally thousands of Halifax bombers. July 1945 saw over 920 in store, rising to 1,527 by the end of the year. How sad to see all those large four-engined bombers that had survived the war succumb to the scrap merchant's torch. It took until 1950 to dispose of all of the Halifaxes before the torch was turned on the Spitfires. How ironic that today these are being rebuilt from scrap for civilian use.

One of the last duties of No 29 MU was the storage of Percival Prentices, the RAF basic trainer between 1948 and 1953. The MU closed in 1962 and the airfield reverted to Care and Maintenance. Some land was returned to its owners for agricultural purposes but the main domestic and technical site remains much as it did in wartime. Now named the 'Angel Centre', it is home to a variety of industrial uses. It is, however, the best-preserved closed airfield in the county and walking around it is like entering a time warp. It remains the perfect memorial to those who lost their lives or were injured flying from High Ercall.

Life in the MU

Some of the memories of Alf 'Jim' Harris, a civilian foreman with No 29 MU now living in Swindon, are recounted above, but before leaving High Ercall it is worth hearing more about his day-to-day life in No 29 Maintenance Unit.

I started with the Air Ministry as a Fitter Airframe (rigger) at the end of 1938, having worked for Gloster Aircraft Company at Brockworth before that. The first airfield I worked on was South Cerney in Gloucestershire with No 3 Flying Training School. They had real planes: Audaxes, Furies and Hinds; all biplanes which we called 'all string and wire'. Gradually, Airspeed Oxfords started coming in and several of us civilians were sent to open maintenance units that were being built. My first was at

Jim Harris and Wally Mitchell in the process of dismantling an Oxford. Most were made of wood and were burned. (J. Harris)

Silloth, No 22 MU, then a brief time at Kirkbride, No 14 MU, until in 1940 I arrived at No 29 MU in Shropshire.

Our transport to High Ercall was by a very well used single-deck works bus. I used to sign in to start at 7.30 am and it was not unusual to see something stranded on the runway that had arrived overnight; usually it was a bomber that had landed in distress. On this particular morning there was a plane on the grass at the far end of the airfield near one of our site offices. Some speculation followed as to 'what it was'. It had a tricycle undercarriage and two engines but we had never seen the type before. Walking round to our hangar entrance I noticed, parked at the back of the crews' rooms, two other aircraft of the same type. I then realised that they had been delivered to us and had been received by the duty night crew. A closer inspection revealed them to be North American B-25 Mitchells, the latest consignment from the US and no doubt delivered by the ATA from Prestwick after we had gone home.

While I was taking off my coat, the phone rang. 'We are ringing from the control tower and would like to point out that the aircraft stuck deep in the mud on the side of the main runway is yours. Move it!' They then added the wind was starting to increase and that the runway was in use. They also warned us that a squadron of American pilots who had been kitted out with Spitfires were going to use our airfield to convert to this type. They would need all the time they could get in on the Spitfires as they had been used to nose wheels rather than tail wheels, and it was suggested we keep a good lookout as we were nearer than the control tower were to the runway.

Myself and a few of the lads piled on to a Clarkson tractor and headed across the grass to the offending Mitchell which was well and truly 'in it' up to the top of the wheel rim. We did have the Ground Handling Notes, an Air Ministry publication telling you all you needed to know to do a daily inspection and how to start and ground-test the engine, but not how to get it out of a muddy runway! Spades to the fore and get digging. We got some short, thick pieces of wood to go under the front of the wheel to drag it up on to something solid. With no towing gear available for this type as yet, we obtained a long piece of thick rope and carefully tying the rope on to each undercarriage leg, we hooked up the tractor and started to pull. However, it was stuck so deep that it would not move on to the wood. It was also in too deep to get it out on its own power and apparently, that had been tried the previous night and had only stuck it in deeper. Plus the fact that by now the prop was very near the ground. The only thing we could do was to get a large ten-ton jack and improvise the jacking pad to lift the one wing high enough to shore it up on wood planks.

We duly placed thick planks of wood under each leg of the hydraulic jack and carefully positioned it under the wing at the position where the jacking pad would go if we had one.

By now the wind had increased and was gusting, the US pilots were flying and not making a very good job of landing with a tail wheel, so everything that should have been in our favour seemed to be against us. The jack was behaving pretty well but we had to jack it high enough to extend the undercarriage leg to its full height before the wheel started lifting. By the time it did so, things were not looking so good for with the jack nearly at its full height, the gusts of wind seemed determined to blow the plane off the jack. The Spitfires taking off close by didn't seem to notice us at all. Then it happened!

Just as we were about to get some wood under the wheel a large gust of wind and a Spitfire going by at take-off revs was just too much. The plane rocked, the jack moved forward off the jacking position and with a very expensive sort of bang, went up through the wing forward of the front spar and appeared through the top of the wing. All eyes turned towards me with comforting thoughts such as was I going to collect my cards on the way out or hide somewhere?

I developed a quick cunning plan which had the approval of all present. We would quickly go through it again but with a lookout on the Spitfires and another poised with the wood whilst a third man got ready to release the jack instantly. It worked! And the wheel was on a solid foundation to move forward. With one man holding a block under the hole in the wing and another on the top gently tapping down the metal skin, we made it look presentable to get it 'home'.

After getting the air traffic controller in the cabin on the end of the runway to keep giving the Spitfires a red light to go round again, we were soon away, steering it with a man on the brakes and a long rope to keep the tractor out of harm's way. After parking it behind the crew huts it was time for Plan 'B'. We were very fortunate that where the jack had gone through the wing, there was absolutely nothing in the way so it just passed straight through without hitting anything. We were thus able to make two inspection covers complete with the required amount of screws. Cut the holes to size, rivet on the back plates, paint the covers and stencil on 'inspection'. The job was done. I often wondered what the future groundcrews thought when taking off all the inspection panels for an inspection and finding nothing inside!

First encounter with a Hudson aircraft

It was mid-afternoon and I was doing paperwork in the office. This was a part of a sizeable wooden hut with a window above the desk looking out on the airfield. The perimeter track was about 30 ft away. My attention was drawn to the 'plonk, plonk, plonk' that was unmistakably an American engine on slow running. Looking up, I saw a Hudson aircraft waiting for attention, so I shouted to the charge-hand Fitter Airframe to see what he wanted. He was soon back with the 'gen'.

The ATA pilot was on his way to deliver the aircraft to a depot to be refurbished but said one engine seemed to be rough

Lend/Lease Hudson, a common sight in Shropshire's MUs. (Lockheed)

and he would like someone to have a look at it. He would leave it with us and ring for a ferry aircraft to take him back to his base. We could let them know when it was ready. This seemed fine so he parked the Hudson outside the hut and left.

My charge-hand engine fitter said he would fix it but wanted it on a hard standing at the back of the crew rooms. So he asked one of the men, Greg, to get it there, which was no mean task as we had no ground-handling kit that would fit a Hudson. The tractor that we had that afternoon was a 'Case', a half-track with a small crane on the front driven on this particular day by 'Old Jess', a retired farmer who was directed to our unit to 'help the war effort'. It was agreed between them that Jess would pull gently with his tractor whilst Greg in the cockpit would steer by using the brakes and with the aid of lookouts to manoeuvre the aircraft between many others, could put the Hudson just where it was wanted. So as they hitched up and sailed off it was going to be just another one of those jobs.

Now at this stage I would like to point out that we had never seen a Hudson before this close and there is a difference between English brakes using air and American brakes using hydraulics. The English brakes have an air pressure gauge on the instrument panel to let you see how much pressure is in the system. However, they managed to get it safely on the hard standing and were putting it at the far end near a fence. Someone shouted 'Stop', which Jess did whilst Greg pulled on the parking brake handle, but nothing happened and the Hudson rolled slowly on. This aircraft had three-bladed propellers and the one nearest to the tractor had one blade pointing straight down. It was directly in line with the half-track and, being made of aluminium, was soft enough to bend. Sure enough, it went 'clack, clack, clack' along the track as it bent backwards. Nothing would now move and we did not have a means of jacking up a Hudson. However, a fitter named Bill said not to worry as he had been on a propeller course and he would fix it.

Jess was extremely worried when Bill told him to drive the tractor out and as it went 'clack, clack, clack' back along the track, the prop bent the other way. Bill, with help, managed to turn it till the bent blade was uppermost as nothing could be done till morning and perhaps no one would notice. Next morning, Bill was missing; he didn't clock in with the rest. Had he chickened out? However, after a while he appeared in the early morning mist, coming across the airfield from the headquarters site with something bulky under his arm. Not stopping at the office he went straight to the Hudson, taking advantage of the mist, to get his plan executed.

I was worried as if it went wrong it would have to be explained away by me, and that would not be easy. My fears grew as I heard loud banging coming through the mist from the direction of the Hudson. I hurried there and found Bill with a couple of engine fitters. One was holding a concrete block at the back of the prop blade while Bill was beating the daylights out of the blade with a lump hammer. He reassuringly said not to worry as he knew about these things!

As an older man, Bill was one of those people you could get advice from about everything. He was so convincing, particularly about marriage and women troubles. So as most of us were young without any experience, he was an asset. Later some of us lost confidence in him when his advice did not work out.

Regarding this blade. After hammering it for all his worth, he reached down into a sack and pulled out a carpenter's vice with large flat jaws and applied it to the prop blade which by now was looking less bent. As he tightened up the vice the blade very slowly bent back to more like its old shape, but a bit more pressure on the vice was required. Bill disappeared again only to return in moments with a short piece of scaffold pole. When fixed to the vice handle it would give untold pressure. The bent blade didn't have a chance; it had to go straight. A couple of strokes with a file got the notches out of the edges and it looked as good as it ever did. But was it in line with the other blades?

Bill knew about this! Off he went and turned up through the mist with a fitter's bench high enough to touch the bottom of the prop. Then, turning the prop, each blade was checked in turn and after checking the blade for cracks it was pronounced a good job. But what about at full throttle?

Bill's men had already taken out the spark-plugs on both engines and had them cleaned and tested at the workshop. As soon as they were refitted, Bill was at the controls shouting 'All clear' and the engines burst into life. Everyone stood well clear as Bill gave it the works. Power up to take-off revs, back and into coarse pitch, fine pitch again, full revs and then back enough to check for a 'mag drop'. Slow running to settle the temperatures down then cut off. Bill said, 'Nothing wrong with that' and went off to have his pipe of 'baccy' and cope with the next problem that would soon turn up.

The ATA pilot arrived and after his ground checks, took off on his delivery flight. Couple of days later he was in again and I asked, 'How was the Hudson?' His reply was, 'You made a good job of that, it was as sweet as a nut. Best Hudson I have flown.' So, for once at least, Bill did 'know about those things', but I think Lady Luck smiled on us that day. We all learnt something from this encounter: that with hydraulic brakes the accumulator has to have pressure kept in it by pumping on the hand pump. It's easy when you know how!

Almost the end

Another of our tasks was to prepare Hurricanes for the war in the Middle East. We fitted them up for various roles and on completion they were despatched to a packing unit at RAF

Sealand for onward delivery to the units they had been allotted to. We had finished several that had all been safely transferred so there was a panic to get the last one away. It was late arriving from Hawker Aircraft at Castle Bromwich but finally we did all the work we had to do for the role it was intended for and then it was test-flown. When the test flight was okay it was put up to the Air Ministry as ready for despatch.

The procedure was, we would get an allotment number and wait for the ATA pilot to arrange to fly it to its allotted destination. First thing in the morning we would prepare all the ones ready for despatch and usually give the engines a short ground run. By around 8 am the phone would start ringing with calls from the various ferry pilot bases to fix a time to pick up the aircraft.

Now the ATA were not allowed to fly if the visibility was below 1,000 yds as they flew visually, usually following roads or railway lines; not at all like all the radio gear we have today. So when I had a call about the Hurricane the chap on the other end said, 'What's the weather like there?' I told him we could not see the intersection of the runways and even the birds were walking so the Hurricane would have to wait till it cleared and when it did, I would ring them.

It was January/February time so the days were short and that sort of weather could hang about for days, which it did. Now I used to report to the test pilots' office after lunch to go through the planes we had for test and the ones that were coming up shortly. On this particular day I did this on the way back from the canteen and as the weather was still lousy, we sat and chatted about this and that when the door opened and the CO walked in. He told us that the Air Ministry had been on the phone about this Hurricane for Sealand and how the situation was now desperate as it was being transferred to the Middle East on the deck of a cargo ship in a convoy that was due to sail; and sail it would, with or without the Hurricane. We explained why the ATA would not take it and that the situation was you could not always see the end of the runway, which was the 1,000 yds required. He suggested we took it there ourselves and that it would be a 'feather in our caps' at the Air Ministry.

In the test pilots' hut, Pete, the younger of the two RAF pilots there that day, had just been promoted from Flight Sergeant to Flying Officer, so at the mess lunch-time there had been a 'few gills' downed which left him in a volunteering mood. Of course he could get the Hurricane to Sealand, but he did not want to be stuck there all night or to find his way back on the train.

We had just been allocated a Monospar aircraft for ferrying duties until such time as it was sent somewhere else. It was an ST-4 fitted with two five-cylinder Pobjoy radial engines and had five seats. Built in 1932, it was a bit worn, canvas covered with cracks that let the draught through, and had the big disadvantage of not having any starter motors, which meant swinging the metal props by hand. Not a very pleasant thing to do on a radial engine with five cylinders! It was a monoplane with a continuous spar that went right through from wingtip to wingtip and was the early forerunner to the single-wing aircraft.

Why do I mention this aircraft? Well, in reply to Pete not wanting to find his own way home, the CO suggested the other pilot, Fl Lt Peter Davies, should fetch him in the Monospar and to take Mr Harris with you in case you have to stop the engines as he is authorized to swing propellers. I rang my office and told them the score so by the time we arrived in the pilots' van, both aircraft were ready. The weather was terrible.

As I was turning over the props for starting I noticed Pete in the Hurricane taxiing out and off down the perimeter track. He soon disappeared in the murk as he 'backtracked' down the runway. Before we started the first engine there was the sound of a Merlin engine at full power as Pete appeared out of the mist only to be swallowed up by it before he crossed the boundary of the airfield.

Having done our ground tests we were off taxiing away out to the take-off point. Turning into wind the full situation dawned on us. We could see very little except a short bit of runway ahead but as Fl Lt Davies said, 'We had better try'. He was in the RAF before the war started and had been shot down in the Battle of Britain, so he knew all about trying. He had been badly burnt before he could get out of his blazing aircraft and, still showing the signs of the fire on his face and hands, he had come to our airfield as test pilot to fully recover.

We were soon off the ground and found that above a hundred feet we could not see the ground, so there was nothing for it but to stick down low and head out to the left of Shawbury till we found the Shrewsbury-to-Chester railway line. There was no radio equipment in the aircraft so it was all visual flying, that is, if you could see anything through the mist. Also the hours of daylight were fast running out.

We found the railway line and headed north towards Chester, where it was clearer in some places but not good at all. Sticking to the railway we caught up with a goods train and I can still see the look on the stoker's face as he turned to get a shovel of coal just as we arrived over the tender! I wonder what he told his family when he got home that night? We were now watching for the line that turned off to the left as that was the line to follow. This ran up the coast to North Wales and passed Sealand on the way. We were keeping our eyes peeled for two tall industrial chimneys as the airfield was close to them and having located them, we made a run in. The landing was okay and we taxied up to the reception office where Pete, with a big smile, stood waiting. He jumped up on the wing as I opened the door and said, 'Come on Jim, in the back. I am flying this thing back.' As he buckled up he shouted, 'I have got my map all ready and we are going home as the crow flies using the compass.'

Pete was still in high spirits as we took off; he didn't seem to worry when I told him we had not checked the compass since we received the plane. On an ordinary day it would not have mattered as High Ercall was on the flat Shropshire plain with the Wrekin sticking up about 1,000 ft and visible for miles. The airfield was about ten miles from it. But this was not an ordinary day and when Pete's watch showed we should be there we could not see anything except murky fog, and it was now around 3.30 pm and getting darker by the minute. Pete's high spirits suddenly disappeared!

We knew we were in the area we wanted to be and we did know the Wrekin was about 900 ft above us and any minute we could be hitting it, but that's about all we knew. I realised that below us was the town of Wellington where my wife and baby son were and how she didn't like me flying; and I could understand the reason why, now I was in this situation. I prayed we would not by chance hit the electric pylons that went near the bottom of our garden and crash into our house. Pete constantly turned the Monospar around but in all directions the situation was the same. 'Well,' he said, 'all eyes looking out as the only thing I can do is to slowly come down.' My heart was in my mouth and my eyes glued to the window. I could see the other two did not look very happy as by now there was nothing on the altimeter except the maker's name.

Suddenly we skimmed the buildings of a railway halt

fortunately going the same way as the lines and I shouted 'Admaston' as I recognised it, on the outskirts of Wellington. 'Keep on this line till we get to the Creamery at Grudgington, then turn sharp left and the OTU gate is just up the road.' We all knew where we were now and as long as Pete stayed low enough to see the ground we would be okay. We went over the gate at the OTU entrance at about 40 ft, skirted round the hangar and as soon as Pete saw grass he put it down. We were just by the control tower so we walked in and rang up for the pilots' van to pick us up and my moving gang to come and move the Monospar back to the hangar on No 2 site.

To approach Admaston from the direction we did, we must have flown along the side of the Wrekin and the Ercall which is next to it. How close we were to them we will never know but we were all thankful to be alive and thought that someone up there was looking after us. I never told my wife how near I was to her that afternoon, but maybe one day I will.

6
PEPLOW
(CHILDS ERCALL)

Though many miles from the nearest coastline, Shropshire at one time had two major naval bases within its boundaries. One was Peplow, lying just south of Childs Ercall, the other was the former Satellite Landing Ground (SLG) at Hinstock. Peplow only came to be a naval shore base at the latter end of the war but had previously served as a major RAF OTU base. In 1942, it was also known variously as Childs Ercall and Eaton-upon-Tern; confusing to say the least!

Originally a small grass airfield, it was developed after 1941 into a major bomber base, with one difference: it had the normal bomber airfield layout of three runways but with a central runway intersection; not ideal when the normal configuration was an equilateral triangle to minimize the possibility of a crash or a bomb shutting the entire airfield. The main runway 04/22 was 6,000 ft long whilst runways 13/20 and 18/36 were both 4,200 ft long. Each was 150 ft wide. Whatever name it was called and whatever role it played, this became one of the largest of the Shropshire airfields.

In early 1941 what was then known as Childs Ercall was deemed a grass-covered Relief Landing Ground (RLG) for nearby Tern Hill. It was used occasionally by the Miles Masters of No 5 Flying Training School and by the Airspeed Oxfords of No 11 Service Flying Training School. It was soon, however, found to be unsuitable for the Oxfords due to their weight and size.

With the need for more bomber crews, a decision was taken to enlarge Childs Ercall to the standard bomber airfield pattern of the time. Work commenced on the upgrade in late 1942, and it involved the requisition of much more land, a fact that the local landowners objected strongly to. These difficulties were quickly overcome and work was allowed to proceed. It involved the erection of five T2 hangars, an instructional area and a technical area.

One building of particular interest contained what is considered to be the forerunner of today's flight simulators, a gunnery and bomb-aiming trainer called the Bombing Tutor Building. This was housed in a specially designed unit and contained several projectors, one of which would project targets onto a white background whilst the other gave a shaft of light with which the trainee would attempt to pinpoint a particular target. When you pressed the 'tit' your imaginary bomb registered on film and any hits were recorded and analysed to give an indication of an air gunner's or bomb-aimer's accuracy. Whilst earlier models were housed in concrete structures, later models were fitted inside Blister hangars as a cheaper and easier-to-erect option. It was the latter that many would-be air gunners were to train on at Childs Ercall.

By the spring of 1943, the airfield was nearing completion. It was destined to become the home of a bomber OTU, No 83, one of the later ones to be formed. The previous year had seen six new OTUs open as Bomber Command struggled to cope with the devastating losses of aircrew and aircraft. However, it was not only the losses that the Command was suffering from, but the fact that many bombs were not hitting their intended targets. Thus an air of apathy had set in among many crews. All of this was to change when the then Commander-in-Chief of Bomber Command, Air Chief Marshal Sir Richard Peirse, made way for his successor, Air Marshal Sir Arthur Harris. He was ably supported by his deputy, Air Vice-Marshal Robert Saundby, and together they were to lay the foundations for the future conduct of a bombing campaign that would gradually do much to bring an end to the war. No 83 OTU was formed at a time when these important changes were taking place.

The OTU was equipped with the Vickers Wellington, a twin-engined bomber affectionately known as the 'Wimpey'. It incorporated the geodetic method of construction designed by Barnes Wallis. This gave it the strength to take a good deal of punishment, as many Wellington aircrew will vouch. The aircraft could fairly claim to have been the backbone of Bomber Command's night raids over Germany in the opening phases of the war. Now, earlier marks were to earn their reputation all over again with the OTUs.

With the official opening of Childs Ercall on 15th July 1943, the advance party arrived to find that it had been decided to use the

A scene all too familiar at the OTUs. A Wellington somewhat in distress. (Imperial War Museum)

OTU at three-quarter strength only. This was due to the fact that no satellite airfield had been allocated, and to have used the airfield to its full capacity without a satellite would have been dangerous due to overcrowding. At the same time it had been decided to change the name of the station to Peplow, in order to avoid any possible confusion with nearby High Ercall.

Shortly after the arrival of the groundcrews, the Wellingtons were flown in by female pilots of the ATA. Coded FI, GZ and MZ, the aircraft were a mixture of Mk IIIs and Mk Xs. In addition, the OTU was to get a Hurricane IIc for fighter affiliation flights and also an Airspeed Oxford for communications and 'taildragger' experience. Peplow now became a station within 93 Group with headquarters at Lichfield in Staffordshire and Egginton Hall in Derbyshire.

The next few weeks saw the arrival of further groundcrews and aircrews. It was at the OTUs that the latter were brought together. There was no prior selection of a crew before their arrival, it being felt that like-minded souls would bond together naturally if left to sort themselves out. Thus upon arrival at Peplow pilots, navigators, air gunners, radio operators etc would all gather in a large hangar and by talking to each other the selection of an entire crew would take place. Only then, when the six men had 'gelled', would the coveted small triangular piece of white linen be issued to slip into the front of their side-caps, signifying aircrew under training.

Then began a series of classroom lectures, both as a crew and in their own individual trades, which went on for about six weeks. This included air force law, drill, navigation, Morse code etc, and only then were the trainees allowed near a Wellington. For the air gunner there was additional training in the teaching dome previously mentioned. There were also ground-rig training turrets which twirled, twisted and cavorted all over the place until the poor trainee became dizzy. The fuselages of crashed aircraft were brought back into use with the pilot sitting in his place and the rest of his crew getting used to their stations. To simulate crashing into the sea there was a damaged Wellington up on blocks from which the aircrews practised getting out and onto the floor of the hangar (which represented the sea) and then into a dinghy within a time limit. The rear gunner often had a difficult time getting out and you would hear the instructor saying, 'Sorry, you didn't make it. You are sunk. Try again.' It was all part of the crew 'gelling' process.

And so the day of actually flying together as a crew approached. In the Flight Office the men were handed their flying clothes: fur-lined boots, flying overalls, sheepskin/leather jackets and gloves. Finally they would appear, looking like Michelin men!

An account of a first flight in a Wellington of an OTU is vividly recorded in *Gunner's Moon* by John Bushby (Futura Publications, 1972):

> It transpired that we would all fly in the same aircraft. In my case being an air gunner we would take turns at firing from the front turret at a sleeve target towed alongside by a Lysander aircraft. The only factor not taken into account was the age of the motley collection of Wellingtons possessed by the school. Once aboard we were seated in a row along a bench clamped to the fuselage side. We all gripped tight as the Wellington lumbered across the airfield, gathered speed, and with that solemn wing-flapping characteristic of the breed on take-off, became airborne. From where we sat there was only one small porthole opposite and through it nothing but a lot of soggy-looking grey cloud. Presumably the pilot knew where he was going. We certainly didn't! This was how we spent our time at OTU, alternating between warm mornings in a stuffy classroom and exciting spells in a Wellington pounding the beat up and down the Lincolnshire coast with always the grey, windswept chops of the North Sea beneath. This was our time at OTU.

For the pilots, it would be the first time that they were to fly an operational aircraft. Having learnt their craft on single-engined aircraft such as the Tiger Moth or Magister or twin-engined aircraft such as the Oxford or Anson, it was now time to move on to the heavy bombers. The course for pilots was very concentrated with both day- and night-flying. At Peplow it consisted of two hours' ground school per day covering aircraft type, engines, dinghy drill, hydraulics, meteorology, navigation, astro-navigation (by the stars), bombing techniques, high and low flying and much more. Initially the flying would be done by the instructor pilot, but once the trainee had got used to the Wellington, he could then occupy the left-hand seat while the instructor sat in the right-hand seat watching the trainee's every movement. Once that hurdle was passed, the entire crew went solo. Life at an OTU could never be called easy.

It was not only potential aircrew and groundcrew that arrived at Peplow in 1943. The coming of the WAAFs was a very welcome sight for them and for the workmen remaining.

First flight. Most pupils took a Tiger Moth flight initially. (Aeroplane)

One of the first girls to arrive was Rita Lovett, as she recalled in a wartime memories project:

In the spring of 1943 I was one of the first contingent of WAAFs to be posted to Peplow. As we were driven into camp we were greeted by cheers from the airmen and workmen on site. We lived, 24 in each, in Nissen huts. We each had a bedspace consisting of a cupboard, a shelf, a hanging rail and an iron bed. The bed had three 'biscuits' which, put together, served as a mattress, plus two or three blankets, two sheets and a hard bolster-shaped pillow. These had to be stacked at the top end of the bed each morning and then laid out again at night. The hut was heated by a central coke-burning stove; the fuel ration was meagre and I can remember collecting cinders from the cinder paths on the site to eke things out. The ablutions were a little way from our hut and consisted of rows of wash-basins and a few baths. You usually had to queue up for a bath and on nights when there was a camp dance you considered yourself lucky if there were no more than four girls in front of you.

We had to be in by 10 pm each night unless on a late pass to 11.59 pm. Monday was domestic night when we had to stay in and do our chores, mending, polishing buttons and shoes etc. WAAF drivers were not supposed to drive lorries over 30 cwt but some of us took tests to enable us to drive bigger vehicles up to three tons. We took it in turns to do night or day shifts, mostly driving the crew-coach. This involved taking aircrews out to dispersals and picking them up when they landed. The station being an OTU meant they were mostly training flights, but before passing out most crews had to fly an operational flight. The crews would be formed at the OTU and would remain together when on their next training station, which would convert them from Peplow's Wellingtons to whatever they were to fly operationally. The first crews I met were British but later intakes were Canadian. The instructors were 'screened', which meant they had completed one or two tours (30 raids per tour) and were being rested from operations. There were accidents of course, where inexperienced pilots and crew were killed or injured crashing into the Welsh hills etc. It was all very sad.

By the spring of 1943 No 83 OTU was fully functional. Week after week, new trainees arrived as the pressure on Bomber Command for aircrew at this time became crucial. One trainee pilot was the then unknown actor, Michael Rennie. He arrived at Peplow in late 1943 to begin operational pilot training. Unfortunately, halfway through the course he found he was not happy about moving on to an operational squadron. This plus continual airsickness made the task even harder for him. In the end he asked to be remustered and was taken off any further aircrew training.

The bad winter of 1942/43 delayed much of the training as snow lay thick all over the county. It was to be late spring before Peplow once again became fully operational, but with increased flying came the inevitable accidents. In comparison with many other OTUs however, No 83 did not suffer as much, but an accident on 22nd September 1943 brought the reality of war very close to home.

Wellington X LN530 was scheduled for a mid-morning exercise. The groundcrew had been busy since early morning refuelling and checking the systems and by 09.30 hrs the aircraft was deemed ready to fly. With the crew briefing over, Sgt D.L. Spence, together with PO A.M. McBride and the rest of the crew boarded the truck to take them to the dispersal where the aircraft and groundcrew were waiting. Clambering aboard, the pilot started the engines and waved 'chocks away'. Moving slowly to the taxi area, the crew carried out the all-important cockpit checks. Finding that everything appeared correct, Sgt Spence called the tower on the radio who told him to line up and take off. With both engines running well, LN530 got airborne and with wheels up, the crew settled down to concentrate on the flight.

Sadly, fifteen minutes later the starboard engine failed and with very little height from which to bale out, PO McBride warned the crew to stand by for a crash-landing. At approximately 10.30 am the Wellington crashed near Ellerton Hall, Sambrook, some sixteen miles north-east of Shrewsbury, killing Sgt Spence and PO McBride. The other three crewmen suffered injuries but were able to resume duties some months later. Eyewitnesses at the time said that the pilot seemed to lose control as he tried to avoid flying into trees. At Peplow, as news of the crash filtered through, many personnel were saddened by this, the first fatal crash at No 83 OTU.

Training continued throughout 1943, the year that the OTUs, 22 in number, reached their peak strength. Along with the usual cross-country flying training came the occasional operation over enemy territory. Since 1942 the OTUs had been contributing crews to main force raids, with more instructors than pupils providing the crews. Some sorties, mainly over Northern France, were undertaken by pupil crews for the purpose of dropping leaflets. These 'Nickel' operations were excellent for giving operational experience.

The first of these operations took place on the night of 17th/18th October 1943. Classed as 'minor operations', the night also saw eight Mosquitos bomb Berlin, with 54 Stirlings and Wellingtons mine-laying in the Friesians and off the Biscay ports. Sixteen OTU sorties were also carried out including the leaflet-drop by No 83 OTU. Despite a light cloud covering they found the designated target and all eleven aircraft returned safely to Peplow.

A visit by the AOC Air Commodore A.F. Ritchie, AFC, boosted morale and confidence within the OTU when he emphasised what a difference the number of aircrew passing through were making to the war. This in addition to the fact that Peplow had won first place in the Group dining hall competition! A tribute to the cooks and mess staff. Three days later, No 83 was again engaged on 'Nickel' operations when three Wellingtons were despatched to the Lille area. Although searchlights and flak were a problem, all the aircraft returned safely with the crews enjoying a well-earned bacon and egg breakfast, the tradition for all returning aircrew. Further 'Nickel' sorties took place on the night of 13th/14th December with no losses.

As the end of the year approached, No 83 OTU could look back with satisfaction on a job being well done. Bomber Command had come full circle and was now turning the tide of the war. Nightly raids by Stirlings, Lancasters, Halifaxes and Wellingtons, together with Whitleys, Hampdens and Manchesters earlier in the conflict, had resulted in the morale of the German nation plummeting. This was the time when the infamous 'Battle of Berlin' was at its height and some OTUs were joining the main bomber forces.

Two days before Christmas 1943 a further two 'Nickel' sorties were carried out. This time the flak was very heavy resulting in one Wellington X being severely damaged. Flak had apparently hit the flaps on the trailing-edge of the wings and without these the aircraft became difficult to handle. Back at Peplow, forewarned, the emergency fire and ambulance crews waited for the Wellington to appear. As its engines were heard, they moved into position alongside the runway. In the aircraft the pilot called for 'wheels down' as the airfield came into sight. He managed to lose height by manipulating the engines, then touched down safely and ran the full length of the runway before stopping. No injuries were sustained and the aircraft was deemed repairable.

Further indications of victory were apparent in January 1944 with the surprise American landings at Anzio. It was also announced that Bomber Command's onslaught against Berlin which had begun in November 1943, was continuing with the biggest bomb-load ever dropped on the German capital. In just over half an hour, 600 Lancasters and Halifaxes dropped more than 2,300 tons of bombs, starting at least 30 big fires.

The new year carried on much the same. Being such a large base in area, personnel were arriving at and leaving Peplow all the time to undertake different duties. For some, Peplow was to be their first posting and their first taste of Service life, as was the case for Sid Willis of Dunstable:

> I arrived at RAF Peplow by train in the spring of 1944 straight from an electricians' course at RAF Credenhill. The first thing I was issued with was a 'sit up and beg' bicycle. I was billeted in a Nissen hut on a site with no hot water; this meant you carried your toilet gear together with your knife, fork and spoon plus mug in a side pack with you everywhere. The only hot water available was in a wash house behind the cook house; you washed there before breakfast and in the evening after coming from dispersal. To reach the dispersal site near the village of

Childs Ercall we used our RAF bikes. One chap, an instrument fitter, could not ride a bike so must have walked miles unless he was lucky enough to get a lift.

The electricians had half a Nissen hut and the instrument fitters the other half. I was matey with Charlie Davis who came from Birmingham. He had his own bike and every week, on his day off, he would cycle to Birmingham to see his wife. One day he was refilling the oxygen bottles on the Wellingtons. There was a fitting on the outside of the aircraft which was connected to cylinders on a trailer drawn by a tractor. Whilst still connected to the aircraft, the NAAFI tea wagon arrived and Charlie, not wanting to miss it, jumped on the tractor and started to move off at a rate of knots until a severe jolt reminded him that he had an aircraft in tow.

One day a Warrant Officer pilot came to dispersal asking if anyone lived in London. He was taking his Wellington to RAF Wing near Leighton Buzzard; from there you could catch a train and be in London in two hours. I called out to a mate, 'Grab your bag, we are going home.' He didn't know what had hit him as we ran to the plane which was revving up and climbed the ladder in the nose. We pulled the ladder up, shut the door and were told to stand in the middle of the plane by the astrodome and away we went. When we landed we asked the pilot to sign our passes as we had left Peplow without anyone knowing.

Eventually, after avoiding awkward questions from officers as to who we were, the pilot told them that our names and numbers had been taken by the duty officer at Peplow, which of course they hadn't. In the end, bull baffled brains and an officer signed our passes. We were still in our working uniform, oil-stained, black plastic buttons and badges and Wellington boots, so we had a wash and shave in the wash-house then washed our boots and pulled our trousers over them. We had a good time in London and on arriving back at Peplow our Corporal reprimanded us for leaving without permission, as he had wasted time asking where Willis and Banner were only to be told eventually that we had gone off in a Wellington! Life at the OTU was not that bad.

Additional duties for No 83 OTU at this time came in the form of Air/Sea Rescue work. This was invaluable to trainee crews as it was often their first time flying over water. Some were successful in finding a ditched crew, some were not, as was the case on 13th January 1944.

The day previous had seen the Eighth Air Force despatch 291 B-17s to Oschersleben and Halberstadt. One hour into the flight the formation was 'jumped' by a large number of German fighters. Nevertheless the sortie continued and reached the target, which was successfully bombed despite thirteen aircraft being lost in the attack. As the rest turned for home several of the bombers came down in the North Sea due to attack damage. No 83 OTU sent four Wellingtons to look for the crews the next day, but the bad weather meant there was no hope of locating them. Reluctantly the four aircraft returned to Peplow, their crews saddened that they had not found their American comrades.

February 1944 saw 38 Wellingtons and four Miles Martinets on strength. The latter had replaced the Lysanders that had previously been with the OTU. The Martinet was the first aircraft to enter service with the RAF which had been designed specifically as a target-tug. A wind-driven or motorised winch was installed in the back of the aircraft to allow six flag and sleeve drogue targets to be carried, more than the previous types of aircraft used for target practice.

Further casualties were sustained on the night of 3rd/4th March 1944. Wellington X LN164 flown by Flt Sgt J. Graham took off from Peplow at 02.27 hrs for a night-training exercise. Whilst climbing away, the port engine failed, leaving the pilot no choice but to attempt a circuit and land. Turning downwind he managed to keep control but whilst landing on the crosswind leg, the Wellington veered through 180 degrees and crashed. The five crew members sustained injuries in what could have been a fatal crash.

A further loss of a Wellington, with one fatality, came shortly afterwards when Wellington X LP568 took off from Peplow at 15.00 hrs with a crew of eight to practice cine-camera gun and evasive flying tactics. Around 30 minutes later, whilst engaged in a severe manoeuvre, the starboard engine failed and Sgt W. T. Cake attempted a crash-landing on Sydall Farm, three miles south of Market Drayton. Unfortunately in doing so he clipped some trees, which caused the aircraft to land heavier than intended. Sgt A.O. Wedin, RCAF, sadly died, and Sgt N.L. Pegg, RCAF, was injured. The rest of the crew survived.

One of the more devastating losses occurred on the night of 19th/20th May. Wellington III BK463 was scheduled for a 'Nickel' drop over France. The crew, FO W.E. Hemingway, FO W. Norman,

Aircrew based at RAF Peplow 1944/45 pictured outside the Sutherland Arms, Tibberton. Third from the left is Flt Lt R. Hooper and third from the right is WO Wally Young. (Ruth Newby)

FO H.E. Dinnage, Fl Sgt W.S. Creber (RAAF), Fl Sgt H.J.W. Stevens, FO R.S. Knapp (RCAF) and Sgt G.D. Cossins had flown together on training exercises for some weeks. Taking off before midnight, the aircraft carried over 4,000 leaflets to drop over Northern France. Whether the drop was carried out is not recorded as for some reason the aircraft crashed at Eps in the Pas-de-Calais, killing the entire crew. All seven are buried in the local war cemetery.

As D-Day approached, bombing of the Northern French coast intensified. Two days before the landings, the RAF dropped 8,000 tons of bombs on German coastal positions centred on Boulogne. 'Nickel' operations also increased with the leaflets suggesting that the Germans should lay down their arms and surrender.

At Peplow a huge security cordon was in place and all 'Nickel' flights and training were suspended for 24 hours. The reason, although guessed by many, soon became obvious as news of the Allied invasion was broadcast over the station tannoy system. Between midnight and dawn on 6th June, troops landed by parachute or glider at key points behind enemy lines. At sea a force of several thousand ships, brought together from widely scattered ports, converged on the invasion coast soon after 5 am. That night Mr Churchill was able to tell MPs that the operation was 'progressing in a thoroughly satisfactory manner. Many dangers and difficulties which appeared extremely formidable are now behind us'.

At this time the mainstay of the bomber OTUs was still the Wellington. Whilst No 83 had always been equipped with the type, some had to labour on with the venerable but very old Whitley. Now, with Bomber Command using only four-engined 'heavies' to bomb enemy cities, Wellingtons were re-equipping all OTUs. In respect of accidents, No 83 OTU fared far better than most. What accidents they did have, however, affected the entire station.

One, in particular, was mourned by everyone. It happened on the night of 23rd July when Wellington X LP567 took off at 23.30 hrs for a night-navigation sortie. With an all-Canadian crew of Sgt L.R. Carter, FO W.D. Watson, Sgt W.L. Blunt, Sgt G.H. Van-Every, Sgt R.A. Johnson and Sgt L.K. Beattie, the Wellington lost radio contact halfway through the sortie and was seen to crash into the sea off the Welsh coast. Five of the crew were laid to rest in Chester Cemetery while Sgt Johnson is remembered on the Runnymede Memorial.

While usually it was the Wellingtons that crashed, occasionally it was the fighter aircraft attached to the OTU for affiliation purposes. Such was the case of Hurricane IIc PG536 which crashed on 27th July 1944. Piloted by FO H. Morrison, it left Peplow at 11.35 hrs for a training flight. One hour later, whilst flying through cloud, it collided with No 41 OTU Hurricane IIc (LF327), piloted by FO W.H. Skelton, RCAF. Both fighters plummeted to the ground at Peplow Grange. The crash was heard at the station but by the time the rescue services were on the scene, nothing could be done to save the pilots. With wreckage strewn around the entire area, it took many hours for the fire to cool down to enable the recovery crews to remove the remains of both pilots and aircraft.

One month later Wellington X JA453 was lost on a night-navigation training sortie which killed three crew and injured a further three. Flown by PO E. Hartstein, the aircraft left Peplow at 20.36 hrs. For several hours the flight went well but at 23.20 hrs the starboard engine lost power. Struggling to keep the aircraft airborne, PO Hartstein warned his crew to prepare for a crash-landing. While desperately looking for a level area of ground on which to attempt this, the aircraft suddenly dived into the ground near Aberporth airfield in Cardiganshire. Three of the crew, PO Hartstein, Sgt F.E. Simons and Sgt R. Lindahl, Royal Norwegian Air Force, were killed, with severe injuries to Sgt D.H. Skelton, RCAF, and two other crew members.

The rapid advance of the Allies after the Normandy breakout saw both the Americans and British push ahead, with Paris being liberated by the French Second Armoured Division under General Leclerc on 25th August. The news was received with great elation at Peplow but sadly an incident on the night of 25th/26th August marred much of the jubilation and celebrations.

Two Wellington Xs of No 83 OTU, HF517 and MF589, were tasked to carry out a diversionary exercise. With take-off scheduled for 01.00 hrs, both crews had eaten supper and boarded their aircraft, joking as to who would be the best crew of the night, with HF517 having an English and Dutch crew and MF589 being all-Canadian. The crew of HF517 were FO E.F.K. Michielson, PO R.S. Junor, PO J.G. Sutherin, Sgt J.E. Clarke, Sgt J. Butterfield and Sgt G.I. Callow, whilst in MF589 were FO E.O. Smith, FO V.H. Bolton, FO N.E. Cousins, Sgt J.J. Poston, Sgt J.C. McMurtrie and Sgt R.J. Sander.

The two aircraft took off and were airborne one minute apart to practise a night exercise termed a 'Bullseye'. This involved a cross-country flight incorporating several different turning points that could be situated anywhere in Britain and was meant to give trainee crews experience that would bind them together into a cohesive unit. Along the route they would probably make a dummy bombing attack on a specified town. At 01.25 hrs on the 26th these two aircraft collided over Prestwood and fell as burning wrecks into the village. Of the twelve crew members, eleven were killed, and the survivor, PO Junor, was found wandering in a dazed condition in Lodge Wood. In the official report following the collision the crash was blamed on 'Failure by both crews to keep an adequate lookout'. The aircraft fell near some cottages and the residents, Mr and Mrs Holt, received severe burns whilst running across a newly tarred road ablaze with aviation fuel. Some weeks later a memorial service was held at Peplow to mark the tragic death of so many crew members.

Whilst D-Day was a success, an Allied invasion over two days in September, the 18th and 19th, was not. Codenamed Operation 'Market Garden', it was an audacious airborne operation that promised to shorten the war by several months. It took place over a small Dutch town called Arnhem. On the night of the 17th, 1,000 troop-carriers and about 500 gliders protected by 1,240 fighters dropped nearly three divisions along the line Eindhoven-Nijmegen-Arnhem. The Allied planners and intelligence services, however, had underestimated the strength of the Germans in the area. The execution of the operation was therefore compromised, not only by faulty intelligence but also bad weather. Sadly the ground forces failed to break through to Arnhem and thus open the 'back door' into Germany. In the attempt, hundreds lost their lives for so little.

During the operation many gliders and their pilots were lost, necessitating the hurried introduction of a programme of glider pilot training. With the war going so well and Bomber Command taking control of the skies above Germany, 28th October 1944 saw the sudden closure of No 83 OTU. Peplow now became the home of No 23 Heavy Glider Conversion Unit as the Wellingtons and most personnel of the OTU moved to other bases. In their place came the Armstrong Whitworth Albemarle, a twin-engined reconnaissance bomber that had been relegated to target and glider towing. Several Horsa gliders also arrived as Peplow entered a new phase in its existence, as WAAF LACW Jean 'Blondie' Smith recalled:

In 1943 I was posted to Peplow as a flight mechanic along with several other WAAFs. We assembled in a hangar for roll-call with a row of airmen behind us. Standing directly behind me was my future husband, Corporal Jim Renshaw. It wasn't long before he was getting to know me better by climbing up beside me as I worked on the engine of a Wellington. In summer when

WAAF LACW Jean 'Blondie' Renshaw (née Smith), Peplow. (Ruth Newby)

RAF Corporal James Renshaw, Fitter IIA, Peplow. (Ruth Newby)

there was a lot of flying, we all had to work late. In the winter, when there was snow, we swept out the hangars then cleared the runways of snow and were rewarded with a rum ration after. In late 1944 we had the task of towing the gliders out with the tractor. Joan Biggs was a flight mechanic in the same hut as me together with Agnes Mulholland, Rusty Thomas, Molly McGeachie, Betty Snee, Sheila Smith and many others.

As we were the first female flight mechanics on the airfield we were mistrusted at first by the men, but after a few weeks it was realised that our small hands could reach the 'fiddly bits' and we were allowed to get on with the job. There were seven men and two WAAFs per gang. We were issued with bicycles for easy access to the hangars which were spread over a large area. We serviced the Albermarles which towed the Horsa gliders; and also the Wellingtons, lovely to work on and repair. We often got the chance to have a test flight once the aircraft had been serviced or repaired, not very high though as they didn't have parachutes. I remember the hangars were very cold with the only relief coming from the NAAFI mobile canteen which sold us mugs of hot tea.

For the first time the khaki of Army uniform intermingled with RAF blue at Peplow. This was because initially the glider pilots were drawn from the Glider Pilot Regiment of the British Army. However, shortly after the ill-fated Arnhem operation, RAF pilots also flew gliders. By October, twenty glider instructors had arrived with RAF pilots for the tug aircraft. Training, including night-flights, began immediately with a steady flow of new personnel arriving all the time. One man recruited for glider training was Peter Winters:

I qualified for my pilot's wings in September 1944 after completing training in America under the supervision of the United States Navy. It was customary for pilots with flying-boat experience such as myself to undergo a general reconnaissance course before joining Coastal Command. When I arrived back in the UK just before my 21st birthday in October, I was sent to the aircrew reception centre in Harrowgate where a week or so later I was astonished to learn that I was to fly gliders. The airborne operation at Arnhem had been a disaster and the Glider Pilot Regiment was short of pilots. There was insufficient time to train others and an immediate solution to the problem was to make use of the reserve of RAF pilots.

An appeal for volunteers to fly 'motorless aircraft', using the official designation, met with little response and so a directive followed. After creaming off the university entrants, who always seemed to enjoy special consideration, the RAF diverted many pilots to gliders. On 30th November 1944 I arrived at Bridgnorth railway station in the pouring rain and after an hour's waiting on the platform, a Midland Red bus transported some 40 pilots, officers and NCOs up the Hermitage and along to Stanmore.

Here we were told that as glider pilots, we would most likely land behind enemy lines and be expected to defend ourselves. A two-week programme had been devised to include instruction in the use of small arms, Bren and Sten guns, rifles and hand grenades, basic infantry training exercises and field craft coupled with a get fit quick routine which excluded the usual home comforts. I do not think many others on the station knew why we were actually there. An air of secrecy prevailed and keeping to ourselves, we created a very sinister presence. Who were these pilots armed with rifles and what were they doing running around the camp at all hours? The rumours began to circulate. No doubt there were sighs of relief when we left to familiarise ourselves with flying the small Hotspur glider, but in early January 1945 I returned to Shropshire to the Heavy Glider Conversion and Operational Training Unit at RAF Peplow where Horsa and Hadrian gliders were towed by twin-engined Albermarle aircraft.

The training operations we carried out were named 'Balbos' after an Italian general who specialised in glider warfare. It was easier said than done even in ideal conditions. My first Balbo was an absolute disaster. Of course the target area was Peplow airfield. Twenty-four Horsa gliders approached from the north and I was at the rear of the formation. A short distance from the airfield I remarked to my second pilot, 'If they don't let us off now we'll all overshoot.' Nothing happened and wasting no further time, I released from the tow rope, gained some forward speed and dived almost vertically towards the ground with full flap. After a reasonable landing, I chose to pull up halfway down the airfield. Some managed to land outside the perimeter fence and others disappeared over the Shropshire countryside. The Station Commander was not at all pleased and made it quite clear that he expected perfection. So for the next five days we practised from dawn to dusk and eventually became proficient.

By the end of November Peplow could boast of having 68 Albermarles together with 48 gliders, both Horsas and Hamilcars. Personnel strength stood at 128 officers, seven WAAF officers, 306 male NCOs, eight WAAF NCOs, 1,301 other male ranks and 312 WAAF other ranks. In order for Peplow to operate efficiently a satellite airfield was hurriedly brought into use at Seighford. Although the period of glider training was very brief, it was very intense. Mr A. Ward, one of the civilians employed at Peplow, was present during this period:

I worked as a civilian electrician at Eaton upon Tern's RAF Peplow. I was a member of a gang of electricians looking after the runway lights. We were mostly on call 24 hours, seven days a week and were responsible for changing the runway lights whilst crews were away flying. When the aircraft came in to land you had an optical illusion that they were coming straight at you till at the last moment they turned away. Another hair-raising job was climbing on top of the hangars to replace the red lamps; the roof used to creak and give as you walked across. All around the airfield there was overhead wiring to feed lights guiding the aircraft onto the runways. Once after a storm some wires dropped onto a barbed-wire fence and didn't blow the fuses but unfortunately electrocuted some cows.

Horsa and Hamilcar gliders were used for training. They landed full of troops who then attacked the firing range which was held by the RAF Regiment. One day we were amused to see the battle interrupted midway for tea and cakes! I can only remember one accident with the gliders. When landing they came in steeply then levelled off to break the speed but this one came in with a long glide, hitting the ground hard and breaking the wheels off. This turned the glider up into the air and it came back down and being wood, it crumpled up. It was full of men but luckily no one was really hurt. The breakdown men chopped it up with axes, loaded it onto a 'Queen Mary' lorry and took it to the dump at the far end of the airfield. It could be dangerous, too, when the gliders were flying. The planes that towed them up released the gliders, then were supposed to drop the tow ropes in a designated area, but a lot strayed.

Another time we were in the operations block putting fluorescent lights onto a solid concrete ceiling when they had a mock gas attack. We had not been warned about this and did not have our gas masks with us. It was a kind of tear gas and was a horrible experience.

The period of the glider school at Peplow was brief as it disbanded on 31st December 1944 and training was transferred to other airfields. The last glider operation was the Rhine crossing in early 1945 and from that time the Glider Regiment was gradually run-down. Peplow was relegated to satellite status and was used by the Airspeed Oxfords of No 21 (Pilots) Advanced Flying Unit ((P)AFU) between 26th January and the end of February 1945. The airfield, with very little flying, became the ideal place for experimental work. No 1515 Bean Approach Training (BAT) Flight moved in from Poulton on 30th January and commenced work on what was a fledgling blind approach aid, the predecessor of today's Instrument Landing System (ILS). Mr Ward once again recalls the period:

> There was a mobile unit at the end of the main runway which sent a signal up the centre of the runway; this guided the pilots in to land. At the other end of the runway there was an angle box on the ground with a green glass and a red glass with a little fan in it. This fan passed in front of the light to make it look as if it was flashing on and off. It could be seen from some distance and if the pilot could see the red part he was too low. It was a very modern system in those days.

It was not, however, all work and no play at this late stage. Victory in Europe came and was celebrated by a much-reduced personnel at Peplow. With the constraints of war now lifted the serious side of flying gave way to a little fun, as Mr Ward recalls:

> Now on a lighter note – I can remember an air display just after VE Day, the highlight of which was a Tiger Moth which was parked on the side of the runway. An old lady went over to it whilst a voice over the tannoy told her to keep away which she chose to ignore. She managed to get into the cockpit and after two attempts she took off and flew round rather precariously then made a horrible landing. The RAF police then went over to have words with her. 'She' then undressed to reveal it was one of the test pilots in drag.

Difficulties with a similar ILS experiment at nearby Hinstock,

Church of the Good Shepherd, Eaton upon Tern, built by the Heatley sisters in memory of their brother, John. It was opened in 1928/29 and used in the war years by RAF Peplow. A memorial window was dedicated to the RAF Peplow men who died in the conflict. The chapel was demolished in the 1970s. (Ruth Newby)

however, forced No 1515 BAT Flight to move and Peplow entered another role, that of a satellite to Hinstock. This was a naval air station which operated Airspeed Oxfords of No 758 Squadron, Fleet Air Arm. A naval advanced instrument flying school, in addition to the Oxfords the school also used Harvards, Ansons and Reliants. Peplow was used as a satellite from 28th February 1945 until No 758 Squadron disbanded on 14th May 1946.

This heralded the end of Peplow's war. It was placed under Care and Maintenance shortly thereafter, and finally closed at the end of 1949. Much of the land was returned to its owners although the runway was retained, part of which is still in use today for light aircraft. The site remained in good condition for many years, but sadly the tower was demolished some years back. The hangars, as usual, remain as sentinels of long ago and in the woods can be found evidence of wartime buildings. Many of the aircrew who trained at No 83 OTU went on to lose their lives in the darkness over the German-occupied countries but, as with many of the other Shropshire airfields, Peplow will always be remembered for a job well done.

7
REDNAL

In early 1942 the French aviation author, Pierre Clostermann, was on his way to No 61 OTU which had recently opened at Rednal airfield. His first impression of Rednal and the satellite at Montford Bridge, vividly recorded in his book *The Big Show* (Chatto and Windus, 1951), was of a heavy snowfall and appalling cold. The Nissen hut he and his fellow Frenchmen occupied had no insulation and keeping warm was a real problem. The two months spent at Rednal and later at the satellite did, however, train Closterman to fly Spitfires. Many others were to learn to fly at Rednal before its closure as the war ended.

Situated one and a half miles north-east of the A5 at West Felton, Rednal was one of the later Shropshire airfields to be built, finally opening in April 1942. Much farmland had to be compulsorily requisitioned, including Haughton Farm immediately to the south of the airfield. The owners had to sell most of their livestock as the dimensions of the new airfield swallowed up their land. The airfield perimeter track ran along the back of Haughton Farm with a fuel storage depot containing 3,000 gallons of 100% octane just a few yards from the farmhouse. Roger Hampson, whose father farmed the land, says they were so close to the airfield that the RAF gave them a specially reinforced steel kitchen table. The orders were that in the event of an emergency, the family were to hide under it!

The winter of 1941/42 was as harsh as the previous one and progress on building the new airfield was slow. With the snow and rain came the mud, and with the opening date set at April 1942 a lot of extra labour had to be drafted in from other counties as well as Ireland. By March, coiled barbed wire protected the perimeter and several brick-built pillboxes had been hastily built lest the new airfield came

Rednal control tower in its prime. Today it is used for paintballing.

under attack. Even though the Battle of Britain had been fought and won by Fighter Command, the Luftwaffe was now concentrating its attacks on major cities, many of which were close to Shropshire.

In the beginning it had been decided that Rednal was to be a parent station with a satellite station at Montford Bridge. For this role Rednal had a Type 518/40 control tower, this being one of the largest types of tower with a wooden first floor and balcony. Inside, several rooms were partitioned off to allow the installation of a meteorological office close to the main control room (most met offices were in a separate building).

Initially the only way to reach Rednal was by road, but this proved impractical when moving large numbers of airmen around. In order to improve travel to the camp, the RAF asked the Great Western Railway Company to run special trains each evening to Shrewsbury, in addition to a request that the Paddington/Birkenhead express stopped at Rednal!

By April 1942, No 61 OTU had moved in from Heston with Spitfires. Most of these were Battle of Britain veterans but to any would-be fighter pilot, they were still beautiful machines. For Pierre Clostermann and his comrade Jacques, they were everything they had dreamt of, as he described in *The Big Show*:

All my life I shall remember my first contact with a Spitfire. The one I was going to fly bore the markings TO-S. Before putting on my parachute I stopped a moment to gaze at it – the clean lines

Disguised pillbox in farm buildings near Rednal airfield in 2007. (Author)

of the fuselage, the beautifully streamlined Rolls-Royce engine, a real thoroughbred. 'You've got her for one hour. Good luck,' called my instructor. Carefully I went through the cockpit drill murmuring the ritual phrase, BTFCPPUR – brakes, trim, flaps, contacts, pressure (in the pneumatic system), petrol, undercarriage and radiator. Everything was all set. The mechanic closed the door behind me and there I was, imprisoned in this metal monster which I had to control. A last glance: 'All clear – contact.' I manipulated the hand pumps and the starter buttons. The airscrews began to revolve slowly and suddenly, with a noise like thunder, the engine fired. The exhausts vomited long blue flames enveloped in blue smoke while the aircraft began to shudder like a boiler under pressure.

When the chocks were removed I opened the radiator wide and I taxied very carefully over to the runway, cleared by snow-ploughs, jet black and dead straight in the white landscape. 'Tudor 26, you may scramble now, you may scramble now.' My heart was thumping in my ribs as I slowly opened the throttle. Timidly I eased the stick forward and with a jolt that glued me to the back of my seat, the Spitfire started forward then moved faster and faster while the airfield swept by on either side with increasing speed. Suddenly, holding my breath and as if by

A Spitfire and pilot of No 61 OTU. The fulfilment of a dream. (Imperial War Museum)

magic, I found myself airborne. I quickly raised the undercarriage, closed the transparent hood of my cockpit, throttled back and adjusted the airscrew pitch for cruising. At last I was in control of a Spitfire.

In the words of Pierre, they were 'two arduous months' at the OTU. The unit consisted of many nationalities who had come to Britain to continue the fight. Belgians, Czechs and Poles were all sent to Rednal to begin their operational training in the same manner as Pierre and his fellow Frenchmen.

As the OTU began its training routine, the inevitable accidents began to happen. While the Spitfires had many hours to their credit and were therefore prone to become non-operational at times, it was the weather and misfortune that caused many of the accidents. Such misfortune befell twenty-year-old Sgt Stanley Paul Lister.

Arriving at Tern Hill from his elementary flying school at Swiftcurrent in Saskatchewan, Canada in 1942, he continued his advanced flying with No 5 (P)AFU before moving over to Rednal and No 61 OTU. He only had to wait two days before his chance came to

'OK, son, she's all yours.' An instructor at No 61 OTU gives a trainee fighter pilot his chance to fly a Spitfire. (Imperial War Museum)

fly a Spitfire for the first time. On Tuesday, 8th September, after a briefing with his instructor, Sgt Lister sat in his aircraft, P7963, at the end of Runway 16 to continue his training. Given clearance to take off he applied full power and began his run down the runway. Those watching his take-off suddenly saw the Spitfire swing to the left. Attempting to correct this problem, Sgt Lister became airborne for a second but was unable to gain any height. Still with his undercarriage down, he struggled with the controls but it was obvious that the aircraft was out of control.

Suddenly, Haughton Farm loomed up as the Spitfire struck a farm building, losing one wing before crashing in the farmyard at 14.45 hrs. The accident had been seen from the control tower and the crash tender and ambulance were immediately sent to the scene. Although the Spitfire was full of fuel, it did not catch fire. Within minutes the rescue services arrived, including a team of medics who carefully removed the pilot from his broken cockpit. Sadly he did not survive for long for, despite the valiant efforts of the doctor, Sgt Lister died minutes later in a corner of the farmyard. He had become engaged less than a week before he lost his life. His body was taken back to his home town of Sandgate in Kent from where he was taken for burial in the military cemetery at Shorncliffe Army Camp near Folkestone. He was mourned not only by his fiancée and family but by many of his fellow

The resting place of Sgt Stanley Paul Lister, killed whilst training at Rednal. (Author)

trainee pilots at Rednal. He was buried in a private grave with a tombstone upon which was engraved: 'His heart for home – His life for country'. Today a plaque marks the crash site at Haughton Farm, placed there by Roger Hampson who, as a small boy, witnessed the crash. Rednal was mourning one of its own.

Just hours before Sgt Stanley Paul Lister crashed, a short distance away at RAF Upper Heyford Wellington Ic DV830 of No 16 Bomber OTU, carrying a crew of four, was about to get airborne, taking off for a combined bombing and navigation exercise at 11.00 hrs. One hour into the flight the port engine suddenly caught fire. The pilot, Sgt J.H. Hall struggled to keep his aircraft airborne whilst looking for a suitable place to land. Seeing Rednal in the distance, he attempted to make the airfield but, rapidly losing height, the Wellington hit a tree and crashed, coming to rest at 14.50 hrs in a ball of flame five miles east-southeast of Oswestry and sadly killing Sgt Hall and injuring the other three crewmen. Again the rescue services from Rednal were called to attend but even prompt action could not save the pilot.

Training continued throughout 1942 with the OTU being linked with a 'shadow' unit, No 561 Squadron. This was only one of several shadow squadrons, the reason being that in an emergency, the combined units could be turned into an operational unit.

A Spitfire II comes to grief at No 61 OTU, Rednal. (A. Thomas)

Christmas 1942 was celebrated in customary style with the officers serving the other ranks before retiring to their own mess. It was a subdued time and the break was short due to the squadrons requiring more fighter pilots to continue to take the war back to the enemy.

Rednal, being so far from the battle front, was spared major attacks, though the major industrial cities of the nearby Midlands were prime targets. Only occasionally did enemy aircraft stray into Shropshire airspace but in the period of heavy attacks on those cities the sounds of destruction could be heard plainly at Rednal. The only recorded incident regarding raiders affecting Rednal was on 27th June 1943 when Spitfires from the combined units of No 61 OTU and No 561 Squadron were scrambled to intercept a raider supposedly over the Irish Sea. They found nothing and all aircraft returned safely.

July saw a fighter hero arrive at Rednal. George F. 'Screwball' Beurling was a superb pilot who had become a legend on the island of Malta. He had applied to join the RCAF in 1940 but lacked the educational qualifications to enable him to be a pilot. He then worked his passage to Britain and joined the RAF where he was accepted for aircrew training. He was untidy, a nonconformist with a shock of hair and a sallow complexion. Although sometimes undisciplined, he passed his flying training with no problems and was soon in the thick of the fighting flying with No 249 (Gold Coast) Squadron. Re-equipping with Hurricane IIas in 1941, the squadron was sent to Malta

George F. 'Screwball' Beurling, Malta fighter ace, pictured far right-hand side, flew from Rednal. (Imperial War Museum)

where Beurling really excelled. He ended his tour on the island with 28 confirmed victories before being shot down and landing in the sea off Malta. Returning to Britain on 1st November 1942, the Liberator in which he was flying crashed into the sea off Gibraltar but Beurling managed to survive. After several months of recuperation, he was sent to No 61 OTU as an instructor in July 1943.

It is no secret that 'Screwball' Beurling hated Rednal and even more so because he was instructing and not operational. Despite several reprimands regarding his 'cowboy-style' flying, he continued to be the nonconformist even to the extent of flying a Spitfire while under the influence of alcohol. Though he flew it perfectly and made a textbook landing, this was too much for the Air Ministry and he was posted from Rednal and instructing in early August. Moving back to an operational squadron, he survived the war and was finally killed delivering an aircraft to Israel in 1948.

In his book *Malta Spitfire* (Greenhill Books, 2002), Beurling described his feelings on being sent to No 61 OTU: 'The instructors at the Operational Training Unit to which we reported for the final stage of pre-combat flying were an all-star aggregation, mostly members of the few to whom the many owe so much, the birds who flew the Battle of Britain. Topnotcher beyond question was Flt Lt Ginger Lacey, DFM and Bar, with 25 German aircraft destroyed to his credit as a Sergeant pilot from the big blitz and the pre-Dunkirk days across the Channel. Lacey was the lad who shot down the Heinkel which bombed Buckingham Palace and was himself shot down by the Jerry rear gunner. He baled out and landed in the grounds of the palace where he was kept for tea by the King and Queen. The others – Baroldi, Powling, Wade, the whole tribe – were out of the same RAF top drawer. Rednal was stiff with medals and if you had added up the sum total of Huns destroyed represented by the staff of the station, it would have run into hundreds.' Just one of the more flamboyant characters to have served at Rednal.

The effective strength of Fighter Command in 1943 was not as great as many supposed. The years before the war had seen an upsurge in fighter numbers but so many pilots had been lost in the Battle of Britain that by October 1940 the Command was grossly under strength. This had to be rectified, the only way being additional OTUs and also

The day begins. No 61 OTU Spitfire, Rednal. (A. Thomas)

Trainee fighter pilot ready to go, No 61 OTU, Rednal. (A. Thomas)

increasing the output of the units already in service. Rednal was one station that felt the increased pressure as the war was carried back to Germany. Although the dogfighting days of the battle were over, operational pilots were being lost in many other ways. Flying over enemy-occupied territory had many dangers and so further flying courses were crammed into the weeks and months.

The pilots that arrived at Rednal had already been through three main phases of training. First there was the ground-based instruction in classrooms. It was here they learnt RAF law, flying tactics, aircraft recognition and so on. Next came the basic flying training on aircraft such as the Tiger Moth or the Harvard. Many students at this stage were sent overseas to Canada, America or Rhodesia where they were safe from enemy attacks and the weather was conducive to flying.

Once they had completed flying training and got their wings, they would then continue flying at an OTU, either fighter or bomber. In the case of No 61 OTU, they would spend their first five weeks at Rednal before moving on to their final three weeks at the satellite at Montford Bridge. Now it was gunnery training, chasing an aged aircraft such as the Fairey Battle which was towing a drogue. This was the occasion when the pilots would be firing live rounds but at other times, an aircraft such as the Miles Master or even another Spitfire would be the target aircraft. In these instances, air-to-air firing would be done by the cine-camera gun. Any hits on the target were recorded on film. Even this had its dangers, as an incident on 18th July 1943 proved.

The morning dawned fine and warm with just a slight haze as an Australian pilot, Sgt J.A. Sharkey, was briefed to fly the target Spitfire for the day. Taking off from Rednal, he gained his operating height and awaited the arrival of Sgt Rinde, a Norwegian, who was to practise air-to-air firing. Noticing his approach, Sgt Sharkey began to fly in a weaving pattern when he suddenly realised that real live bullets were hitting his aircraft. Diving away and discontinuing the exercise, he landed safely only to discover several bullet holes around the cockpit area. With the arrival of Sgt Rinde back on the ground it was found that he had mistakenly pressed the gun button on his joystick and not the cine-camera gun button. It is not recorded just what conversation took place between the two pilots!

In another incident, a Belgian pilot lost his life on 22nd August 1943, just another training day for the pilots of No 61 OTU. (Two weeks before, the unit had witnessed the arrival of several new pilots including a large Belgian contingent.) It was around 16.35 hrs that PO Jean Noizet and his friend, PO Henri Maurice Goldsmit, got airborne in Spitfire IIs P7304 and P7444 respectively to practise dogfighting. This involved tail-chasing each other in an attempt to keep the other within their sights as well as flying head on and breaking to either port or starboard. Witnesses on the ground described the two aircraft hitting each other with the result that one, P7304, lost a wing. This caused his Spitfire to enter a steep dive while the Spitfire of Henri Goldsmit, although damaged, was controllable. With its engine screaming, PO Noizet's aircraft ploughed into some woods at Hincks Plantation near Lilleshall. In one terrific explosion the entire aircraft broke into pieces as the impact drove the Merlin engine into the ground, resulting in a large crater. For Jean Noizet, death was instantaneous.

As was the policy at this stage of the war, the RAF recovery team just cleared the surface wreckage, leaving what was buried deep in the ground. What was defined as the remains of the pilot were taken for a military funeral at Brookwood Military Cemetery in Surrey. Henri Goldsmit had managed to crash-land his Spitfire at Halfpenny Green airfield and although badly shaken, was not injured. He continued to fly but was killed whilst on an operation over Holland in November 1944.

The post-war period generated a new brand of archaeology, that of wartime aircraft recovery. All over the country groups of amateur archaeologists research, pin-point and excavate crash sites, both German and British. In Shropshire one such group was the Wartime Aircraft Recovery Group who began an excavation on the site where PO Noizet had crashed. Safe in the knowledge that he had been accorded a military funeral, it came as a shock when the group found what they suspected were human remains. Keeping to the law of the land, further excavation was stopped and the police and the RAF were informed. With the arrival of the local coroner, the remains were taken to RAF Shawbury where they were examined, eventually to reveal a complete skeleton minus a foot. With the body parts removed from the crash site, excavation was allowed to continue, eventually uncovering several personal effects including PO Noizet's ID card, pieces of a letter from a girlfriend and a shoe.

In the meantime, in 1948, the remains that were interred at Brookwood had been repatriated by the Belgian authorities to the military cemetery at Evere. It was thought that this was the end of the story but a chance article in a Belgian newspaper regarding the new excavation came to the attention of Paul Noizet, the brother of Jean. Once again the process of repatriation of the body began, with the help of the RAF and the Belgian authorities. Finally, on 15th March 1978, Jean Noizet was buried with full military honours in a grave at Evere with members of his family in attendance. A Shropshire historian, Michael Davies, has thoroughly researched the incident and in 1995 took to the air in a Tiger Moth and made a low pass over the crash site 52 years after the fatal collision. He was also instrumental in placing a commemorative plaque at the entrance to Rednal airfield.

The remains of Spitfire P7304 were taken for display at the RAF Museum at Cosford where they remained for several years. However, despite assurances from the then curator that it was to remain a permanent display, it was dismantled and stored. It is now with the Wartime Aircraft Recovery Group at Sleap where it remains a fitting tribute to a pilot who died so far from his homeland but who now rests in his country of birth. Michael has written a book entitled *The Limitless Horizon*, an in-depth look at the incident which has yet to be published.

Jean Joseph Albert Noizet, No 61 OTU, Rednal, killed 22nd August 1943. (M. Davies)

Henri Goldsmit of No 61 OTU, Rednal. (M. Davies)

With training continuing apace in 1943, many of the early Spitfires were slowly being replaced by newer marks. The Miles Masters continued to be used for dual flying instruction but it was the needs of Fighter Command that ensured that as many trainees as possible moved quickly from the OTU and on to operational squadrons. With D-Day coming closer, many of the trainees from No 61 OTU would witness the Allied invasion from the air.

Many airfields during the war were subjected at one time or another to film crews descending upon them. Most were military archive film units but occasionally a civilian film would be shot at an operational airfield for authenticity. Such a fate befell Rednal on 13th October when a crew from Denham Studios arrived to make a film detailing the part the RAF played in the fall of Greece in 1941. Several Gloster Gladiator biplanes flew in to Rednal together with a Wellington bomber that was to act as a camera ship. (It was intended that many of the airmen and women stationed at the base would act as film extras, something about which there was certainly no hesitation.) Filming was scheduled to take place over several months with several of the instructors taking the opportunity to fly the ancient aircraft. However, two incidents in the air saw an abrupt end to the project.

The first occurred on 4th November when Flt Lt H.D. Flowers crashed one of the aircraft whilst landing in a dense fog at Rednal. The second incident was far more serious. Flt Lt R.G. Kleinmeyer, a New Zealander, and Flt Lt K. Baghe were instructors at Rednal. They were chosen to fly the two Gladiators, K7927 and K8045, for air-to-air photography and on 24th November were airborne to carry out a sequence of events for the camera. Whilst changing formation from echelon to line-astern they collided, both aircraft suffering major damage. So much so that the pilots decided to take to their parachutes and abandon the Gladiators. They both suffered injuries upon landing and the aircraft crashed just a few hundred yards apart near the village of Penrhos. In the event the film, destined to be called *Signed with their Honour* or *The Air War in Greece* never did see the light of day and is probably lurking in some forgotten corner of a film buff's studio.

Although the Allied armies made their historic landings on five beaches on the Normandy coast on 6th June 1944, they remained in battle against a determined German force for ten weeks. During this period many casualties befell the Allies, which required a mass evacuation programme. A tight security cordon was placed around Rednal with all but compassionate cases of leave cancelled. No one was allowed to enter or leave the base unless strictly authorised. The reason for this became all too clear a short time later as American C-47 Skytrains landed at Rednal with many casualties on board, both American and British. Once the casualties were unloaded they were taken to various military hospitals in the area. The airlift began on 3rd July, with one of the busiest days being 5th August when nine C-47s landed, each carrying 24 wounded. From this time on it was not uncommon for a similar number of aircraft to land each day.

In addition, badly shot up aircraft returning from bombing missions were glad to see the runways at Rednal. Such was the case with an American B-24 Liberator which crashed short of the airfield in September 1944. The pilot had seen Montford Bridge and had attempted a landing. Realising that he was not going to get down due to the small size of the field, he aborted the landing and headed for nearby Rednal. Sadly the aircraft did not make it and crashed at Sharawardine, killing all but one of the ten-man crew.

The same month saw a tragedy unfold when a Martin Baltimore of the Empire Central Flying School crashed on take-off killing two of its passengers and injuring a further three. It finally came to rest at Tedsmore Hill near West Felton where it broke in two. One of the dead was Wg Cdr Wilkerson, a survivor of 46 bombing operations as a

A student pilot of 61 OTU on approach to Rednal. (CH 6455)

PO G.C. Walsh (pictured on left) arrives at No 61 OTU dispersal with a safer form of transport. (Imperial War Museum)

Halifax pilot. The inquiry into the crash later established that the groundcrew, being unfamiliar with the type, had inadvertently failed to notice that the overnight rudder locks had not been removed from the aircraft. It further stated that this was also overlooked by the pilot. Today a simple wooden cross marks the crash site.

The end of 1944 brought hope that the next year would see the end of the war. On 1st January 1945 a last-ditch attempt by the Luftwaffe saw them employ over 800 aircraft to attack Allied airfields in France, Belgium and Holland, but the enemy was in full retreat on every other front. Despite the optimism, life at Rednal continued as before with trainee pilots still completing the eight-week course. Since its inception, No 61 OTU had used Spitfires for training but the New Year saw the arrival of North American Mustang IIIs, transferred from No 55 OTU. This American Rolls-Royce Merlin engined fighter was to join the ranks of the RAF's best fighters and would prove a better aircraft than the aged Spitfires. With a top speed of 442 mph at 24,500 ft, it became a popular mount with the trainees. The aged Miles Masters were also exchanged for North American Harvards in the role of dual instruction.

During this latter period of the war several German POW camps were set up in Shropshire, with the prisoners mainly engaged on agricultural work under strict supervision. One of the camps was at Oswestry and it was here on 17th February that a number of prisoners attempted to escape. Once it was realised what had happened and the alarm was raised, the county went onto red alert. At Rednal, security was once again tightened and a rota for airfield perimeter patrols was introduced. This did not stop a German prisoner from entering the camp unnoticed, however, with the intent of stealing an aircraft to fly to Germany and freedom.

The day after the general alert dawned frosty and clear. The groundcrews, including WAAFs, were getting the aircraft ready for the day's flying. Among the latter was Margery Rosser who recalled vividly her encounter with what she called 'a gorgeous, tall, blonde German' sitting in one of the Mustangs: 'I popped out to the plane at around 06.30 hrs. I know it was winter as the wings were very icy and I was slipping about. I climbed up to fill it with fuel, pushed the cockpit open and there he was. I screamed and the whole squadron came rushing to me including the Group Captain, the officers and all the chaps I worked with. The German was a very innocent-looking chap. He was asleep but soon opened his eyes when I screamed.'

With the arrival of the station commander the German got out of the Mustang and clicked his heels. He could not speak English and those around him could not speak German. However, the station commander invited him to the officers' mess for a drink to await the arrival of the military police. He insisted that Margery accompany him to the mess and, feeling rather embarrassed, she duly did so. With the arrival of the

'How did I do?' A familiar scene at the Shropshire OTUs. (Imperial War Museum)

The memorial to Jean Noizet placed at the entrance to Rednal airfield by Michael Davies. (Author)

military police the German bowed and clicked his heels to her before being taken away. Maybe it was a case of love at first sight! Later that day it was announced that all the escapees had been recaptured.

This proved to be the last excitement for Rednal for with victory just around the corner, the airfield and its satellite were taken into Care and Maintenance on 20th June 1945. The next day No 61 OTU comprising the CO, Gp Cpt Miller, 131 officers, 189 NCOs, 1,011 airmen and women plus the Mustangs were posted to RAF Keevil.

Rednal had done its task well but there was no use for it in the peacetime RAF. It languished for many years, gradually falling into disrepair until the site was finally returned to the original landowners. One of its last tasks was to provide a haven for a lost American pilot flying the new Meteor jet aircraft when it suffered a mechanical problem and made an emergency landing at the disused airfield.

Part of the airfield was retained and is now the home of the Classic and Vintage Aeroplane Company. This was also used for a test flight of a miniature Global Challenger balloon of which the larger version was to have carried Richard Branson and Oswestry's Per Lindstrand around the world. Sadly, this was not achieved. The superb control tower and the woods around it are now used for of paintballing, a sad end for a building that has so much history.

At the entrance the memorial is a poignant reminder of just how many young lives were lost flying from RAF Rednal.

8
SHAWBURY

One of the major airfields in today's RAF, the future of Shawbury as a helicopter training base looks assured. In all weathers the 26 Eurocopter Squirrel HT1 and six Bell Griffin HT1 helicopters of the Defence Helicopter Flying School are airborne to train aircrew for all three Services. Shawbury has always operated in a training role stretching from the First World War through to today. Its other claim to fame is that it was the start point for a series of record-breaking round-the-world flights during 1944.

Situated close to the village of Shawbury, it is one of the oldest military airfields in North-west England. Its origins lie in the First World War when in 1915, with an expanding Royal Flying Corps (RFC), new sites away from any danger of aerial attack were sought.

Shawbury wartime control tower pictured in 2007. (Author)

From the beginning it was intended that the new grass airfield should be a training depot, such was the RFC's need for new pilots. A period of requisitioning took place, much to the annoyance of the local farmers, before the arrival of McAlpines to begin a process of levelling the ground, clearing fences and filling ditches before laying out a grass runway. Due to the lack of labour at the time, arrangements were made to bring Irish labourers to the site who together with German POWs, ensured that the station was built in record time.

By the summer of 1917, Shawbury was deemed ready and its first duty was to become the headquarters of No 29 Training Wing, an Australian Flying Corps (AFC) unit. The Wing controlled five squadrons, three at Shawbury (Nos 10, 29 and 67) and two at nearby Tern Hill (Nos 34 and 43) which had been built around the same period. The entire Wing was commanded by Major A.W. Tedder; now more commonly known now as the 'Father of the Royal Air Force'.

No 29 Training Wing flew various aircraft, with the major one appearing to have been the Avro 504. In addition to the squadrons, an Aeroplane Repair Section was formed on 1st September 1917 whose duty was the receipt of all new aircraft, the issuing of them to the squadrons and maintenance and repair. This Section was based in two of the seven timber hangars that had been erected, the Aeroplane Repair Section carrying out a role that continues at Shawbury today.

Aerial shot of Shawbury during wartime. (via M. Jones)

Another aerial shot of Shawbury during wartime. (via M. Jones)

November 1917 saw the first Americans arrive to join the British and Australian trainee pilots. With this increase in personnel, further accommodation was built as well as extra canvas Bessonneaux hangars for the aircraft. The station continued its training role until the Armistice was signed on 11th November 1918. Over the next year very little changed and its future seemed assured as it was named as one of the wartime airfields on the list for retention. This promise, however, proved to be false as the flying units moved out, giving an indication that all was not to be. Though the airfield continued its duty as a storage unit and the new Airship Construction Service arrived, by January 1918 most personnel had left and the buildings began to fall into decay. The newly formed RAF finally left in 1920.

By this time very little was left of the station. It fell to the distant rumblings coming from Germany during the 1930s for the site to be looked at once again as the expansion plans for the RAF got under way. Reconstruction began in the spring of 1937 but this time, Shawbury was to be twice its original size. Once again the problem of requisitioning further land began as plans emerged for the station to become home to a Flying Training School (FTS) and a Maintenance Unit (MU). The latter would be housed in large hangars to be built around the perimeter of the airfield to allow natural camouflage such as trees to conceal them. These were to be 'B' Type hangars, each one 273 ft long and 162 ft wide with a height of 60 ft, with offices or workshops adjoining and running alongside the length. These were supplemented by a smaller Aeroplane Repair Shed, while scattered around the airfield at six dispersed sites were Lamella and 'L' Type hangars. A station headquarters, barrack blocks, messes, technical blocks etc were all built and the grass runways were reseeded, one of them being 4,000 ft long.

It was rumoured that the FTS would use the main central part of the airfield while the storage of aircraft would occupy the perimeter areas. When still far from completion in February 1938, No 27 MU was established as the first civilian-manned storage and repair unit under military control. Accordingly Wg Cdr C. Hanson-Abbot, MBE, arrived to command this unit whilst the arrival of the first Shawbury CO, Gp Cpt H.P. Lalo, DSO, DFC, in May 1938 heralded the start of Shawbury's long and illustrious career.

By 1939 No 27 MU was on a war footing and ready to begin the storage, maintenance, modification and overhaul of all types of aircraft held as reserves for flying units. Among the first to arrive were Hawker Harts and Audaxes, Bristol Blenheims, Fairey Battles, Gloster Gladiators and Miles Magisters. On the main site, No 11 Flying Training School (FTS) became established when they brought their complement of eighteen Harts, eighteen Audaxes and four Gloster Gauntlets to Shawbury on 16th May 1938 from Wittering.

Air Ministry policy was changing and with the exception of the Harts, the biplane open cockpit training aircraft were soon to be

A fine photograph of an OTU Bristol Blenheim. (Bristol Aeroplane)

The prototype Oxford V. Many were flown from the Shropshire airfields. (J. Jarrett via T. Hughes)

replaced by the Airspeed Oxford. The Oxford was the RAF's first twin-engined monoplane advanced trainer. One of the new types ordered over the expansion period, it was a military development of the Airspeed Envoy. The initial production contract was for 136 aircraft to be built at the Airspeed factory at Portsmouth Airport. By the outbreak of war, nearly 400 had been delivered with the original Oxford Is intended for aspects of aircrew training. For gunnery training, the aircraft was fitted with an Armstrong-Whitworth dorsal turret.

The length of the FTS course pre-war was 22 weeks but when it became apparent after the Munich crisis that war was inevitable this was cut down to sixteen weeks and then again to ten weeks. Pupil flying hours were reduced from 100 to 72. By May 1940 Shawbury's aircraft strength still stood at 45 Harts, 40 Audaxes, 63 Oxfords and thirteen Battles, the latter being used by the Advanced Training Flight. The transfer of No 11 FTS to No 21 Training Group on 6th May 1940 saw the single-engined aircraft returned to No 18 MU at Dumfries. Shawbury now became a Group II (twin-engined) school with an establishment of 108 Oxfords.

It may appear odd that even at the opening stages of the war, biplane trainers were still in use for single-seat training. This was primarily because the aircraft that in 1936 had been designated the

Shawbury pictured in 1970. (RAF Shawbury)

special single-engine trainer with modern characteristics, the de Havilland Don, had not lived up to expectations. Designed as an advanced trainer mounting a dorsal turret, due to changes in policy the original order for 250 in July 1936 was cut down to 50 of which only 28 were delivered as complete airframes. Those that did fly with the RAF had the turret removed and were used only in a communications role. Hence the time to replace the aged biplanes did not come until the North American Harvard and the Miles Magister were in service.

The other method of training pilots was the Link Trainer, of which Shawbury had two. With no radios in the training aircraft, pupils could only stay within sight of the ground. Thus the Link Trainer was the only way to practise instrument flying.

The weather of 1939/40 severely hampered flying training. Still operating from grass runways, the heavier aircraft were constantly turning the grass into mud. As yet, no relief or satellite landing ground had been allocated to Shawbury and the entire site, full of aircraft for training and storage, had reached its capacity. This situation may well have led to the first Shawbury casualty of the war when Acting PO G.H.H. Coates took off in Oxford P1845 from a rather wet runway in conditions of mist and occasional rain. Several minutes after take-off and with the aircraft not visible from the airfield, a loud explosion was heard and the worst fears of those on the ground were realised. PO Coates had flown into the Wrekin and was killed.

The command of No 27 MU passed to Wg Cdr E.H. Eldridge in July 1940. Although eventually twelve hangars were to be made available for storage and maintenance, two of the Lamellas were not yet ready. This caused considerable problems for the MU as every available parking space for aircraft was used. One of the sites had two 'D' Type hangars and a naval Pentad, these being used specifically for aircraft assembly. So close were the aircraft parked to the perimeter of the airfield that certain roads running alongside were closed with a five mile barbed-wire fence placed around the entire airfield.

This build-up of aircraft did not go unnoticed by the Luftwaffe. Although by 1940 enemy aircraft were roaming over the West Midlands cities carrying out reconnaissance, it was the blitz down south that was taking the brunt of the attacks. However, some aircraft did venture into Shropshire, with the first air raid siren sounding on 25th June 1940. Though it was a false alarm, it was a taste of what was to come for Shawbury, the result of which was the decision to build further gun emplacements for airfield defence.

The FTS was now known as a Service Flying Training School (SFTS) and with a change of signature came a signal stating that the output of pilots should be increased. The pupil population at Shawbury increased overnight to 200, an amount that saw the station bulging at the seams. Accommodation was at a premium, so much so that many pupil pilots were given the luxury of staying in the officers' mess. Similar problems were apparent at the MU when by March 1940 it was holding some 600 aircraft, with more coming from the factories every day.

The military situation in France deteriorated rapidly and a signal was received to clear all the Hurricanes, Battles and Blenheims as quickly as possible in a last-ditch attempt to stop the German progress across Europe in its tracks. In May 1940, 176 aircraft were despatched from the MU; in June, despite the withdrawal of the BEF from France, that figure rose to 67 a day. Further dispersals with hard standings were required for with the bad weather, aircraft parked on grass gradually became bogged down. Despite this, as an interim answer to the problem, sixteen large fields around the airfield were taken to store aircraft until they were required by the squadrons.

Thursday, 27th June saw night-flying in progress at Shawbury. With the flarepath lit for aircraft flying circuits and bumps, the brightness attracted a lone enemy aircraft to commence a chance attack. The only

Shawbury pictured on 27th June 1940 showing bomb scars.

areas under warning that night for enemy raids were Middlesborough, Norwich, Ipswich and Portsmouth. They were all under a red warning whilst Shropshire was still yellow. At 00.55 hrs, a different engine sound was heard just before four bombs were dropped from a considerable height, landing near some of the technical buildings. Three more landed several yards outside the airfield perimeter, breaking a few windows in Shawbury village. Damage was caused to several buildings on the station plus several parked cars. No loss of life was incurred although some personnel were hurt by flying glass and debris. The enemy aircraft, after what seemed like minutes but was really seconds, turned away and was lost in the night. Ten minutes after the raid, the sirens sounded and the warning code was changed to red! What had been made clear was that air raid shelters were needed for personnel should any other attacks occur. It was also decided that when night-flying was in progress, the flarepath should be reduced to a single row of Glim lamps and the airfield location lights extinguished entirely.

Standardisation of aircraft for No 11 SFTS came in August 1940 when the last of the biplanes were sent away leaving 72 Oxford Mk Is, 43 Mk IIs and a single Fairey Battle. With the Battle of Britain continuing down south and the loss of so many pilots, the need for more became even more critical. With this in mind a signal was received from HQ 21 Group stating that the time taken to train new pilots had to be reduced. Consequently the initial training and advance training courses were brought down to six weeks, with each course being increased from 40 to 50 personnel. Once again the lack of accommodation was to prove a problem and was only solved by moving the WAAF quarters and building many wooden huts for the trainees.

It was not only the SFTS that was feeling the increased pressure at this decisive period of the war. Due to the earlier enemy attacks, it was felt that despite the quantity of aircraft to be stored and the demand on the civilian workforce, the parking of aircraft should be sparse lest a hangar be hit in any further attacks. The Ministry of Aircraft Production issued new regulations the same month for the parking of aircraft at the MUs. It stated that aircraft of one type were to be distributed over at least four sites; not more than three Spitfires or Hurricanes were to be parked together; and a maximum of 30 aircraft were to be stored in camouflaged 'E' or 'L' Type hangars, with a maximum of fifteen if uncamouflaged. It went on to lay down a maximum of eight aircraft in 'D', 'J' or 'K' Type hangars; no more than

Wartime guardroom from one of Shawbury's maintenance sites in 2007. (Author)

six 'large' aircraft in each 'C' Type hangar; open-air parks were to be 400 yds apart from hangared dispersals; open-air parks were to be 800 yds apart; aircraft parked in the open should be 100 yds apart reduced to 50 yds if partially concealed by trees or camouflage netting; and no petrol was to be left in aircraft in hangars or open-air parks.

Still the problem of the grass runways was apparent at Shawbury. In the short term, No 27 MU occasionally used the concrete runways and hard standings at High Ercall, but this obviously could not be permanent for that station had its own problems with aircraft storage. Someone, somewhere, realised that the situation was going from bad to worse and at last arrangements were made to give Shawbury a Relief Landing Ground (RLG), though this would not happen until the end of 1940. Meanwhile the station once again came to the attention of the Luftwaffe during September.

On the night of the 5th, enemy raids commenced soon after 20.30 hrs with the main targets being in South Wales, the Midlands, Manchester, Liverpool and the West Riding. At 21.40 hrs the sirens sounded in Shawbury accompanied by the sound of enemy aircraft. The lights were doused at the airfield but at 22.20 hrs, three explosions were heard just around the perimeter. As the noise of the explosions died down flames and smoke were seen coming from the MU dispersal. The emergency services were quickly on the scene but found no damage to the hangars, the bombs having dropped some distance from them. At that time of night all the personnel had gone home and so there was no loss of life.

Luckily there was no loss of life several weeks later either, on the 25th, when night-flying was in progress. The two Oxfords airborne at the time were recalled rather hurriedly! The sirens had sounded in the village and the station status had changed from yellow to red when an enemy aircraft was seen to be in the area. This was one aircraft of a force of about 100 that had crossed inland between 10.00 hrs and 01.00 hrs heading again for South Wales and the Midlands. As the landing lights were extinguished on the airfield, two incendiary bombs were dropped to the north-west. Several minutes later the aircraft returned and dropped a further stick of bombs. Most fell outside the boundary and again, no damage was sustained. The enemy force, however, suffered badly with the official record stating that 26 enemy aircraft were destroyed, along with eight probables and twelve damaged.

The only other attack of any significance happened on the night of 14th November when a lone aircraft machine-gunned the buildings. This may well have been an aircraft that had previously dropped its bombs on Coventry and was just looking for another target of opportunity to shoot at.

The 14th was the night of the devastating raid on Coventry but there were also other heavy raids on the Midlands industrial targets, as John Vaux recalls: 'One night early in 1941 there was a heavy raid on a city to the north. The drone of enemy aircraft was almost continuous as they headed towards the searchlights, flak and the red glow of fires. However, it soon became evident that not all the aircraft were taking part in the raid for two or three were circling Shawbury trying to find us. Then down came the incendiary bombs, all falling to the north-east of the station where there was a large collection of parked aircraft; Blenheims, Beauforts, Wellingtons, Beaufighters and others. Soon they were all black against the firebombs which lit up the whole area. Yet not one hit an aircraft. Had this happened the resultant blaze would surely have brought down heavy HE bombs onto Shawbury and its hangars. As it was we escaped – just. It was a near thing as we saw next morning for some of the bombs had been burning within a few yards of the parked aircraft. It was not our time on that occasion.'

With the increase in trainees and an accelerated training programme, it was announced that at last Shawbury was to get its RLG. The site chosen was a large field two miles to the north-west known as Bridleway Gate. Once inspected and found to be suitable, permission was obtained from HQ Flying Training Command on 19th September to begin work on preparing the site. The plan included levelling the ground and removing obstructions, together with the building of a Bellman hangar, (though this never materialised), three Nissen huts and hard standings for vehicles etc. This was very basic but owing to the urgency dictated by increased courses requiring more aircraft, it was essential to bring Bridleway Gate into use as soon as possible. With plans approved by September 1940, the RLG was officially opened on 1 January 1941. Sixteen days later an Oxford, L4559 of No 11 SFTS, became the first aircraft to use it when forced to make an emergency landing.

Christmas 1940 was bleak and cold. Owing to the state of the runways, very little flying was done over the period allowing most to spend the festive period off base. With Christmas over, the training began again with increased urgency. The Battle of Britain had rapidly depleted the number of operational fighter pilots and late 1940 and early 1941, with the battle over, was a time allocated to replenishing the pool.

At the same time No 27 MU still had problems of overcrowding. During December 1940, 79 aircraft of various types were stored and 70 were issued to the squadrons. The new year saw this increase to 88 and 177 respectively. By March, 530 aircraft were being held by the Unit, a figure that Shawbury's storage facilities could not contain. So great was the demand for space that fields several miles away were requisitioned for use, the aircraft arriving on lorries. Twenty new and quickly assembled Ministry of Aircraft Production hangars built of steel and corrugated iron and known as Robin hangars, were constructed on these sites. It was suggested that nearby Elmdon airfield, now Birmingham International Airport, be used for storage but with the testing of Stirlings and Lancasters being carried out on that site, only a few aircraft were stored there. The problem was further exacerbated when heavy snow fell in January 1941 making Bridleway Gate unusable.

Although far away from the battle front, Shropshire had many anti-aircraft and searchlight sites established for the defence of the Midlands. Both from time to time needed a calibration process to measure deflection of fire and beams etc. In January 1941, No 6 Anti-Aircraft Co-Operation Unit (AACU) arrived for such duties. It provided a calibration service for the Army manning both ack-ack and searchlights and operated a variety of aircraft such as Leopard Moths, Dragons, Blenheims and Lysanders. When eventually the unit became No 7 AACU in May 1942, the aircraft were standardised to Miles Masters.

Several months earlier Shawbury had been allocated another RLG. This was at Bratton, just north of the town of Wellington. In essence, like Bridleway Gate it was just a large grass field, but with the minimum amount of work and the use of farm buildings it became habitable. With the threat of a glider-borne invasion around this time, scrap cars were strewn across the landing area. By late November when this threat had subsided, they were removed to allow the RLG to be used.

A local resident recalls the building of Bratton and describes how two elephants were conscripted to the military to assist in the process:

When we walked to school, this would be around 1942/43, the planes used to be parked wingtip to wingtip alongside the road. When they started up the noise was deafening. We witnessed several crashes, both serious and odd bumps. Two in particular I remember seeing. They crashed in flames near to the Gate Inn public house. The second was when we saw a single-seat aircraft, possibly either a Hurricane or Spitfire, fail to take off. It went through the hedge opposite a house called Wayside on the road from the Gate Inn to Longdon upon Tern. It came to rest blocking the road and instead of going to school we went to see the crash. The pilot climbed out unhurt and as we got near he told us to 'go away'. He then kicked the tail of the plane, climbed back through the hole in the hedge and walked off across the airfield.

My school friends from those years will remember also being given rides in the rear of the Oxford planes when they were being moved around. The sentry posts dotted around the perimeter of the airfield provided play places for us after the war. Now all the buildings and hangars are gone. Several of the buildings were used by families to live in after the war when housing was scarce. I can confirm that elephants were used to try and clear the felled trees when the airfield was being built. They were from a local circus and were named Salt and Saucy, and were housed at the big house where the guardroom was adjoining the airfield. (A report in the *Wellington Journal and Shrewbury News* of February 1940 told of the Bratton elephants but due to wartime censorship just mentioned that it was 'somewhere in Shropshire'.)

Heavy snow shut down Bratton shortly after it was ready. Those Oxfords that were using it already and were parked around the airfield ready for the next day's flying had to be dug out of the mud and parked in drier areas. There were days when no flying could take place from the parent station or the RLGs due to bad weather. When there was flying, bad conditions led to many accidents as the following few incidents record:

> 08.06.1940 – Airspeed Oxford, R6246. Engine failure, hit cottage at Muckley Corner, Lichfield, whilst making emergency landing; written off.
>
> 23.09.1940 – Airspeed Oxford, N4769. Collided with N4637 at Shawbury and crashed; written off.
>
> 23.09.1940 – Airspeed Oxford, N4537. Collided with N4769 at Shawbury and crashed; written off.
>
> 08.10.1940 – Airspeed Oxford, R6326. Night landing, Shawbury, undershot and hit trees; written off.
>
> 09.12.1940 – Airspeed Oxford, R6287. In circuit at night, Shawbury, stalled and spun in; written off. Instructor PO W.J.B. Wadie and pupil u/t R.B. White both killed. The latter lies in St. Mary's Churchyard, Shawbury.
>
> 09.01.1941 – Airspeed Oxford, R6296. Precautionary landing in snow at Bredenbury, between Bromyard and Leominster, Herefordshire; hit trees on attempted take off; written off. FO J.R. Law, instructor, died of his injuries on 17.01.1941 and lies in St. Mary's Churchyard, Shawbury.

By this time No 27 MU was receiving crated North American Harvards from the USA which were to be reassembled. The North American Aviation Company Ltd took over one of the hangars for this purpose. The Harvard was a badly needed advanced trainer from which most pilots graduated to the Spitfire. As part of the Lend/Lease agreement with the USA, over 5,000 were to be sent to Britain in the hope of speeding up the training courses. This was not a popular aircraft for the local people as its characteristic rasping note caused by the propeller could be heard all over the county.

With the arrival of spring and better weather, both RLGs came back into use, to the relief of all at Shawbury. However, five days after reopening, a huge fire engulfed Bridleway Gate when a fuel bowser was taking fuel from the storage dump. This virtually shut the RLG again for a limited period. In order to expedite the training programme further, arrangements were made to continue night-flying from Chipping Norton, the RLG to Little Rissington. This, however, was also

St Mary's Churchyard, Shawbury. The final resting place for many British and Commonwealth airmen. (Author)

After the war, many German airmen buried in local churchyards were exhumed and taken to the German war cemetery on Cannock Chase. Here an RAF party from Cosford and Shawbury carry a former enemy to his final resting place. (MOD)

found to be waterlogged and so the plan was changed to use Lindholme. Although training began there on 22nd February, two fatal accidents together with bad weather forced the detachment to be recalled to Shawbury. By April, Bridleway Gate was once again deemed serviceable although the aircraft returned to Shawbury every evening lest they became stuck in the still-wet grass overnight.

A change in command at No 27 MU took place the same month when Wg Cdr C.M.P. Hartley handed the reins over to Wg Cdr Elbridge. It had been a difficult time for the former, with an ever increasing demand for storage and despatch. There were now six dispersal areas capable of holding a large number of aircraft together with large holding sites within the airfield perimeter. Shortly after the new CO had settled in, arrangements were made to store aircraft at Hardwick Park. Classified as No 37 Satellite Landing Ground (SLG), it had a 3,000 ft grass strip and was capable of storing 65 aircraft. Yet again the weather intervened but another problem arose when it was realised that the SLG was shared with the Army for manoeuvres. It did, however, remain in use for the MU until February 1945.

The only site deemed safe for night-flying was Shawbury. This, however, could not accommodate all the courses and with neither of the RLGs suitable for the purpose, it was imperative to find somewhere else. One site under consideration was the RLG used by RAF Penrhos named Llandwrog in Caernarvonshire. This was made available to No 11 SFTS and a servicing party left by road on 11th June 1941 to prepare for the arrival of eight Oxfords of No 4 Flight. Having settled in both ground and aircrews, the trainers were about to start flying when a signal was received that no aircraft were to take off due to the Oxfords not being recognised and therefore liable to be shot down by the ground defences or friendly night-fighters! It took some time for a system to be worked out whereby the Oxfords were not to fly above 1,000 ft and were to contact Valley control, the sector station for the area, when night-flying. The system seemed to work and now at last Shawbury had two RLGs and a night-flying RLG.

If evidence were needed that Shawbury was overcrowded and that No 11 SFTS was suffering badly from a congested airfield and pressures of maintenance, the months from April to September 1941 saw nineteen Oxfords lost in various crashes. Sadly the accidents also saw loss of life, one in particular when an LAC going solo for the first time was killed when his Oxford, L4575, broke up in mid-air. He lies in St Mary's Churchyard, Shawbury.

Although 53,136 flying hours had been achieved by the SFTS during

1941 with an establishment of 81 Oxfords, this had not been accomplished without tragedies. It was hoped that the long-expected hard runway promised for Shawbury would drastically reduce the accident rate. Prior to this, however, the training had to continue using grass airfields and strips with more RLGs needed to meet further demand. Scheduled for September, the start of the runway-building programme did not help the situation and severely curtailed both day- and night-flying. For a limited time from September until October, Cranage in Cheshire was made available to the SFTS. In addition, and for the same limited period, the Cranwell RLGs of Fulbeck and Wellingore were used, together with nearby Childs Ercall (Peplow), the satellite of No 5 SFTS based at Tern Hill. By December it had been found necessary to add yet another RLG for the SFTS, this being Wheaton Aston just across the border in Staffordshire.

Shawbury itself had become equally as busy with the station strength standing at 1,856 RAF personnel, 340 WAAFs, 41 Army officers and nine Free French Air Force pilots by the year's end. However, No 27 MU was holding 229 aircraft, fewer than for many months.

By the end of 1941 it had become apparent that it had been a bad year for all concerned at Shawbury, and that 1942 could not be allowed to pass in similar vein. A review and a decision that had its origins back in 1940 was to ensure that the past year was not repeated.

By mid-1940, due to weather and other limitations at the training airfields in this country, it had been decided that the majority of flying training would be carried out overseas, known as the Empire Air Training Scheme (EATS). One of the first countries to sign up was Australia. Most training schools did not go overseas until mid-1941 but No 21 Group, within whose remit No 11 SFTS worked, did not go at all. In addition to Australia, countries such as the USA, New Zealand, Canada and Rhodesia trained many thousands of pilots who would eventually return to Britain and to an advanced training unit before moving on to an operational squadron. In total, this scheme provided the RAF with a staggering 50,000 trained aircrew each year.

No 21 Group signalled that No 11 SFTS was to become No 11 (Pilots) Advanced Flying Unit ((P)AFU), whose task was to take trained pilots coming from the EATS and advance them to the operational stage of flying. In order for the backlog of trainees still with No 11 SFTS to move on quickly, good use was made of the hard runways at nearby High Ercall because of the waterlogging again at Bridleway Gate and Bratton.

The remaining pupil pilots of No 11 SFTS spent a second Christmas at Shawbury. The custom of the officers serving the other ranks was upheld before they returned to their own mess. In order to get the remaining personnel of the SFTS through their course, January 1942 saw Perton near Wolverhampton and Wrexham become additional RLGs – with work continuing into the New Year on the hard runway, Shawbury saw very little flying, hence the need for so many RLGs.

The end of the year, however, did bring a very unusual occurrence at the airfield, as John Vaux recalls:

> One day the station air raid sirens sounded and two Wellingtons with full RAF markings flew very low over Shawbury. No gun was fired as the two aircraft circled us and then flew off to the east. Consternation! They were being flown by Germans, obviously captured after Dunkirk.
>
> I was in RT control at the time, a cement bunker next to HQ, when it all happened. The phone rang – 'Air Raid Warning Red – Air Raid Warning Red'. So I rang the gunposts and called up the four Armadillos, converted trucks with a crew of four, a radio and a machine gun, on the radio. Phone rang again – 'Stand Down'. I began to reverse all my calls. Phone rang again – 'Air Raid Warning Red – Air Raid Warning Red'. I started all over again and had just finished when the phone rang yet again. 'Stand Down – Stand Down'. I did it all once more. Many questions were asked as you can imagine. I only hope the two Wellingtons were shot down by equally confused German gunners but somehow I doubt it.

The New Year also saw Gp Cpt R.J. Divers, MBE, arrive to command Shawbury while Wg Cdr E. R. Hoare, OBE, became the CO of the MU. No 11 SFTS was officially renamed No 11 (P)AFU on 1st April with No 1 Course comprising 50 pilots, followed by a similar number on No 2 Course on 18th April. Unfortunately they had to wait until June before the hard runway was finished, a state of affairs that saw the Oxfords still using the many grass RLGs and satellites. The condition of the grass, however, was certainly not a factor in the first fatality of the new unit. Sgt Pilot A.R. Whitington had taken off from one of the grass strips in Oxford AS766 in clear weather on 2nd May. It is not possible to state exactly what happened but the aircraft was seen to dive vertically into the ground at Hadnal. Sadly, Sgt Whitington died instantly.

At last, on 5th June 1942, the two reinforced concrete runways became operational. Runway 05/23 was 4,400 ft long and 01/19 was 3,950 ft long. It was not the training unit which first used the new

Cartoon drawn by John Vaux while stationed at Shawbury and its satellites.

facility but No 411 (Grizzly Bear) Squadron of the Royal Canadian Air Force. They flew their Spitfire Vbs in from Digby on the day the runways were opened, the first operational squadron to use Shawbury. They stayed for two days before returning to Digby, then came back on 5th August for three days before returning once again to Digby.

The construction of the new runways had seriously affected the day-to-day operations of No 27 MU. It became necessary for aircraft destined for the MU to land at High Ercall, the home of No 29 MU. The home unit's pilots then flew them into Shawbury or one of the RLGs when an opportunity arose. Likewise, aircraft prepared for despatch were flown to High Ercall to await the ATA pilots to take them onwards. Yet another RLG (No 21) had been taken over by 20 April, this time at Ollerton. This was capable of taking about 50 aircraft dispersed around its perimeter.

Another RLG that was in the process of being built for storage was Hodnet, which was different in that it covered two sites; one was used for storage whilst the other was used for taking off and landing. When aircraft were to be despatched, the main Shrewsbury road had to be closed to allow them to taxi from the holding site to the grass area. Opened in June 1942, it was taken over by No 27 MU in July. At the same time the RLG at Ollerton was handed over to the Royal Navy to become HMS *Godwit*. An ever-expanding maintenance unit, No 27 now handled such diverse aircraft types as Battles, Beaufighters, Bermudas, Horsa and Hotspur gliders, Magisters, Martinets, Mosquitos and Oxfords.

Controls of a Horsa glider being rebuilt at Shawbury in 2007. (Author)

The middle of 1942 saw two further airfields in the county in the process of construction, both of them to be of satellite or RLG status. One was at Condover, the other at Montford Bridge. The former with its three runways rapidly became the most important RLG for Shawbury. Intended to be a full satellite airfield to Atcham, with the arrival of the Americans there it was re-allocated to Shawbury as an RLG. Prior to the opening of Condover, it was to the smaller Montford Bridge that a detachment of Oxfords from No 11 (P)AFU flew in July 1942. They trained there for a month before moving to the now completed Condover.

The rest of the year saw Shawbury and its satellites and RLGs continue in much the same routine of training. At the end of 1942 Winston Churchill stood in the House of Commons and, in a speech about the El Alamein victory, said: 'It is not the end. It is not even the beginning of the end. But it is perhaps the end of the beginning.' The signs were optimistic that the Allies were very much on the offensive. This was borne out by the fact that so many aircraft were now being despatched by No 27 MU. Shawbury itself was just as busy with 113 Oxfords on strength. In January six pilots were taken from the AFU to form No 1534 Beam Approach Training Flight. Formed on the 16th of

Horsa glider under rebuild at Shawbury. (Author)

the month, the BAT Flight provided training in beam approach techniques for radio-assisted landings (an early type of instrument landing system), with each pilot from the AFU undertaking some ten hours' beam flying.

Condover now became the main RLG for Shawbury, together with Perton and Wheaton Aston. These were to become virtually self-contained units during 1943, with Bridleway Gate and Bratton seeing less use due to the continued problem of waterlogging. The hard runways at the main RLGs allowed flying training to continue in most weathers, which in turn meant that more pupils passed through the AFU. In February 1943 the flying groups were dispersed thus:

> No 1 Group – Shawbury
> No 2 Group – Shawbury
> No 3 Group – Shawbury
> No 4 Group – Condover
> No 5 Group – Perton
> No 6 Group – Wheaton Aston

Instructional flying hours for February amounted to a colossal 10,838, with better maintenance of aircraft giving an increase in the numbers of aircraft available. Thankfully the number of major incidents had dwindled by the end of the year to just two. Sgt B. Pernaux and his pupil Sgt W. Lauder were sadly killed when Oxford AT677 crashed at Rhosmedrh at the end of a cross-country exercise; while two more pilots, Fl Sgt T. Gersw and pupil Sgt T.F. Mills, died when Oxford LW730 crashed to the ground shortly after take-off from Condover. An increase in aircraft brought the station strength to 138 Oxfords, five Ansons, one Tutor and a Magister with 1,146 male personnel and 433 WAAFs. However, 1944 would see big changes at Shawbury, with an event that would underline its place in the history books.

With very little use being made of Bridleway Gate, the RLG was closed for flying on 10th January 1944, its future use being that of a fuel dump. A change in policy saw No 11 (P)AFU move to Calveley at the end of the month after many years of success and despair at Shawbury. The unit was to continue the admirable job of training pilots to an advanced level until the end of the war. No 5 (P)AFU from Tern Hill would take over Condover as a new RLG and with these changeovers all completed by the end of January, Shawbury entered a new phase in its life as the home of the Central Navigation School (CNS). The CNS was primarily for the training of navigation instructors as well as holding specialist courses for developing navigation techniques. It consisted of 42 Wellington XIIIs, four Stirling IIIs, a Proctor, a Magister and a Lockheed Hudson: far fewer aircraft than had been previously stationed at Shawbury with the AFU.

Staying at Shawbury was No 27 MU which, with further hangars allocated to it since the departure of the AFU, was now also stockpiling Horsa gliders for the forthcoming invasion of Europe. Stirlings, no longer front-line bombers, were also arriving for storage, taking up more room than smaller types of aircraft. Large numbers of Mosquitos were now being built which meant that Shawbury was receiving them daily for storage until allocated to squadrons. At the same time many Fairey Battles, the first monoplane bomber for the RAF, had also come to the end of their operational lives and were being received at the MU for dismantling and scrapping. As an indication of how the types of aircraft had changed, August 1944 saw 79 Mosquitos and 37 Miles Martinets, used as target-tugs, arrive out of a total of 120 aircraft. Over the same period 58 aircraft were issued to the squadrons. Even at this late stage of the war there was no let-up in demand for the services of the MU, with both Shawbury and its RLG at Hodnet as busy as ever.

The School of Air Navigation was formed at Manston on 1st January 1936 out of the Air Navigation Schools at Andover and Calshot. After further changes of location, No 2 School of Air Navigation was formed at Cranage from an element of the first School which had moved to Canada to help with aircrew training. The Central Navigation School (CNS) then formed at Cranage with Ansons, having about 60 on strength. However, by the time it arrived at Shawbury in early 1944, conversion to Wellingtons and Stirlings had taken place, together with several communications aircraft. Commanded by Gp Cpt N.C. Ogalvie-Forbes, the CNS soon got under way, with four Wellingtons leaving for an extended navigation exercise to India. Although the world was still at war, the idea was to give senior officers in the Indian theatre of operations up-to-date information about modern navigation and radar aids. A very detailed report was submitted on return giving every detail of all the airfields visited en route. On 2nd June Stirling LK849 left for a long-distance flight to Canada followed by a similar flight to Iceland over 29th and 30th August. These flights accumulated much information and it was decided that a round-the-world flight was possible and should be attempted to test navigational equipment. This became known as the 'Aries' series of flights, and is described in Chapter 14.

Command of the station passed to Gp Cpt A.I.L. Saye, CB, OBE, AFC, in June 1944 as normal training continued whilst the series of long-distance flights were taking place. The last few months of the war saw No 27 MU continue to store aircraft that were surplus to requirements at this late stage. The RLG at Hodnet closed in February 1945, with the reputation of a job well done and accompanied by much relief for the motorists of Shrewsbury now that the road would no longer be shut. The MU was now specialising in Mosquitos for delivery, as well as war-weary veteran aircraft either for storage or more often, dismantling for the scrap merchant to collect after the removal of radios, radar and engines. It was an ignominious end for so many first-class aircraft. The Mosquito was to serve with the RAF for many peacetime years and this kept the MU busy with radar modifications etc.

In May 1945 Wg Cdr Hoare was posted from No 27 MU to be replaced by Wg Cdr C.F. Howard. He was to see the war out at Shawbury, as was Air Commodore P.H. Mackworth, CB, CBE, DFC, who arrived as the station CO in September 1944. The 8th of May 1945 was Victory in Europe Day and a station parade was held to celebrate the fact. After an address by the CO, a comic football match was played followed by a celebratory film performance in the Astra cinema. In the evening an all ranks dance was held ending with a bonfire and firework display which included a processional parade of Nazi effigies, a fitting end to the demise of the Third Reich.

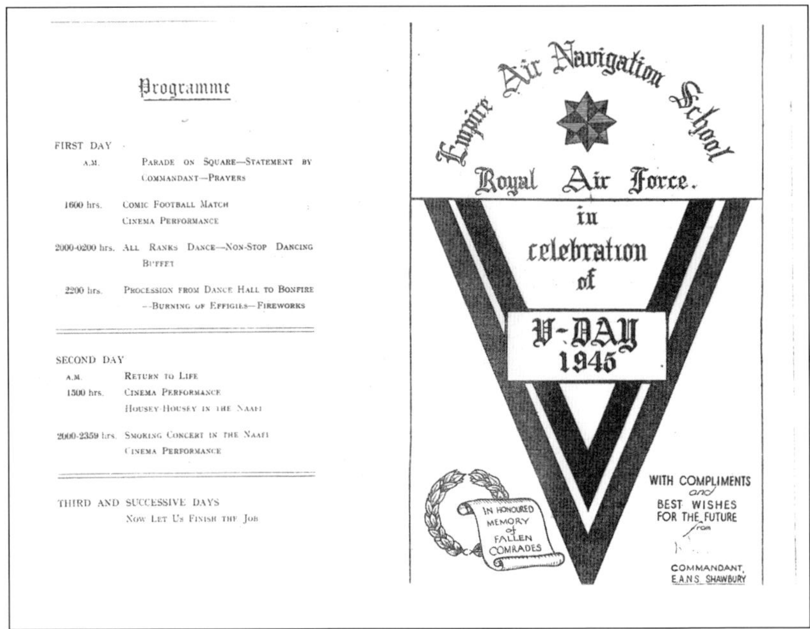

The Empire Air Navigation School programme at Shawbury celebrating victory in 1945. (RAF Shawbury)

No 27 MU finally closed its doors on 30th June 1972 after many years of excellent service. With it went about 1,000 civilian jobs but, in 1979, Marshalls of Cambridge (Outstations) Ltd won the contract to service the Bulldog and Chipmunk training aircraft, re-employing many of the former workforce. In October 1996 the existing contract was replaced by another with FBS Ltd, a company formed between Flight Refuelling Aviation, Bristow Helicopters and SERco. This contract covers engineering and supply of aircraft, much the same duties as were carried out by No 27 MU.

The tradition of training was carried on during the post-war years, and continues today with the Defence Helicopter Flying School. This tri-service school is tasked with training over 400 students each year, including pilots, crewmen and post-graduate students. Formed on 1st April 1997, it operates on a round-the-clock basis, such is the need for helicopter crews. Shawbury is also the home of the Central Air Traffic Control School, tasked with training over 550 students per year in the art of air traffic control.

Post-war Shawbury. A Wessex helicopter is lowered into place as a gate guardian. (via M. Jones)

Refurbished Dakota at Shawbury in 2007 (static display only). (Author)

The rebuild of an American Waco Hadrian glider is progressing well at Shawbury. (Author)

Many front-line aircraft are held in reserve at Shawbury, just as with the wartime MU. No 6 Army Air Corps (Volunteers) Flight was formed in 1993 and equipped with four Gazelle AH1 helicopters. Its role is to provide communications, transport and exercise support for both regular and territorial units in Land Command. Finally, the Westland Apache Maintenance and Support Unit was formed in June 2002 to manage the temporary storage of the Army Apache Battlefield Helicopter.

With such a large workload, the future of the airfield, hopefully, is assured. Though a long way from the main battle front, Shawbury served the RAF well and deserves its place in the history of the Second World War.

The wartime station flag hangs in Shawbury church. (Author)

9
SLEAP

Although Sleap (pronounced 'Slape') was not built until halfway through the war, it has survived many other larger stations in the county and even today continues as the home of the Shropshire Aero Club. Although categorised as a satellite airfield, it probably saw more use than some of the smaller airfields and large satellites.

Work began in the winter of 1941 but bad weather was to interrupt progress. Three miles from Wem, it was built as a satellite to Whitchurch Heath (Tilstock) with the intended completion date of August 1942. Finally opened on 15th January 1943, it came under the umbrella of 93 Group Bomber Command. Not a lot happened until the Whitleys of 'C' Flight of No 81 OTU transferred from Tilstock and, combined with ground instruction, the usual pattern of cross-country flights began in earnest. Known as 'the flying coffin', the aged Whitley still had a good role to play in training bomber aircrew. One of the ground training establishments was used to train bomb-aimers and air gunners. Called an AML Bombing Teacher and Turret Trainer, the example still at Sleap is difficult to access due to the years of growing foliage, but it is the only known survivor in which the original target screen is still visible. One wonders just how many aircrew sat inside the 'Teacher' to perfect their aim.

There were distractions from the routine of training such as the incident that happened on the night of 4th/5th April 1943. On that particular night Bomber Command had amassed a force of 577 aircraft to attack Kiel. This was to be the largest raid on Kiel so far and would consist of Wellingtons, Halifaxes, Stirlings and 203 Lancasters. Over the target they found thick cloud and strong winds, making accurate bombing impossible. After dropping their bomb-load the force turned for home. As the Lancaster force approached the English coast they were told that, due to fog over the Lincolnshire airfields, they would have to divert to any airfield they found open. Two of the Lancasters

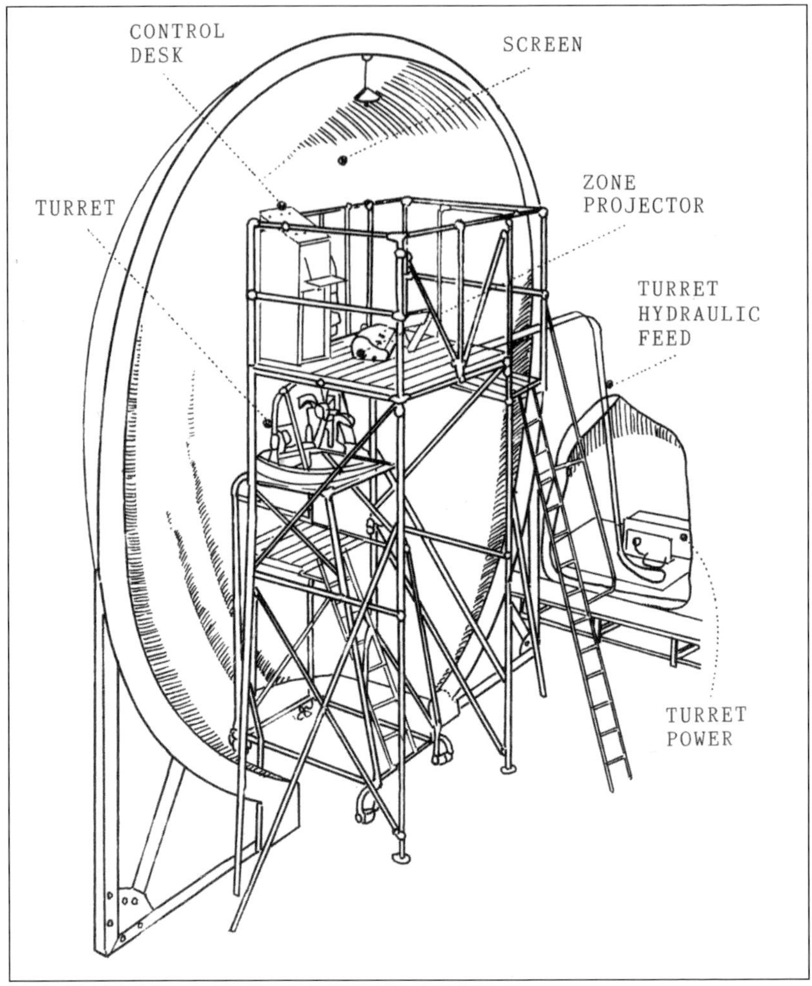

Drawing of the unique standard free Gunnery Trainer at Sleap airfield. (C. Samson)

travelled inland and found Sleap basking in moonlight. Although perhaps considered rather small for aircraft the size of a Lancaster, they managed to land successfully. After the pilots had enjoyed a night's sleep and a hearty breakfast, the aircraft were refuelled and managed to take off for their home bases.

It did not take long before tragedy came to the satellite. Whitley V EB405 took off from Sleap on a night-navigation exercise on the night of 2nd/3rd May 1943. The flight and training procedure went well until the pilot attempted to land. After two failed attempts the Whitley crashed in flames at Loppington, three miles from the airfield, at 04.20 hrs. Sgt H.J. Spiers, Sgt H. Leather, Sgt J.J. Brown, Sgt J.W. Scott and Sgt W.A. Capel sadly lost their lives. This was the first real tragedy for Sleap, but there were to be many others.

The detachment at Sleap was commanded by Wg Cdr Carter and his immediate second officer, Sqd Ldr Lockwood. They oversaw the first 'Nickel' sortie when several Whitleys dropped bundles of leaflets in the Amien and Caen area of France during June. Sadly they were also in command when the first of two dreadful accidents occurred at Sleap.

FO K.N. Laing, RCAF, Sgt T.W. Fair, RCAF, Sgt T.R. Armstrong, RCAF, Sgt R.G. Henderson and Sgt Guile had spent the early evening of 26th August 1943 in the briefing room. After an evening meal the crew boarded the transport that was to carry them to the dispersal where Whitley V LA937 had been checked out by the groundcrew and was waiting. Clambering aboard and settling down, they prepared for a night-navigation exercise. Taking off at 20.50 hrs, the training went well. Returning to Sleap at around 03.00 hrs, the pilot lined the Whitley up on the main runway. At the crucial moment, as the aircraft came over the threshold, both engines faltered, possibly due to lack of fuel. Desperately trying to control the aircraft, FO Laing touched down but the aircraft veered off the runway, crossed the grass and crashed into the control tower.

On duty that fateful night in the tower were AC1 Ferguson, ACW2 J. Viney, a WAAF, and the Chief Flying Instructor (CFI), Wg Cdr D.S. Robertson. As the Whitley left the runway and crossed towards the tower, the duty crew could only watch in horror as it careered towards

No 81 OTU Whitleys lined up for the day's flying, April 1943. (David Birrell)

A Whitley of No 81 OTU is connected to a trolley-AC prior to starting. Sleap 1943. (David Birrell)

'We nearly caught the train!' A Whitley overshoot at Sleap, 1943. (David Birrell)

them. With a terrific crash it ran into the ground floor of the tower and burst into flames. The cockpit area of the aircraft was totally destroyed on impact, killing the pilot, FO Laing and the bomb-aimer, Sgt Armstrong. The other six crewmembers all received injuries when the impact threw them forward. The three personnel in the tower had to be taken to hospital and several groundcrew standing close by were also injured.

The Whitley was a write-off and the collision had caused a lot of damage to the tower. After several hours the fire crew managed to douse the flames enough for the crash crew to pull what was left of the aircraft clear of the tower. The damaged tower was then repaired temporarily, allowing it to be

PO D. Stewart Robertson before becoming CO of Sleap. He was then flying Whitleys with No 81 OTU. (David Birrell)

back in service the following morning and training to continue.

The rest of August saw no further incidents. A full military funeral was held for the two aircrew killed, who were buried in Chester (Blacon) cemetery. Many station personnel from Tilstock and Sleap attended, together with family members of the two men. It was a sad and solemn occasion. Just seven days later an entire crew from Sleap were killed in another crash.

Whitley V AD679 took off from the airfield at 20.15 hrs on 2nd September 1943 in the company of eight other Whitleys for a 'Bullseye' exercise. Sgt W. Hall, Sgt A.L. Culley, Sgt W. Harrison, Sgt I.F.W. Pears and Sgt A.C. Strolin were in the second aircraft to become airborne and for some time the exercise went well. As the crew were approaching the outer limits of Hertfordshire, the searchlights around the capital suddenly lit up, turning night into day in the cabin of the aircraft. It is thought that Sgt Hall was dazzled by the glare of the searchlights causing him to fly into high ground at Finch Lane, Bushey. In one single explosion the entire crew died. The official report stated that in

Wing Commander D. Stewart Robertson with his crew at Sleap. (David Birrell)

Aircrew of 'A' Flight No 81 OTU, Sleap in 1943. (David Birrell)

attempting to take evasive action from the searchlights, the pilot exceeded the safe limitations of the mainplanes. The bodies of the crew were taken to their home towns for burial.

If ever history was to repeat itself it did so on 7th September when a late-night training exercise began and ended in tragedy. Preparing to take off from Sleap at twenty past midnight was Whitley V BD257 with a crew of FO R.W. Browne, FO E.L. Ware, RCAF, Sgt W.D. Kershaw, Sgt E. Young and Sgt S. Williams. It had begun well with the crew checking all systems before beginning to taxi to the runway. After checking his crew were ready for take-off, FO Browne released the brakes, applied full power and BD257 began to gather speed. As it was just about to reach its maximum speed the Whitley suddenly veered off the runway and tore across the grass, heading for the control tower.

The night duty crew in the tower that night were Cpl N.W. Peate and four WAAFs – ACW2 K.M. Ffoukles, ACW2 V. Hughes, ACW2 B. Hall and LACW A.B. Jowett. Looking from the top floor of the tower they knew by the sound of the engines that something had gone wrong with the take-off. Almost instantly they saw the Whitley heading for the control tower and began to run for the back of the visual room where the stairs were. Sadly it was too late as the aircraft hit the tower

Sleap control tower in 2007. Signs of the two fatal collisions are still apparent in places. (Author)

and exploded in a ball of flame. Four of the aircrew died instantly and it was a miracle that Sgt Williams, the air gunner, survived. Two WAAFs, LACW Jowett and ACW2 Hall, both of the meteorology section, died in the inferno whilst the other three personnel together with Sgt Williams were rushed to Cosford Hospital with severe burns. It was a tragic coincidence that within the space of two weeks, eight people had died in similar circumstances. Yet again the victims were given a full military funeral before being laid to rest in various cemeteries. It was to be a long time before Sleap got over such tragedies.

September saw the station strength stand at 591 men and 91 WAAFs. Still a satellite of Tilstock, Sleap was also a home for many returning aircraft and for those diverted due to weather conditions, such as the B-17 Flying Fortress that landed when its home base was covered in fog on 24th September. It was generally a bad day with poor visibility across the country. The B-17 was taking nineteen ferry pilots to various airfields when it was forced to land at Sleap. Grateful to land safely, the crew and ferry pilots enjoyed the station hospitality until the next day when conditions improved.

The rest of the year followed the normal training pattern with night-navigation and 'Bullseye' exercises. Two accidents in November saw two aircraft lost but no loss of life. Whitley V Z9322 ran off the runway on 6th November and shut it for three days, whilst on 9th November Whitley V T4153 swung off the runway, causing its undercarriage to collapse.

Many were glad to see 1943 draw to a close for the cost over the year in human lives at Sleap and Tilstock had been grave. This was the year in which the bomber OTUs reached their peak with 22 such establishments in existence. The end of 1943 also saw the end of No 81 OTU at Tilstock and a new era for Sleap when a signal was received transferring Sleap and its parent station from 93 Group to 38 Group Bomber Command. With 1944 heralding several airborne operations which it was hoped would bring a swift end to the war, more glider and tug pilots were needed and after the establishment of a new heavy conversion unit at Tilstock, all glider training was transferred to Sleap.

Still known as No 81 OTU, its ageing Whitleys were now expected to tow Horsa gliders. With a crew of two and capable of carrying 20 to 25 troops, it was the RAF's first operational troop-carrying glider. Its success as such is measured by the fact that 3,655 were produced by various companies, all of them in wood. First used in the invasion of Sicily in July 1943, the Horsa went on to take part in the D-Day and Arnhem landings.

Whitleys of No 81 OTU with Horsa gliders, summer 1944. (David Birrell)

View of a Horsa glider from the astrodome of the towing Whitley. (David Birrell)

Airborne from Sleap in 1944 – Horsa gliders towed by Whitleys. (David Birrell)

Paratroopers preparing to board a Whitley for an exercise, Sleap 1944. (David Birrell)

With Sleap now under the command of the former CFI, Wg Cdr Robertson, Whitleys towing gliders became a familiar sight in the skies above Shropshire in the spring of 1944. The Horsas would be lined up along the runway and the Whitleys made ready for the tow. With the tow rope attached to both aircraft, the Whitley would taxi to the runway and the slack rope would slowly be taken up. Once both aircraft had lined up it was full power on the tug until the Horsa became airborne before the Whitley. This involved skilful flying for both pilots lest the glider reach a height above which the Whitley could not cope. For the glider pilot, it was the turbulence caused by the tug aircraft that was difficult to control. They would sometimes find themselves at the end of a taut rope one moment and the next almost level with their tugs with the rope hanging in a huge loop below and behind them. For the passengers in the glider it was equally unpleasant as again turbulence from the tug aircraft caused the Horsa to move in a surging motion when the tow rope tightened or slackened. Flying a glider could be just as dangerous as flying a powered aircraft.

The remaining months of 1944 were spent in similar vein. By this time the serviceability of the Whitleys was being questioned. Many days saw over half of the OTU aircraft grounded because of engine or mechanical problems. Spares were becoming increasingly difficult to

'Lift-off.' A Horsa glider gets airborne from Sleap in 1944. (David Birrell)

A Horsa glider lands at Sleap in August 1944. (David Birrell)

locate and at a time when airborne operations were paramount to ending the war, thoughts were turning to their replacement.

Before this happened, however, an exercise held in April 1944 proved that the training and hard work was paying off. Nine Whitleys and their gliders took off to take part in a cross-country exercise. All nine successfully clawed their way into the air, completed the short flight and landed safely back at Sleap in a massed landing. Never before (or since) had the airfield seen so many aircraft landing within minutes of each other. No doubt many pilots on that training exercise were to go on to take part in D-Day and the Arnhem landings, with the realisation that perhaps at last, the end of the war was in sight.

A repeat of a massed landing took place during the day of 16th November 1944. Bomber Command had been tasked to bomb three towns near the German lines which were about to be attacked by the American First and Ninth Armies in the area between Aachen and the Rhine. Some 1,188 Bomber Command aircraft carried out the attacks by night whilst USAAF bombers attacked German cities by day; 1,239 American aircraft, mainly B-17 Flying Fortresses, carried out raids in the same area before turning for home. A fog was lingering over Britain upon their return and a total of 62 aircraft were diverted from Molesworth, Grafton Underwood and Great Ashfield to Sleap and Tilstock. Thirty-one were accommodated at Sleap and the rest made the short hop to Tilstock. For the catering section at both airfields it was quite a challenge!

The time was fast approaching when the Whitleys would have to be replaced and one of the last training sorties carried out by the type was at the end of November. The next month saw them being replaced by Wellingtons and at the same time Tilstock returned to being the parent station as No 81 OTU was redesignated No 1380 Transport Support Conversion Unit. Still using the aircraft in a pilot training role, the unit was to continue its vital job at Sleap until 28th December 1945 when the station went into Care and Maintenance. It remained this way until 1958 when it became a satellite to Shawbury. Once again the RAF blue uniform was seen at the airfield. Another purpose it was to serve in peacetime was that of training air traffic controllers, part of the Central Navigation and Control School. After a refurbishment and the laying of a hard runway, Vampires and Jet Provosts were the usual occupants until once again the RAF gave up the airfield in 1964.

It was a traumatic war for Sleap and although classified as a satellite airfield, it saw action and tragedy comparable with many other airfields in the county. Today it is the home of the Shropshire Aero

Airborne from Sleap in 1944, Whitleys of No 81 OTU pulling Horsa gliders. (David Birrell)

Wing Commander D. Stewart Robertson, DFC, takes the salute at a parade at Sleap in March 1945. (David Birrell)

Horsa gliders dispersed at Sleap during early 1945. (David Birrell)

Club who use the wartime control tower as their clubhouse. Looking around the walls one can see photographs of wartime Sleap, reminding visitors of just how important a part it played during those years. Close to the tower is the Shropshire Wartime Recovery Group. The building they occupy displays aircraft remains recovered from various aviation 'digs' around the county. It is a treasure trove of wartime memorabilia and, again, is a reminder of Sleap and its personnel.

10
TERN HILL

The oldest military airfield in Shropshire, Tern Hill is one of the few so far inland to have been part of the Battle of Britain when during the period of June to October 1940 its fighter squadrons achieved some success in shooting down the enemy. Its main function, however, in line with most of the airfields in the county, was training, a duty that is still performed. Although perhaps living in the shadow of nearby Shawbury, there are men and women around today who are proud to have served at Tern Hill.

Situated one mile south of the junction with the A53, this large flat area of over 300 acres was requisitioned by the War Office in 1916. The contractors laid out two 1,000 yd grass landing strips and built various units. Accommodation was in wooden huts and with no electricity, heating by a single coke stove and no proper cooking facilities, life was extremely hard for these early airmen. However, by late 1917 the site was deemed habitable and by December, Nos 34 and 43 (Reserve) Squadrons of the RFC arrived to begin training. They flew the usual selection of aircraft around at that time, Avro 504s and Sopwith Camels. Joined by Nos 30 and 33 Squadrons of the Australian Flying Corps, No 4 Training Depot Station (TDS) became fully established but moved quickly to Hooton Park. Tern Hill now became No 13 TDS and, with a change of role, a bomber training base. Several units rotated through Tern Hill but by this time the First World War had ceased and all thoughts of military training were beginning to wane.

The airfield languished until a huge fire in March 1919 destroyed two of the main hangars and rapidly spread to the rest of the station. This hastened the end of Tern Hill's First World War activities and the site was sold in 1920 as a 'potential sporting estate'. It remained this way until the RAF began to look at sites ready for expansion. Tern Hill was once again requisitioned and work began to enlarge the site to enable it to become a major airfield. However, fire once again struck on the night of Wednesday, 9th October 1936 when a coke fire caused flames to spread over a huge area of the camp destroying much that had already been built. This held up work for some considerable time but extra workers were bussed in to ensure that the site was ready for occupation as soon as possible.

Although far from completion, January 1936 saw the airfield open allowing No 10 Flying Training School (FTS) to bring their Hawker Harts, Audaxes and Avro Tutors in to begin the training role. The Empire Air Day that year, held on 23rd May, had the first public showing of the new station and its units. A throwback to the Hendon Pageant days of the 1920s, the Empire Air Days were a way of showing the nation the calibre of its air force. It was important for the RAF, whose very existence at the end of the First World War had been increasingly under threat, to be seen as an essential part of the defence of the empire. There were just two Empire Air Days before the outbreak of the Second World War but they showed the public their air force and what it was capable of. The 1937 Empire Air Day saw 18,125 people flock to Tern Hill.

Like Shawbury, the airfield was to support a maintenance unit as well as flying units. The contractors moved in to construct two 'D' Type and one 'C' Type hangars on the south-east side of the airfield. Three dispersal sites were also constructed amongst the trees with two

Still operational. Tern Hill's wartime control tower in 2007. (Author)

Wartime T2 hangar remaining at Tern Hill in 2007. (Author)

Lamella hangars on each. The building work was hampered by bad weather but such was the urgency to get the MU up and running that the personnel already on site had to sleep in the hangars, there being no hutted accommodation yet built for them. Part of No 23 (Training) Group, the MU opened on 1st July 1937. Almost immediately it began receiving Lysanders, Wellingtons and Swordfish. It was redesignated No 24 EU (Equipment Unit – aircraft repairs and maintenance) before the establishment of Maintenance Command on 1st April 1938, thus becoming No 24 MU. Like Shawbury, it was encompassed within 51 Wing with its headquarters at Broughton Hall, Flintshire. Tern Hill was now set to go to war.

By the outbreak of war on 3rd September 1939, 354 aircraft were resident at No 24 MU. For the flying school it meant more aircraft cramming in more flying hours than before. No plans at this time were formulated with regard to hard runways. Like most of the Shropshire airfields, Tern Hill suffered from the weather preventing flying when the grass was sodden. Despite Sir Hugh Dowding, the Commander-in-Chief of Fighter Command, stating in 1938 that, 'We must have these [hard] runways at every fighter station if we are to be able to operate fighters by day and night during the winter', nothing much was done. At this opening period of the war the training stations were certainly as important as the fighter stations with the demand for more pilots. Yet still the subject of hard runways was being debated. Experiments carried out at Cranfield where hard runways had been constructed proved that they were preferred by most pilots and that they were the answer to concentrated night-flying which would otherwise have been impossible. There were also other factors in favour of this yet Tern Hill would not get hard runways until the end of 1941.

From the beginning, accidents occurred with the flying school, redesignated No 10 FTS on the outbreak of war. Many of the biplanes, Ansons and Harvards on strength were to be lost. Indicative of how and when, the following are just a fraction of them.

> 02.05.1939 – Hawker Audax K5146. Engine failure, crashed in making an emergency landing up a slope at Whitmore, Staffs.
> 05.10.1939 – Hawker Hind K5401. Taxied into Anson L7069 at night, Tern Hill. Repaired by unit.
> 05.10.1939 – Avro Anson L7069. Parked Tern Hill, hit at night by taxiing Hind K5401. Slight damage repaired by unit.
> 09.11.1939 – North American Harvard N7104. Stalled off steep turn, spun into Hinton-on-the-Green, Worcs. Written off.
> 17.01.1940 – Hawker Hind K6772. Landing Tern Hill skidded on frozen ground into boundary hedge. Repaired by unit.

Avro Anson – the ferry pilots' taxi. (MAP)

21.03.1940 – North American Harvard N7060. Mid-air collision with Anson N5039 near aerodrome. Written off.

By 1940 No 10 FTS was beginning to run efficiently. The harsh winter of 1939/40 had severely restricted activity at Tern Hill but with better weather the speeding-up of courses began. With the war raging in the south of the country, very little happened to interrupt the training schedule. However, the enemy had been making nightly infiltrations to the Midlands, a fact that the Air Ministry took into consideration when it was decided that Tern Hill should become a 9 Group Sector Station for the defence of the industrial Northwest. It was further decided that a detachment of Blenheim Ifs should be based at Tern Hill for night defence of this area. No 29 Squadron, based at Digby, was signalled to send two Blenheims each night, returning to Digby in the morning. From a task of North Sea escort duties, July 1940 saw the role of the squadron change to that of night-fighting. For daylight defence, a detachment of No 611 (West Lancashire) Squadron, also from Digby, arrived with their Spitfire IIas. The squadron had just returned from covering the Dunkirk withdrawal and operations were now to become intensive.

Nightly, the Blenheims of No 29 Squadron would be on stand-by until scrambled when raiders were picked up crossing the East Coast by the coastal radar stations. Many were fruitless patrols but the night

A Harvard T2B. This was the aircraft most pilots flew at service flying training schools. (MAP)

of Sunday, 18th August was to prove it a wise decision to base the aircraft at Tern Hill.

Now known as 'the hardest day', it was the day enemy aircraft attacks increased on a huge scale. Two major assaults were made against targets in southern England together with numerous smaller actions. The day saw 100 German aircraft destroyed with 136 British aircraft either destroyed or damaged in the air and on the ground. One of those enemy aircraft destroyed was a Heinkel He 111.

The day dawned mainly cloudy with occasional showers. All the major assaults continued but as dusk approached they petered out. The country braced itself for further attacks during the night.

They were not long in coming for as darkness fell, the Luftwaffe sent 92 aircraft drawn from KG 1, 2, 3, 27 and 53 to bomb targets at Sheffield, Leeds, Hull, Colchester, Canvey Island and Sealand. The raids were carried out effectively but once the bombs had been dropped, aircraft split up to make their own way back to France.

Sitting in the crew room at Tern Hill was the duty pilot for the evening, PO R. A. Rhodes and his observer/navigator Sgt 'Sticks' Gregory, so nicknamed because he played the drums. Just before midnight they were scrambled to patrol the Liverpool area when enemy aircraft were reported to be around. Their Blenheim carried the first developments of airborne radar, which sometimes proved very unreliable. However, the crew's eager eyes soon spotted an He 111 south-west of Chester, probably one that had previously bombed Liverpool.

Cautiously coming up behind the enemy, PO Rhodes realised they had been seen as the enemy bomber began to weave around all over the sky. Then began a long chase until the Blenheim finally came within range and pressing the 'tit', PO Rhodes raked the bomber with his bullets. Suddenly flames could be seen coming from one of the engines as the Heinkel side-slipped into a dive and crashed into the sea 25 miles off Spurn Head.

Returning joyfully to Tern Hill, the Blenheim crew were congratulated by all personnel who had turned out to welcome them home. The Luftwaffe records show that only one Heinkel did not return that night, it being one from KG27. The records state that the aircraft failed to return after a night sortie over Liverpool. Whilst their exact fate is uncertain, Oblt Siegel and three NCOs were reported missing and it may well have been this aircraft that gave victory to PO Rhodes and Sgt Gregory. Although routine patrols continued, very little further contact with the enemy was forthcoming. Sadly PO

Heinkel He 111. The most common enemy plane to be seen in Shopshire skies. (ATB)

Rhodes was to lose his life just a week later at the age of nineteen. He is remembered on Memorial Panel 9 at the Runnymede Memorial near Windsor, a war memorial dedicated to recording the names of those RAF and Commonwealth aircrew who have no known grave.

The second occasion on which success came to a Tern Hill unit was on 11th November 1940. No 611 Squadron had been at readiness all morning. Bored that nothing was happening, the pilots were playing football or reading or dozing in the sun when the ring of the telephone at dispersal sent everything flying. Called to scramble, they found the enemy in record time and managed to shoot down two Do 17s and in the ensuing battle claim two probables and one damaged. When they landed back at Tern Hill there was a signal from the CO, Sqd Ldr J.E. McCloud, congratulating them on their success.

Shortly after, the No 29 Squadron detachment returned to Digby to be replaced by No 306 (Torun) Squadron. This was the first Polish squadron to be based at Tern Hill and it also had the first Hurricanes to be seen there when they flew in from Church Fenton. The third Polish fighter squadron in the RAF, it was commanded by a British CO, Sqd Ldr D.R. Scott. Declared operational on 8th November, routine patrols began to be flown. The first contact came on the 13th when an enemy aircraft was attacked over Birmingham. This followed an attack on the Austin Motor Works at Longbridge. No result came from the contact and although targets in the Midlands were still being attacked and routine patrols still being flown, no further contact with enemy aircraft was made.

Polish airmen at English lessons before joining one of the Shropshire OTUs. (Crown)

Further expansion took place at No 24 MU with the acquisition of land between Stoke Heath and Buntingsdale. It now had several dispersed sites catering for different types of aircraft. Site 'A' repaired and refurbished Spitfires and Lancasters while site 'B' catered mainly for Spitfires. Site 'C' consisting of two hangars stored Fairey Battles and Tiger Moths, and site 'D' was for any other types with various degrees of damage. Some aircraft taken from this site were beyond repair and were used for a variety of purposes such as instructional airframes and decoy aircraft.

With an increase in enemy activity during the darker evenings from 10th September, No 29 Squadron now based four Blenheims at Tern Hill. During an early evening patrol on Saturday, 21st September Blenheim If L1507 was fired upon by ground defences at around 21.05 hrs. Not knowing if any hits had registered, the pilot, Sgt V.H. Skillen, shouted to his observer, AC D.W. Isherwood, that he was going to land as quickly as possible. Coming in over the threshold of Tern Hill, in haste, he collided with a floodlight alongside the runway. Neither man was hurt and the Blenheim was deemed repairable.

Two further Blenheim Ifs, K7135 and L6741, were damaged on Wednesday, 16th October when on a dull morning, a Ju 88 flew low over the airfield at 07.21 hrs and dropped four 250 kg high explosive bombs and six incendiaries. Turning their aircraft swiftly around, the enemy returned and began to strafe the airfield. Immediately a fierce fire broke out in a 'C' hangar in which aircraft were undergoing maintenance and being stored. The blaze eventually spread to neighbouring buildings, in which one civilian employee was badly burnt. Another civilian and four station personnel were slightly injured by flying metal. Two of the Blenheims inside were damaged together with several other types being stored. Although all the aircraft were repairable, the hangar was totally destroyed by the fire with another nearby damaged. Being early morning most of the civilians had not yet arrived for work, which contributed to the fact that although there were injuries, not one person died as a result of the raid. With 'C' Type hangars both expensive and time-consuming to rebuild, a single Bellman hangar was erected in its place. This one hangar remains today as a memorial to the injured.

No 10 FTS was now flying Oxfords and Harvards. At least this was a great improvement on the aged biplanes. What was lacking was the experience of instructors at this early stage of the war. Only the most experienced pilots and aircrew were fit to serve as instructors but most of them were already in the front line of battle. Whilst this problem affected Bomber Command more than Fighter Command, both needed trained pilots which No 10 FTS and many others were trying to provide. The bad winter of 1940 did not help but by this time No 10 FTS had been disbanded and moved to Moose Jaw, Saskatchewan in Canada where it continued its training role under the auspices of the Empire Air Training Scheme.

In its place came No 5 FTS from Sealand, using the Miles Master, a two-seat advanced trainer made of wood and plywood covered. However, they arrived at a time when flying was impossible due to a waterlogged airfield. This continued for many weeks and although some flying was undertaken from other Shropshire airfields, it became very obvious that if the increasing demand for pilots continued, something would have to be done about a hard runway. The same problems were affecting No 306 Squadron. Desperate to make contact with the enemy, their daylight patrols achieved very little. With the heavy enemy attacks being carried out at night, thoughts turned to changing the role of the squadron to night-fighting.

With a busy Tern Hill, accidents were never very far away. The 26th of November saw a collision between a Hurricane and an Anson occur. The Hurricane of No 306 Squadron was being taxied by the CO, Sqd Ldr D.R. Scott, when it collided with an Avro Anson of No 5 FTS. Sqd Ldr Scott was hospitalised whilst the two pupils in the Anson received just bruises. Later in the day, however, two airmen died in separate accidents. Miles Master N7427 crashed at Gardenfields Farm, Cuddington, killing LAC P.G.W. Paul, while another Master, T8397, crashed at Uffington killing LAC W. Bethel. A sad month for the FTS and for Tern Hill. There were to be four more fatal accidents in December, ensuring that it was a very sombre time for all.

The arrival of a new CO for No 306 Squadron and a visit by Marshal of the RAF, Viscount Trenchard, in January did help to raise spirits a little. In his address he stated that the Service thought that Tern Hill was a credit to the RAF and that a hard runway would soon become fact. Sqd Ldr D.E. Gillam, DFC, AFC, then gave an address on behalf of his new squadron, saying that they would soon be introducing night-fighting to their operations.

From the very beginning of the night offensive, lone Hurricane and Spitfire pilots had taken to the skies in an endeavour to find and shoot down night intruders. These solo attempts found little success but by the end of 1940 and beginning of 1941, a specialist number of fighter squadrons began to be trained in night detection. One such squadron was No 306 which, with its black-painted Hurricanes, carried out many night patrols from Tern Hill. One night saw thirteen such patrols, sadly without any contact with the enemy. In order to help this increase in operations, the RLG at Chetwynd was officially taken over by Tern Hill.

It was also felt that a Polish airman should now be in command of a Polish squadron. In March 1941, Sqd Ldr T.H. Polski replaced Sqd Ldr Gillam and immediately No 306 Squadron began its first offensive sorties across the Channel escorting large Blenheim formations on bombing operations. All of this was in addition to the night-fighting, making No 306 a very busy unit. The demand upon the Poles began to show, with several accidents. PO Bielkiewicz crashed and was killed on 13th February, and the same day saw Sgt Jasinski slightly injured when his Hurricane crashed. By April it was apparent that the squadron had taken on too much and it reverted back solely to night-fighting with a move down south to Northolt, now regarded as the official home of Polish squadrons. In their place came the Hurricanes of No 605 (County of Warwick) Squadron which arrived on 31 March. They stayed for one month before leaving for Baginton. After the relative comforts of Martlesham Heath they had found Tern Hill 'uncomfortable' and were glad to vacate it.

April was also to prove a bad time for No 5 FTS when nine airmen were killed in flying accidents; a busy time for the station mortuary. Still flying the Oxford, the Mk II had now been introduced. This particular mark was intended purely for pilot training and was known more popularly as the 'Ox-box'. No 5 FTS, like the other flying training schools, was under great pressure to increase its output of trained pilots. The news that at last a hard runway was to be laid at the station meant that even greater demands would be placed upon the unit.

No 24 MU, busier than ever, took over the SLG at Hodnet. Known as SLG 29, it too was soon full of aircraft such as Wellingtons, Hudsons, Ansons and Oxfords. Very basic in its 'creature comforts', the aircraft were dispersed amongst the trees and around the area surrounding Hodnet Hall. It was also used by the Masters of No 5 FTS for circuit training, becoming a very busy SLG during 1941 and 1942.

Several fighter squadrons were rotated through Tern Hill although only for short periods. They were still based there for the defence of the Midlands, though most never made contact with the enemy. One of the more unusual units was No 403 (Wolf) Squadron of the RCAF. They arrived on 19th March from Baginton where they had formed, flying the Curtiss Tomahawk. This was an American-built fighter aircraft ordered by France but not delivered before France was overrun. The

RAF therefore took over the order and received 140 Mk Is, 110 Mk IIas and 635 Mk IIds. Originally formed as an Army Co-operation unit, the Tomahawk was never a favourite with No 403 Squadron and upon arrival at Tern Hill they converted to the Spitfire Ia. They worked up on the type before becoming fully operational and moving to Hornchurch in Essex to become part of Fighter Command.

No 131 (County of Kent) Squadron arrived from Catterick in August 1941 to replace them. Commanded by Sqd Ldr J.M. Thompson, DFC, the Spitfire Is stayed one month before moving on to Atcham and leaving Tern Hill devoid of any fighter squadrons. With the German army nearing the gates of Moscow by late summer 1941, some of the heat had been taken off the large enemy attacks on the Midlands. After the bombing of Pearl Harbor on 7th December, the United States entered the war when Andrew May, the Chairman of the House of Representatives Military Affairs Committee announced: 'There is no doubt that within a few hours, Congress will give the President whatever authority he needs to prosecute the war all-out.' At Tern Hill the news was broadcast over the station tannoy and greeted with jubilation. This was in addition to the construction of a hard runway, beginning in October, which although hampering flying at the time was welcomed by all.

No 41 Maintenance Group had now become the parent of No 24 MU at Tern Hill and also No 27 MU at Shawbury. With both being close geographically, they were also linked in other ways. On occasions they were to use each other's RLGs and SLGs and at the same time, both units grew to enormous size. Aircraft were still being flown in daily to be prepared for issuing to the squadrons, many of them now larger and therefore taking up more room than their predecessors.

No 5 FTS continued the gruelling task of training whilst the runway construction was going on. This was to continue over the Christmas period until finished in early 1942. Throughout the next year very little happened to interrupt the routine with the exception of accidents. The hard runway allowed increased night-flying to take place, although No 5 FTS had for some time been using what was known as the day/night scheme.

Several methods of simulating night-flying were in place at Tern Hill. One of them was the single stage (flarepath) scheme for which the pupil wore special goggles and was only able to see the flarepath and his instruments. Further methods consisted of the aircraft being fitted with blue screens and the pupil wearing amber goggles, and vice versa. Most of these, with the exception of the synthetic method conducted in

A busy scene at Tern Hill, 12th May 1942. An Oxford of No 286 Squadron, a Turbinlite Havoc and a Handley Page Harrow Transport named 'Boadicea'. (A. Thomas)

purpose-built units, were dropped during 1942 in favour of practical night-flying.

On 13th April No 5 FTS became No 5 (Pilots) Advanced Flying Unit ((P)AFU). This was in line with other training establishments where pilots arrived for advanced training from the Empire Air Training Scheme. Both single- and multi-engined training was continued with the arrival of several Hurricanes, a far faster mount than the single-engined Masters. The difference in speed and performance between the two allowed those pupils with aptitude and good potential to fly the same type of aircraft that they would once assigned to a regular squadron. They stayed until mid-1943 when the unit reverted to Miles Masters.

No 24 MU was transferred to 43 Group in April 1942. Although receiving various types from time to time, their main task was the repair of Lancasters and Spitfires. The former were also repaired at the nearby Avro works at Langar, working on a similar principle to Tern Hill. Those undergoing repair would be divided and taken apart in four sections – nose, mainplane, fuselage and tail. After overhaul or repair they would be reassembled (but not necessarily mated with their former parts), wheeled out and test flown before returning to a regular squadron. The workshops at Tern Hill were busier than ever

A Turbinlite Havoc I from High Ercall pictured at Tern Hill. (A. Thomas)

with the Lancaster repair and assembly continuing until 1945. A civilian worker at the MU, Albert Ward knew the process well:

At Tern Hill they used to bring Lancasters that had crashed and repair them. Where the Borstal is now, they rebuilt the engines. They used to have a test bench up which ran 24 hours a day testing the engines before they put them back into the aircraft. Going back a bit, I remember when they were building the runways; the Irish labour camp was right opposite our house. The other thing that sticks in my mind was when I was standing on the A41 and a German plane and one of ours were having a dogfight over our heads. We were standing there like fools listening to them. You could hear the bullets hitting the fields. The German plane was eventually shot down and the pilot was buried in the cemetery at Stoke upon Tern. Another time a plane came over as I was going to work. I thought, 'Funny, he is low.' Then there was an explosion as it had bombed the airfield. The bombs had come down among the hangars but only hit one of them. He then came round again and machine-gunned the entire area. There were plenty of crashes with the trainers, with one crash at the back of my brother's farm. It tipped the corner of the thatched cottage and ran into the hedge. I think it was a Harvard.

In 1943 the only apparent change to the training routine was that No 5 (P)AFU now had Harvards in addition to the Oxfords and Hurricanes. Sadly, in January the Chief Flying Instructor, Wg Cdr A.W.M. Finny, died in a flying accident. Apparently his aircraft got into an uncontrollable spin and whilst his pupil was able to bail out, Finny remained in an attempt to control his aircraft and was killed in the ensuing crash.

A rather foolish incident during 1943 ended in the death of an airman. Aircraftman Johns, one of the military personnel attached to No 24 MU, took it into his head on 29th August to fly one of the aircraft. Whether he had previous flying experience is not known but somehow he took an aircraft and managed to take off without permission. It is reported that he performed several aerobatic manoeuvres before diving into the ground outside the airfield perimeter and killing himself. His death saddened the station and ensured that security was tightened up lest this should happen again.

Training continued in 1944 with the usual crop of incidents, but with the war going the way of the Allies much of Britain, including Shropshire, had been turned into an armed camp. General Dwight D. Eisenhower in finalising plans for D-Day visited many locations thoughout the country. Military exercises were taking place every day and many methods of deception were being put into place. Airborne landings by parachutists and glider troops were being rehearsed daily, many over the skies of Shropshire. At Tern Hill the security cordon thrown around the station tightened. It would contine this way until some days after 6th June 1944: D-Day. On that day, as the drama unfolded, the entire personnel of No 5 (P)AFU and No 24 MU stood and listened to the announcements being made over the radio and relayed via the station tannoy. The demand for certain types of aircraft was intense for the MU but they and the rest of Tern Hill coped admirably. At nightfall the world knew that it was on the final path to victory.

Christmas 1944 was celebrated with far more optimism than those that had gone before. However, it was tinged with sadness by the news that the popular American bandleader, Major Glenn Miller, had gone

Squirrel HT1 helicopter of the Defence Helicopter Flying School seen at Tern Hill in 2007. (Author)

missing over the English Channel on a short flight to Paris. Many personnel had danced to his music at camp dances or listened to the regular broadcasts on the American Forces Network and the BBC. Though he never brought the band to Shropshire, many had travelled to nearby concert halls to see and hear the American Band of the AEF.

In May 1945 a signal was received to disband No 5 (P)AFU. It was replaced by No 9 (P)AFU from Errol which immediately retained the No 5 (P)AFU title. It was this unit and No 24 MU that were to celebrate victory at Tern Hill.

The task of training pilots continued into peacetime with No 6 SFTS becoming resident in 1946 and remaining until 4th August 1961. No 24 MU was joined in March 1951 by No 30 MU from Sealand, both units returning to the latter airfield in February 1959. No 6 SFTS was due to convert to the Jet Provost but due to the short runway, the School moved to Acklington on 4th August 1961. Its place was taken by the helicopters of the Central Flying School (CFS) but with Shawbury named as the main peacetime helicopter training base, the CFS moved and Tern Hill was placed under Care and Maintenance. It remained this way for several years but today the Squirrel and Griffin

The remaining residents of Tern Hill – No 632 Volunteer Gliding School. (Author)

helicopters of the Shawbury-based Defence Helicopter Flying School use Tern Hill as a satellite.

The airfield is in constant use for training and is also the home of No 632 Volunteer Gliding School flying the Grob Vigilant powered glider. This outfit enables a succession of Air Cadets to experience their first taste of flying. The domestic site has been taken over by the Army and is the main base for the Royal Anglian Regiment. The large 'C' Type and Lamella hangars are reminders of the wartime period when Tern Hill was not only a main flying training school but also a very important and busy maintenance unit. It is hoped that with the future of Shawbury assured for the foreseeable future, Tern Hill will also remain an important satellite training base.

11

TILSTOCK (WHITCHURCH HEATH)

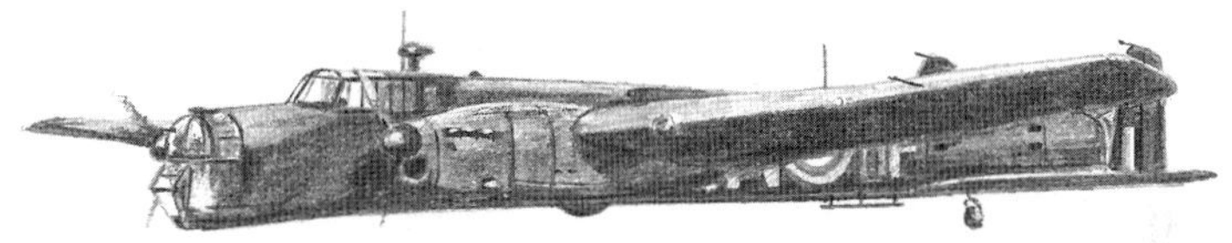

Depending on their geographical location, some of the Shropshire airfields were known by several names. One of them was Tilstock, often referred to as Whitchurch Heath but known locally as Prees Heath. Both of those villages were close to Tilstock and alongside the A41 main road approximately three miles south of Whitchurch. To most airmen after 1942, however, the airfield was Tilstock – the change of name coming about not least because confusion caused a momentous error when Whitleys destined for RAF Whitchurch were sent to RAF Whitchurch in Hampshire – and many are proud to have the name imprinted on their minds.

One of the later airfields to be planned in the county, it was built by Alfred McAlpine and originally named Whitchurch. It was built to a standard bomber pattern with three runways but like Peplow airfield, it had the rather unusual central runway intersection. The three runways were 03/21 (6,100 ft), 33/15 (4,200 ft) and 25/07 (3,600 ft), with all three having a width of 150 ft. The main A41 road cut right across the landing area and was thus closed for the duration of the war. Three T2 hangars were constructed together with the usual domestic and technical buildings. Not usual at the majority of the Shropshire airfields, however, a Battle Headquarters was built amongst the trees at the end of Runway 33/15. Had the airfield been occupied by enemy forces, control of the main functions and defences would have been moved to this semi-sunken reinforced concrete building.

Officially opened on 1st August 1942, the first airmen to arrive travelled the short distance from Ashbourne in Derbyshire. They were part of No 81 OTU and although formed at Ashbourne on 10th July

The 'bull nose' of a Whitley bomber seen at Tilstock. (Crown)

1942, the unit did not receive any aircraft until they moved to Whitchurch. These were Vickers Wellingtons but the OTU was not to have them for long as once installed at the airfield they were exchanged for the venerable Whitley.

One of the mainstays of Bomber Command during the early years of the war, the Armstrong Whitworth Whitley was relegated to a training role from 1942 onwards. It is chiefly remembered for its many 'Nickel' raids but prior to 1942 it carried the night offensive to Germany. With a crew of five and an all-metal, stressed-skin construction, the last Whitley bombing operation was a raid on Ostend on the night of 29th/30th April 1942. A former Whitley pilot recalls, 'The Whitley was a sturdy aeroplane with few vices, if any. It could take a lot of punishment and was a pleasure to fly if a trifle on the slow side, but well liked by those who had to fly them on operations. There was a marked tendency to swing to port on take-off because of the engine torque created by the two 1,000 hp Merlin engines which powered it. But swing was experienced to some degree in most aircraft and easy to counter by coarse use of the rudder or by opening the port throttle in advance of the starboard one in the early stages of the take-off run.'

The changeover of aircraft was swift and once the unit had become established, the training of crews began. As with all OTUs, from the beginning accidents were going to occur, many sadly with a loss of life. Such a tragedy brought the realisation of war to Whitchurch shortly after the arrival of No 81 OTU.

The early evening of 30th November 1942 saw Whitley V EB339 prepared for a night-training exercise. The crew, Sgt T.J.T. Evans, Sgt L.C. Lawson, Sgt J. Overend and Sgt Whitebeard had been briefed and were sitting in their positions in the aircraft going through the all essential cockpit checks. By 00.45 hrs they were cleared for take-off with the aircraft beginning its roll down the runway at 00.50 hrs. Lifting off successfully, for some reason the pilot found it necessary to return to base. Whilst turning the aircraft around, the Whitley crashed into some trees 450 yds short of the runway. It immediately burst into flames killing Sgts Evans, Lawson and Overend and severely injuring Sgt Whitebeard, the rear gunner. Though this was the first major accident for the OTU since its formation on 10th July, it had a profound effect on all personnel at Whitchurch.

Like several other OTUs, No 81 was initially at three-quarter strength. However, with the establishment of a satellite airfield at Sleap and the fact that by February 1943 the unit had 54 Whitleys on strength, they could at last boast of being a full OTU.

The Whitleys were known to most crews as cumbersome and not very comfortable although the handling characteristics were reasonable. With no real heating, flying in them during the winter could be very unpleasant. The one redeeming feature with the version that No 81 OTU flew, the Mark V, was that it was the major production Whitley powered by two Rolls-Royce Merlin X engines. The fuselage had also been lengthened by 15 in. Altogether 1,476 Mark Vs were manufactured with the last one being delivered on 6th June 1943.

With the damage the Germans had inflicted on the civilian population and our towns and cities, this wanton destruction was to bring on their heads a terrible revenge. It felt only right that the crews in training wanted to inflict this revenge as quickly as possible. First, though, it was they who faced a rigorous schedule of training, with the usual cross-section of nationalities.

'Our course was common to any such group of its time,' recalled a pilot of an unknown OTU,

Englishmen, Irishmen, Scots, Welshmen and various other European nationalities all thrust together with one intention, that of getting back at the enemy. First though it was a series of classroom lectures which went on for the next six weeks. Theory of aerial gunnery, formation flying, simple ballistics, hydraulics, air force law and so on. On chilly mornings and warm afternoons we listened to the instructors imparting their knowledge, some good, some bad. After lessons we would go out and watch others who had passed before us getting into their aircraft to carry out what they had been taught. Men in thick white sweaters under their battledress and fleece-lined boots would clamber into aged aircraft and prepare to take off on exercises. What were ops really like? What did it feel like to see flak or to have searchlights find you and turn your darkness into eternal light? Then the aircraft would run up with the whole evening vibrating with engine noise. Making their way to the runway the crews would be checking all their equipment and hoping that it would work for the entire exercise. The pilot would be hoping that one of his engines did not stop in flight and the navigator would be hoping that this time he would be able to plot a course correctly. All of this was to come to us very soon but for now we could only learn and watch and hope we would soon be doing the same.

The official Air Ministry account of those early years (*Bomber Command*, HMSO) put it somewhat differently:

In the spring of 1940/41 the Wellingtons, Whitleys and Hampdens were still new and comparatively untried aircraft. Before their appearance on the scene the men of Bomber Command had been flying far less powerful aircraft such as the Handley Page Harrow, the Hawker Hind and the Vickers Wellesley. These carried a crew of two or at the most three, which meant that most of the responsibility fell upon the shoulders of the pilot. With the bigger aircraft, however, carrying crews of four, five and six, the necessity for closer team work soon became apparent. A further stage in flying training known as operational training was then introduced. A bomber, unlike the fighter, is flown not only by the pilot but also by the air observer, the wireless operator and the air gunner. They form a team and the success or failure of the flight depends on the closest and most intimate co-operation of all on board. The captain and second pilot do the flying; the observer navigates and drops the bombs; the wireless operator helps the navigator and with the air gunner does the fighting. To rewrite the old saying, their motto is and must be, 'United we fly, divided we fall'. More than anything, teamwork is the secret of their success.

So just what would 1943 bring? It began rather badly for No 81 when a training exercise in the late afternoon of 11th January came to grief. Unusually it was a screened pilot, navigator, wireless operator and five-pupil aircrew that were briefed to fly Whitley V LA766. Crewed by WO D.R. Roberts (RCAF), Sgt C.E. Aron, PO R.J. Binham, Sgt A.T. Strachan, Sgt D.B. Lister, Fl Sgt R. Smeaton, Sgt M.J. Buckle and Fl Sgt W.H. Stewart (RCAF), it left Whitchurch at 16.07 hrs for an evening cross-country exercise. The Whitley crashed at 20.50 hrs some 23 miles from base in the county of Denbigh. Tragically, all eight crew were killed in the crash which has remained unexplained to this day.

Despite the terrible loss felt by all personnel, the first of several 'Nickel' raids took place on 6th February 1943. Classed as 'minor operations', the target was Paris. The OTU aircraft were not flying alone but as part of a force that included 52 Wellingtons and twenty Halifaxes engaged on mine-laying between St Nazaire and Texel. The No 81 OTU Whitleys returned safely although enemy aircraft and flak were sighted on the way back, as the interrogation officer's report states:

Report of Nickelling Operation
Night Leaflet Operation Paris

Dropped 240,352 leaflets on Paris at 22.57 hrs to 23.07 hrs. Operation was carried out at 31,000-34,000 ft with 10/10 cloud over the target area. 3 enemy aircraft were sighted over the Channel and in the vicinity of Le Treport but made no attacks. Meagre and inaccurate flak was encountered at the French coast. All aircraft and crew returned safely.

The method of disposing of the packets of literature was basic and simple. The leaflets were loaded into the fuselage in open cardboard boxes with a given number of packets in each box, each packet being held together by an elastic band. When over the dropping area, the wireless operator, navigator or rear gunner just had to take out one packet at a time, remove the elastic and stuff the packet down the flare chute. The leaflets would be immediately dispersed on emerging into the slipstream. Gently they would then flutter down and cover large areas in paper.

Things were by now turning desperately sour for Germany. By the end of the year the official historian at Tilstock had written:

> Bomber Command under the vigorous leadership of Air Marshal Harris had shown, not only to Britain's allies but also to her enemies, the tremendous potential power of the long-range heavy bomber force.

More output was required from the OTUs to meet the insatiable appetite of Bomber Command. Tour-expired aircrew posted to instruction rapidly learned that flying pupils in old, tired aircraft was as hard as being operational themselves. The problems incurred in time-expired Whitleys and Wellingtons cost many lives as 25% of the trainees were killed before they could pass out as aircrew. Included in this percentage were many personnel from No 81 OTU, including PO D.P.R. Wild who had the misfortune to have his parachute open prematurely.

Whitley V LA769 departed from Whitchurch at 21.32 hrs for a night cross-country exercise which was to incorporate practice bombing and infra-red photography. Shortly before 02.27 hrs a con-rod in the starboard engine seized and PO Wild instructed the other two members of the crew to bail out. Leaving his position he moved to the escape hatch in order to abandon the aircraft, but in doing so somehow his parachute opened. Realising he could not now jump, he untangled himself from the canopy and went back to the cockpit hoping to control the Whitley enough to crash-land. Although he succeeded in reaching the airfield, he lost control at the last moment and the Whitley crashed alongside the runway, PO Wild being killed in the ensuing fire.

February and March were 'Nickel' months with several trips to Rouen and Lille. Thousands of leaflets were dropped telling the French people to take heart that the Allies were winning the war and warning the occupying forces that the fight was being lost. March also saw the beginning of the nationwide 'Wings for Victory' campaign. Every town and city in the country was urged to take part and collect money to be put towards the war effort. This morale-raising idea caught the imagination of everyone and Whitchurch, like most of the county's airfields, was to participate in parades through town centres to encourage people to part with their hard-earned money. The parades also gave the local populace an idea of just how much was owed to the gallant airmen and airwomen.

Amongst all this civic duty, April was to prove a devastating month for No 81 OTU and Whitchurch. The first tragedy occurred on the

The Raven Hotel, beloved 'watering hole' for Tilstock airmen. (Author)

10th of the month when Whitley V LA771 crashed during a training exercise. Taking off at 10.22 hrs, it appeared to climb too steeply resulting in a stall. Sixty seconds later the aircraft hit the ground and burst into flames killing Sgt W. Berry and injuring the other three sergeant trainees. The next day Whitley V EB342 left Whitchurch for a night cross-country flight. At 03.30 hrs a message was received at the airfield that the pilot, Sgt A.C. Browning, was going to make an emergency landing near Moxall Farm, Acton, a mile from Nantwich in Cheshire. Nothing further was heard until the wreckage was found some time later. Sadly, Sgt G.E. Davies had been killed, whilst injuries had been sustained by Sgt Browning, Sgt J.F. Hallett, Sgt J. Smith and Sgt Bragg. Two days later an entire crew were lost when Whitley V EB346 left Whitchurch at 21.39 hrs for a night navigation detail. Some two hours into the flight the port engine failed and although it was possible for a Whitley to fly on one engine, at 23.44 hrs control was lost and the aircraft crashed nine miles west-north-west of Great Driffield. The seven members of the crew – FO L.H. Page and Sgts Harrison, Sibbery, Frapwell, Martin, McCartney and Levitus – were all taken for burial in their home towns and villages.

Yet again, on the 17th, Whitley V LA768 crashed whilst on a night-training exercise. A reason has never been given for the crash but it cost the lives of Sgt R.C.S. Findley and Sgt H. Derbyshire and severe injuries were suffered by Fl Sgt Whitley, Sgt Hill and Sgt Randall. The final tragedy came on the 28th when Whitley V EB341 carrying out a night cross-country exercise began to lose glycol from both engines. The pilot, FO D.C. Bradshaw attempted to make for Twinwood Farm airfield in Bedfordshire but the aircraft came down just short of the airfield. Both FO Bradshaw and his co-pilot PO W.T. Shannon survived the crash, only to lose their lives a month or so later carrying out a bombing raid on Köln.

May did not begin much better when an entire five-man crew were lost when Whitley V EB405 took off from the satellite airfield of Sleap at 22.35 hrs on a night-navigation exercise. On its return it attempted two landings until finally it crashed into trees at 04.20 hrs and burst into flames near Wem. Just one further accident was to occur during May. On the 13th, Whitley V EB338 took off at 18.05 hrs only to lose the use of the port engine twice before finally crashing at 18.55 hrs eighteen miles west of Derby. Of the six-man crew, only Sgt G. Belec, RCAF, lost his life. He rests in Ashbourne Cemetery. For Whitchurch and No 81 OTU this was one of the most difficult periods in its existence.

With confusion over its name still causing concern, the airfield became Tilstock on 1st June. A sad incident took place on the 21st when Whitley V EB402 lost power and the order was given to abandon the aircraft by the captain, Sgt E.T. Jones, RCAF. The other five crewmembers successfully left the aircraft but Sgt R.H. Hanson had the misfortune to land in the River Dee where his parachute dragged him under the water causing him to drown. Meanwhile, Sgt Jones managed to land the Whitley halfway down the runway at Hawarden airfield but realising that he would not be able to stop within the runway perimeter, he pulled the undercarriage up to slow down, thereby wrecking the aircraft.

One month later, Whitley V BD411 flown by Sgt Bugg with Fl Sgt Homer, a trainee, lost its port propeller and crashed out of control a few miles from the airfield. Having survived this accident, Sgt Bugg was to lose his life in another No 81 OTU crash, that which happened on the night of 13th/14th July. He was flying Whitley V LA831 when the aircraft suddenly dived into the ground at 04.15 hrs, killing the six-man crew. Wreckage was strewn over a large area, much of which was recovered at the time. One engine was later given to the Cosford Aerospace Museum but has since been donated to the Shropshire Wartime Aircraft Recovery Group at Sleap airfield where it can be seen today.

Clearly, the summer of 1943 was not a good one for Tilstock. It seemed as though every other week saw empty beds where crews had not returned from training flights. The station mortuary, small in size, was in constant use over the summer months. Many families were to receive the standard telegram telling them of the loss of a father or son. Sadly, No 81 OTU was no different to any of the other OTUs; they all had their share of tragedies.

'Nickel' raids continued throughout the summer period and many commented that it was safer to carry out one of these than to fly training sorties. By September the station strength stood at 1,405 airmen and 314 WAAFs. August was to fare better with just one major accident, although this was to involve ground personnel as well, but the first two weeks of September were once again bad for the OTU. With much of the flying being done from Sleap due to overcrowding at Tilstock, the deaths of so many airmen and airwomen brought the realism and horror of war to the airfield (see Chapter 10, Sleap).

Despite the tragedies the relentless training programme continued. With Sleap becoming as busy as Tilstock, night and day the skies above Shropshire would throb to the sound of aero engines. This pace of training would see further incidents though none ended in deaths. The last was to occur on 20th December when a communication Airspeed Oxford of the OTU was forced to land at Great Bullamore Farm near Newport due to severe turbulence. Though the aircraft was a write-off, the five-man crew survived with just one serious injury.

The year 1943 saw the bomber OTUs reach their peak strength with 22 of them in existence. Despite all the tragedies and aircraft losses, Bomber Command was now delivering an unprecedented assault on German cities. For Tilstock and No 81 OTU the time for change was approaching. With Christmas celebrated in the usual style, 1944 beckoned and with it a new role for the station.

On 1st January 1944 Tilstock and its satellite transferred from 93 Group to 38 Group. The role of the unit was now glider tug training in preparation for the invasion of Europe. The arrival of Gp Cpt G.H.W. Gibson, DFC, from Mildenhall to command heralded the start of the training which initially was done on the old Whitleys of No 81 OTU. Several Horsa gliders arrived and training commenced with a new sight appearing in the skies above, that of a Whitley towing a glider.

This was not to be the only new sight as the advance party of No 1665 Heavy Glider Conversion Unit arrived from Woolfox Lodge to take up residence at Tilstock on 23rd January, when two special trains drew in to the local station bringing around 700 personnel ahead of the arrival of several Short Stirling bombers. This was the first four-engined monoplane bomber to enter service with the RAF. It served Bomber Command well but by the middle of 1943 had quickly become out-moded as a heavy bomber. Its main use from 1944 was as a glider tug, a role in which it served with distinction.

There now commenced daily training flights at low level across wide expanses of open countryside. Teams of navigators were trained to find and photograph certain bridges and landmarks, experience that would be needed for the accurate despatch of gliders over the war zone. In addition, containers were dropped at specific pre-marked targets to simulate dropping supplies to troops, a role that would become all too prevalent later in 1944.

Despite the changes, accidents still continued. On 14th February Whitley V LA936 was involved in a taxiing accident with Whitley V EB666 due to the failure of the brakes on the latter aircraft. The next day, Whitley V DT420 crashed killing all the crew, and later in the month another Whitley crashed at Snailbeach with the loss of five New Zealanders whilst towing a Horsa. By good fortune the glider had cast off seconds before and was able to make a safe landing.

To give the reader an idea of just how much activity was going on at Tilstock during February and March, the station diarist faithfully recorded it all:

SERVICING WING

GENERAL – This month has been a period during which No 1665 HCU have begun to settle down to their new station and No 81 OTU have also begun to become more acquainted with the problems of glider towing. From the servicing point of view No 81 OTU have preserved their relatively high serviceabilty in spite of grave warning of troubles that would be incurred on Whitley aircraft due to glider towing. No 1665 HCU have shown a very fine increase in their serviceability and a more rapid turn out of inspections, which, although a great achievement, can still be improved.

FLYING HOURS AND SERVICEABILITY – The flying hours total 2,245, of which 964 were done by Whitleys and 975 by Stirlings. The flying hours show a substantial increase on the previous month due to three reasons, the settling down of the Stirling unit, the part change-over from Stirling I to Stirling III, and a high percentage of fine weather. The Stirling serviceability also shows a substantial increase due partly to the change-over.

STRENGTH OF AIRCRAFT – The present holding of Stirling

aircraft is 50 but this is misleading as it is anticipated very shortly that all Stirling I aircraft will be flown away from the unit and the strength will then be reduced to 35 maximum. All except one of the Whitley aircraft allotted away have now left and the holding at present is 26 against an establishment of 27.

ACCIDENTS – This month has been marred by a number of accidents one of which was fatal.

As D-Day approached, General Browning, the commander of the airborne forces, arrived at Tilstock to give a morale-boosting talk to the pilots under training. In it he expressed admiration for the work being carried out by both units but gave no hint as to when the first airborne operation would take place. This came when a tight security cordon was put in place for Tilstock and a signal was received that no flying or training was to take place from 4th June until 7th June. Over this period the great assault began, with aircraft carrying troops and aircraft towing gliders filled with troops becoming headline news.

With this increase in operations July became a very busy month for the station. Apart from the station strength of 31 Stirlings, 28 Whitleys, eight Ansons, seven Oxfords and a Spitfire for fighter affiliation duties, Tilstock was often a haven for aircraft returning from the Continent either shot up or with mechanical problems. This brought into operation the 'Darkie' procedure which was used for aircraft in distress and which needed to land as quickly as possible. A system of direction finding in which an aircraft could call for a homing using the call sign 'Darkie', it was mainly operated by WAAFs from a building in the middle of nowhere. Whilst they could not transmit or speak

A Short Stirling of No 1665 Heavy Conversion Unit at Tilstock. (Shorts Plc)

Workhorse of the Shropshire OTUs – a Whitley bomber. (Crown)

directly to the pilot, once they had received a 'Mayday' signal from an aircraft that was lost or had no navigation aids they were able to guide the pilot by giving out the vectors to the station controllers in the sector operations room. The controller then passed these to the pilot to enable him to land safely. Many a crew was grateful to the system that brought them home safe and sound.

Over the next few weeks after D-Day, Tilstock was to accommodate many different types and sizes of aircraft. The 'Sandra' lights, three searchlights whose beams were directed to form a cone over the airfield, were illuminated on numerous occasions to assist aircraft in landing, together with sodium flares to allow the pilots to see the end of the runway. It was not uncommon to see both fighters and bombers, RAF and American, sitting around the airfield in various degrees of distress.

One particular Stirling of No 1665 HGCU was certainly in distress when it ended up straddling the main A49 road. Two versions have been given for this mishap. One was that it overran the short runway and went through the perimeter fence, which was only wire mesh, and the other that it was on the perimeter track when the wind caught it and swung it over the fence onto the road. Whatever version is the truth, the puzzled groundcrew had the job of getting it back on to the runway!

Even in late 1944 the enemy was still active on occasions as the crew of a Stirling of the conversion unit found in a frightening incident. The pilot, Fl Lt Carpenter, with his pupil pilot PO Nettlefield and air gunner Sgt Whitbread were on a training flight cross-country sortie. At 22.25 hrs in conditions of light cloud with bright moonlit periods, the crew were flying on autopilot with the navigation lights on when they suddenly realised that they were being fired at. Bullets could be seen hitting the aircraft and the attack was observed to be coming from dead astern. The pilot immediately told PO Nettlefield to take out 'George',

Fitters work on a Short Stirling at Tilstock in 1944. (Imperial War Museum)

the autopilot, but by this time the attack was over. Meanwhile the port outer engine had cut and flames were seen to be coming from the port inner engine.

With Fl Lt Carpenter taking control of the aircraft, it soon became apparent that the Stirling was losing height. After ordering the rest of the crew to bail out, the pilot moved to the escape hatch himself and jumped. As his parachute opened he saw the enemy aircraft, a Ju 88, above him just entering the cloud. A flash on the ground indicated where the Stirling crashed. The subsequent inquiry into the incident stated that the crew did not keep a sufficient eye out for enemy aircraft. It was said that, had they been fully alert, they would have seen the exhaust glow of the Ju 88 and could therefore have avoided being a target. It was known that the enemy was targeting training areas and this incident highlighted the dangers of not being aware and alert all the time.

Four Hawker Hurricanes arrived in August to assist the Whitleys and Stirlings with fighter affiliation. The same month arrangements were made for USAAF hospital aircraft to land, bringing back wounded Allied soldiers from the battlefront on the Continent. Being a relatively quiet area, the Midlands was the site chosen for many American hospitals to be built. Daily these hospital aircraft arrived and a close

Tilstock tower. Left to right – CFO Squadron Leader R. Glass, DFC, CO Wing Commander G.H. Gibson, DFC, Flying Controller Squadron Leader G.T. Yuill. (Imperial War Museum)

liaison with the local ambulance service was set up to transport the injured to the 15th, 16th, 83rd and 87th General American Hospitals.

As autumn approached it was obvious to everyone that victory was within sight despite the ill-fated Arnhem operation. With the loss of so many tugs and gliders during the assault, the training programme was accelerated. This once again brought further crashes involving deaths and injuries. More aircraft were diverted to Tilstock after bombing sorties, one particularly eventful day being 16th November when 62 B-17s were diverted from Molesworth, Grafton Underwood and Great Ashfield after a daylight raid on France. Some 560 aircrew had to be accommodated both at Tilstock and Sleap. Several weeks later, 34 B-24 Liberators were diverted from Bungay to Tilstock, causing something of a headache for the duty officer!

December, at last, was to see the end of the Whitleys as several Wellington X aircraft flew in for No 81 OTU. Most air and ground crews were not sorry to see the Whitleys go as maintenance on this old aircraft had become a problem. Many had to be cannibalised in order to keep a certain number airworthy.

The forlorn-looking control tower at Tilstock in 2007. (Author)

Although it was obvious to all that the end of the war was fast approaching, No 1665 HCU received six Halifaxes to form a conversion flight. The older Stirlings were replaced by the newer Mk IVs and even at this late stage of the war, changes were ahead for Tilstock. No 1665 moved to Saltby in Lincolnshire and No 42 OTU arrived to take their place. They had been flying the twin-engined Albermarle at Ashbourne but were now to convert to Wellingtons, some of which had arrived to replace the Whitleys, as part of No 81 OTU.

In April 1945, the station strength was given as 187 officers and 1,695 other ranks. With victory in Europe in sight, the need for military OTUs began to diminish. There was, however, still a need for conversion units for transport aircraft and No 1380 Transport Support Conversion Unit was formed out of what remained of No 81 OTU.

Victory was celebrated at Tilstock with civic parades and much partying. Over four years the OTU had trained thousands of aircrew, many of whom were to lose their lives on operations. Now, with peacetime restraints, the airfield became surplus to requirements. It went the normal way of Care and Maintenance but was used occasionally by the Territorial Army, the Naval Reserve and the Auxiliary Air Force for exercises. By mid-1950 it had fallen into disrepair and much of the land was returned to its former owners. It did not die completely, however. Today it is operated as a light aircraft airfield by R. T. Mason Esq of Twemlows Hall, Whitchurch. Renamed Whitchurch, part of the concrete runway, 15/33, remains, together with the control tower, the latter looking forlorn and prone to vandalism. The hangars are used for farm storage and lurking in the woods can still be found the odd building. Tilstock, Whitchurch Heath or whatever name it was called, had done its task of training aircrew well.

12
MINOR AIRFIELDS, SATELLITE AND RELIEF LANDING GROUNDS

Bratton

Situated two miles north of Telford, this large area of open grassland was constructed with the aid of two circus elephants named Saucy and Salt. Their strength enabled small trees and hedges to be removed quickly, allowing the Irish labour force to move in and complete the

A naval officer's life was good in those days! No 758 Squadron, Fleet Air Arm, relax at the satellite airfield of Bratton in 1944. (Reg Howard)

work of levelling etc. Intended to be a Relief Landing Ground (RLG) for Shawbury, it suffered the same problem as the parent airfield, that of waterlogging over the winter periods. It was used by the Oxfords of No 11 SFTS but only when dry conditions prevailed.

Ready for occupation by October 1940 and with the threat of an airborne invasion still apparent, the large grass landing area was covered in scrap cars and large metal objects. These were cleared by spring 1941 to allow limited usage. When the better RLGs such as Condover and Wheaton Aston came into use, Bratton became surplus to requirements. The site was transferred to No 5 (P)AFU Tern Hill for use by the school's Miles Masters. It was also used by the Oxfords of the Royal Navy airfield at nearby Hinstock. It closed in 1945 and reverted to agriculture. The few buildings constructed are today used by the local farmer.

Bridleway Gate

Named after the farm from which the land was requisitioned, Bridleway Gate is unique in that while most other RLGs had permanent lights installed to warn of obstructions when night-flying took place, here the owners of a cottage situated on the airfield perimeter were asked to leave a light on in one of the upstairs bedrooms to act as a warning and a beacon for trainee pilots.

Once again, this RLG was built to take some of the pressure off Shawbury and fine days would see the Oxfords of No 11 SFTS practising circuits and bumps. Although it was one of the larger RLGs with a three grass runway configuration, the use was very limited. It closed for flying on 10th January 1944 and became a fuel dump. The stockpiling of jerrycans eventually reached 327,502, this number gradually reducing as the Allied invasion of Europe marched on. Prior to 6th June it was used for military exercises in which parachutists and containers were dropped from aircraft flying from Tilstock.

Reduced to Care and Maintenance on 25th October 1945, the Blister hangars were removed and the site returned to its owners. Only a few concrete bases remain today to remind us it was once an airfield.

Brockton

One mile north of Sutton Maddock, this Satellite Landing Ground (SLG) opened on 2nd July 1941. It was decided early on that it would not be so much a training airfield as a storage depot for aircraft from Cosford. Known as No 30 SLG, the natural camouflage of the trees, hedges and undergrowth meant it was ideal to hide aircraft away from prying eyes. Even the Robin hangars were camouflaged to look like a farmhouse from the air.

Initially the aircraft stored on the site were Wellingtons, Whitleys and Blenheims but later on it became a storage depot for many diverse types. The two runways were first strengthened with Sommerfeld tracking, which was later replaced by the stronger square mesh tracking to accommodate large aircraft landing and taking off. It continued in use until 1945 when it reverted to fields. The Brockton airfield headquarters was made into a private bungalow which survives today.

Chetwynd

More commonly known as the baby of Tern Hill, Chetwynd became more than its intended role as an RLG. It was built to relieve congestion at Tern Hill where No 5 SFTS were engaged in training pilots. More use was made of Chetwynd whilst the construction of the hard runways at the parent airfield was undertaken but the grass, like that at many similar RLGs, was often waterlogged. This rendered the site unusable for long periods.

Situated two miles north-west of Newport, the site officially opened on 13th September 1941. It was used for both day- and night-flying, the latter responsible for the first accident which occured on 17th October. Taking off from Tern Hill, an instructor and LAC W.C. Vocking attempted a landing at Chetwynd in Master W8562. Sadly it crashed in the darkness, killing LAC Vocking. This was the first of three such incidents. Six days later Master W8569 also crashed at Chetwynd, killing LAC H.R. Johnson. Another six days saw Master N7450 crash, again killing the trainee pilot, LAC B.N. Lee. Chetwynd was beginning to get a bad reputation.

Tom Gatward was a Leading Aircraftman (LAC), the same rank as those that had perished: 'When we got there we had to pitch tents as it was a month or so before they completed the Nissen huts, which we then moved into. The flying was on the other side of the airfield and we had to walk across it to get our lunch and meals. The cookhouse was on one side and we were on the other side by the road that runs from Pickstock to Sambrook. We were stationed there permanently and the aircrew used to come in from Tern Hill by bus. They came down each day; some were on refresher courses, some were training. We had Miles Masters and a couple of Hurricanes plus a couple of Spitfires for pilots that had been on general operations and wanted to refresh their flying. For night-flying we used paraffin flares. I remember all of a sudden one night this huge aircraft appeared and tried to land. It was a Wellington and it overshot the end of the runway and ended up over the Sambrook road. It ran into a potato field and stopped just short of the river. All the fuselage was piled up with potatoes. I think it was flown by Frenchmen because they asked, "Are we in France?" to which we said, "No, you are in Shropshire!".'

More permanent use of the site came in 1942 when 'E' and 'F' Flights of what had now become No 5 (P)AFU were based at the RLG. Again, with a wet spring, very soft patches of grass runway plagued the flying programme with many aircraft becoming stuck in them. Night-flying was done with the aid of a sodium flarepath which replaced the goose-neck flares, while the trainees either had a blue screen attached to their aircraft or wore tinted goggles, both designed to simulate night-flying. The station diarist commented on the use of such ideas: 'Day-night flying is rapidly proving its value as a training feature in that an increasing number of pupils are flying solo at night after only one dual night landing.'

Despite its problems, Chetwynd continued as an RLG for Tern Hill for the rest of the war and into peacetime. The Tiger Moths and Harvards of No 6 FTS became a familiar sight from April 1946 onwards. They were replaced by Percival Prentice trainers which were in turn replaced by Percival Provosts in 1953, until the advent of the jet-powered trainer, the Hunting Jet Provost. With the latter aircraft the FTS moved to Acklington in August 1961 whereupon the RLG was used by the helicopters of the Tern Hill-based Central Flying School. With the closure of the latter in 1976, Shawbury became the parent station, a situation that remains so today. The helicopters of the Defence Helicopter Flying School are still a common sight around Chetwynd where they practise circuits and bumps. Do not trespass on the site as it is still in the hands of the MOD.

Condover

Some called it a 'wretched place' but Condover was planned as a satellite to Atcham, a higher elevation than an RLG. Just how close it came to being one is indicated by the fact that the first aircraft to land on the incomplete airfield was a Miles Master flown by the CO of Atcham, who had flown over especially to see how progress was being made. He found an airfield far from completion but did not need to worry as it never did become a satellite to Atcham but an RLG to Shawbury.

Completed by early 1942, it opened on 21st August when the Oxfords of No 11 (P)AFU flew in. Part of No 4 Group, it received three concrete runways, a fact very unusual for even a satellite airfield. Maybe it was the sight of a hard runway that attracted a Lancaster to land in an emergency after being shot up over Germany. It arrived in the middle of night-flying and had to be dragged from the runway to allow training to continue.

The nearness of the Stretton Hills claimed several victims from Condover. One of the WAAF drivers, Mrs Margaret Edwards had to attend to several crashes as well as her other driving duties: 'When you went in in the morning you looked on the board and whatever duty was on the board, you did. Sometimes I had to fetch men from the railway station, sometimes drive an ambulance and sometimes take German and Italian POWs to their work on the local farms. Occasionally I did flarepath duty. We didn't have any runway lights at Condover and you had to take out lanterns. If that was your job you picked up a Bantam Carrier, a low-loading vehicle, fetched the engineer who sat with you and you had to put these lights all along the runway. If the wind changed you had to get the man again and fetch them in.

'I went to several air crashes from Condover. There was one I went to in which I was first on the scene. A Canadian on his first solo, in a Master I think, had flown into the Lawley (a nearby hill). He was too low and was killed outright. I was on ambulance duty that night.

'We had a Lancaster come in one day. The airfield was not nearly big enough for it but it had dropped its bombs out at sea and when it started to come in it was so huge that I thought it was never going to make it. I was sent out to take the crew to the officers' mess. When I got there one of them said to me, "Would you like to have a look in our ship?" I got in and it was terribly hot and stuffy. I have never forgotten that landing. The Canadians gave me some chocolate which all the girls tried to get off me!'

The airfield reverted to being a satellite for Tern Hill in January 1944. No 5 (P)AFU received Harvards as the end of the war approached, with Condover remaining operational until June 1945. It was then earmarked to become a Beam Approach satellite for Hinstock and also a store for over 300 aircraft. However, nothing became of this plan as Condover went into Care and Maintenance until 1961 when it was sold off by the Air Ministry.

Condover control tower in 2007. (Author)

The old control tower at Condover. Some say there are ghosts here. (Author)

The Wrekin hill seen from Condover airfield. (Author)

The hard runways were taken up and many of the buildings demolished. Today the site is occupied by a riding school but the control tower remains, though in a sorry condition. Looking out from the second level of the tower one can see the hills in the distance, the graveyard of many aircraft and men, and imagine Oxfords flying around the circuit.

Hinstock (Ollerton)

It was a ship without water! So far inland it is hard to imagine why this airfield should be called 'His Majesty's Ship *Godwit*'. The Royal Navy did, however, call their shore establishments 'HMS' and it was the Fleet Air Arm (FAA) that put Ollerton to good use as an instrument flying school.

Situated one mile north-north-west of Childs Ercall, it is a difficult site to find today. Once you have found it, its presence is signified by the superb Naval three-storey control tower that has been made into a desirable residence.

When the land was requisitioned from local landowners in 1939 it was first known by the name Sayerfield. Classed as No 21 SLG by the Ministry of Aircraft Production, it was also known as Ollerton. Two grass runways were laid and the site was destined to become a storage depot for No 37 MU based at Burtonwood. However, when it opened in April 1942 it was No 27 MU at nearby Shawbury that flew in Battles, Masters and Magisters for storage. Not until 1942 did Ollerton really come into use.

At that time the Royal Navy were looking for a site in a quiet area of the country in which to base an instrument flying school. It was agreed

The magnificent Hinstock Hall became the officers' mess for No 758 Squadron, FAA at Hinstock. (Reg Howard)

with the Ministry that Ollerton could be taken over and the station promptly became HMS *Godwit*. It also changed its name to Hinstock lest Ollerton be confused with Tollerton in Nottinghamshire. A new building programme began which took most of 1942 and the spring of 1943 before Hinstock was officially commissioned as HMS *Godwit* on 14th June under the control of RNAS Stretton. The Fleet Air Arm marked out one runway to represent an aircraft carrier and a man with two bats brought the aircraft in as if they were out at sea. Quite a few of them did end up in the sea, i.e. outside the marked landing area with one particular landing ending in a bad crash that killed the pilot.

It was Naval uniforms that were now seen around the lanes of Shropshire as No 758 Squadron, Fleet Air Arm, arrived with the

An Airspeed Oxford of No 758 Squadron, FAA at Hinstock in 1944. (Author)

A Stinson Reliant alongside a naval Pentad hangar at Hinstock in 1944. (Reg Howard)

venerable Oxford. The aircraft of this unit were easily identified by their display of yellow triangles on the fuselage and wings. White or sky/pale blue code letters were usually applied alongside.

The advance party of No 758 Squadron, known as the Beam Approach School, arrived at Hinstock on 15th August 1942. It changed its name to the Blind Approach School shortly after arrival and by April 1943 it was known as the Naval Advanced Instrument Flying School, a title it kept until disbandment. Under the command of Lt Cdr J. Pugh and later Lt Cdr J. Watson, the unit specialised in trials of ground and airborne equipment used in blind landings. Detachments were located at Crail, East Haven, Fearn and Yeovilton. Training was initially done in the Link Trainer, and the expected time schedule for passing out from the course was eight days. Thus, many FAA pilots were to pass through HMS *Godwit* before moving to a ship.

By June 1944, 40 Oxfords were in use, together with Tiger Moths and Masters. HMS *Godwit* was now divorced from RNAS Stretton and had become a stand-alone airfield. Several other units were to use the station for brief periods including Nos 702 and 734 Squadrons, FAA. The latter was known as an engine-handling unit and was equipped with Whitley GR VIIs which were used as 'flying classrooms', in which pilots could be instructed in Merlin handling techniques.

With the larger aircraft it became necessary for Hinstock to have a satellite. The recently RAF-vacated Peplow (Childs Ercall) proved suitable and the Whitleys used this to good effect. Commissioned as HMS *Godwit II*, in addition the unit also took on several Lancasters as Chief Petty Officer Ron Swinn recalls: 'The Fleet Air Arm took over RAF Peplow and in naval manner named it HMS *Godwit II*. The CO

'E' Flight of No 758 Squadron, FAA at Hinstock in 1944. Sub Lt Reg Howard is in the middle row, second from right. The CO in the middle is Lt Cdr Shotter. (Reg Howard)

gave orders that any married personnel could use the deserted buildings as sub-standard married quarters. My wife, son and daughter lived in the regulating office on the WAAF sub-site, away from the main camp, but some of the chaps lived in the NAAFI building.

'I was in charge of a Lancaster bomber, an ex-Royal Canadian Air Force aircraft, NG232. This we converted into a flying classroom for Royal Navy Observers. We could take up a dozen or so at a time, as against two in an Oxford or Anson aircraft. This flying classroom was a casualty of a stupid young Sub Lt whilst I was doing maintenance on a fuel tank between the two engines on the port wing. The aircraft had been jacked up to take the weight off it whilst I removed a large piece the size of two house doors. I left the aircraft thus whilst I went to RAF Cosford for a spare fuel tank. When I returned the Sub Lt had

Sub Lt Reg Howard at Hinstock in 1944. (Reg Howard)

moved the Lancaster to get his car into the hangar! This move had twisted the spar making it bend out of shape. The aircraft was written-off and never flew again. The main camp was at Hinstock and I recall a couple of Naval airmen stealing the station fire engine to transport them into town. Unfortunately they pranged it on the way back and I believe it made the local papers at the time. They were really in hot water.'

When No 758 Squadron disbanded at the end of the war, the replacement, No 780 Squadron re-formed at Hinstock on 28th March 1946 as an advanced flying training unit. Equipped with Oxfords, Harvards, Fireflies and Tiger Moths, it also had a few Lancasters that were based at Peplow. HMS *Godwit* finally closed in February 1947 in favour of the Navy taking Peplow over completely. This they did for two years before the base went into Care and Maintenance. The superb tower conversion to a bed and breakfast residence at Hinstock and the associated equestrian centre will ensure that HMS *Godwit* will never be forgotten as the ship without water.

Hodnet

Opened on 12th June 1941, Hodnet, also known as No 29 SLG, was under the control of No 24 MU at Tern Hill. It was different to most SLGs due to the fact that it was two sites, separated by the main Shrewsbury road. Aircraft were taxied from the holding area across the road to the flying field. From 1942 it was used by No 27 MU from Shawbury, mainly for the storage of aircraft such as Masters and Martinets. It closed in February 1945 and today the storage area is Hodnet cricket ground.

Monkmoor

Possibly the oldest of the Shropshire airfields, Monkmoor had connections with the inter-war years, known as the 'halcyon days' of flying. It was opened as an Aircraft Acceptance Park in 1918 but saw little use as such. However, the Alan Cobham era saw it become the home of Berkshire Aviation Tours, the first of the Cobham county displays. During the Second World War it was taken over by No 30 MU in 1940 as a salvage dump for crashed aircraft. Known as a 'smash and grab' yard, parts were often taken from aircraft dumped there to be used again. It closed in 1945 and today is an industrial site unrecognisable as a past airfield.

Montford Bridge

Montford Bridge held special memories for the late television commentator and superb pilot, Raymond Baxter, for it was here that he was to meet his wife of many years. He was an instructor with No 61 OTU training Spitfire pilots to become operational airmen. When he left Montford Bridge, after what he said were the happiest six months of his life, he returned to operational flying.

Another personality to have perfected his flying technique at the airfield was Pierre Clostermann. Having spent five weeks at Rednal learning the basics of flying, the last three weeks of the eight-week course were spent at Montford Bridge. The entire eight weeks were laced with the tragedy of losing comrades. He recalled his feelings in his book *The Big Show*: 'Those were, at OTU, two arduous winter months. Course succeeded course, flying hours accumulated rapidly, aerial gunnery exercises over the snow-covered Welsh hills quickly mounted up in my pilot's log-book. Not without losses and tragedies, however. One of our Belgian comrades' Spitfires exploded in mid-air during an aerobatics practice. Two of our RAF friends came into collision and were killed before our eyes (Spitfires P8429 and P7921). Then Pierrot Degail, one of the six Frenchmen on the course, crashed one misty evening into an ice-covered hill-top. It took two days to reach the debris through the snow. His body was found in a kneeling position, his head in his arms like a sleeping child by the side of his Spitfire. Both his legs were broken and, unable to move, he must have died of cold during the night.

'The burial ceremony with military honours, was moving in its simplicity. Jacques, Menuge, Commailles and I carried the coffin, wrapped in the tricolour. God, how sad and weighed down we were under the thin icy rain. The slow procession, one by one, before the pit filled with the sound of shovelfuls of

Raymond Baxter was an instructor at Montford Bridge. (Imperial War Museum)

The neglected control tower at Montford Bridge in 2007. (Author)

British soil falling on the poor kid. At Montford Bridge, a small satellite airfield lost in the hills, we continued our training.'

At the end of the three weeks, which ended near New Year's Eve 1942, Pierre and his comrades awaited their posting: 'New Year's Eve came and went, very quietly and slightly sad in that remote corner. Then came the day of posting. Commailles, Menuge and I were to leave for Turnhouse in Scotland to join 341 Squadron, Free French Fighter Squadron 'Alsace' then in the process of forming. The die was cast.'

No 61 OTU was to be the main unit to use Montford Bridge for the rest of the war. May 1944 saw five Piper Cubs of the US Army's 83rd Artillery Division arrive for the purpose of transporting wounded US military personnel from the European battle front to the American hospitals in the county. A detachment of Oxfords from No 11 (P)AFU at Shawbury used the airfield as an RLG in July 1942 pending the opening of Condover and Oxfords of No 6 AACU were at Montford Bridge from May 1943 until the summer of 1944.

With the end of the war No 61 OTU moved to Keevil and the airfield became a sub-site to No 34 MU for the scrapping of Masters and Hotspur gliders, the latter from No 5 GTS at nearby Shobdon.

The year 1946 saw the MU employ German POWs to assist in the work of breaking up aircraft. In September larger aircraft such as

216

Mosquitos, Lincolns and Wellingtons were being sold for scrap after the removal of certain equipment. By July 1947 the MU had moved out and Montford Bridge went into Care and Maintenance.

The airfield was remembered by Grafton Primary School who incorporated a Spitfire in their school badge. The lonely control tower looks out over a vast stretch of the airfield and the remains of the tarmac perimeter track are still visible. When one thinks of the different types of aircraft broken up here and the fact that today not one example of certain types survive, is it not sad that future generations will only have photographs to tell the story?

Weston Park

One of the more unusual SLGs was Weston Park. Situated on the south-west fringe of the park surrounding a stately home, the flat parkland appeared the ideal place to store aircraft. Known as No 3 SLG, June 1941 saw Spitfires from No 9 MU at Cosford dispersed amongst its foliage. In grounds that were laid out by 'Capability' Brown, the landing area was so large that it enabled a Wellington bomber to make a test landing and take-off.

From 1942 it became an SLG to No 27 MU at Shawbury and a year later an SLG for High Ercall, which desperately needed space to store their 700 aircraft. From early 1944 it was a satellite to RNAS Hinstock and was used by the Oxfords of No 780 Squadron Fleet Air Arm. Closed in 1945, it is used today for balloon displays and the occasional air display.

13
THE *ARIES* PROJECT

In 1944, with the anticipated ending of the European war, British thoughts turned to the Pacific theatre of operations where America and her allies were in conflict with the Japanese. With no end in sight to this Asian war, it was felt that we could, and should, help America defeat Japan just as America had helped us to defeat Nazi Germany. This would entail very long-distance flights in varying climates, which would require accurate navigation as never before. Although the navigational aids installed in the aircraft of Bomber Command from 1943 onwards were far more accurate and dependable than during 1941/42, if the RAF were to fly over vast stretches of the Pacific Ocean, even these may not suffice. The extreme climates were also a worry for there was very little information on how these would affect the performance of an aircraft.

We have read in the Shawbury chapter of the move of the Central Navigation School (CNS) from Cranage in Cheshire to Shawbury in March 1944. Their arrival brought a further selection of aircraft to the station, consisting of Wellingtons and Stirlings together with a Proctor, Magister, Hudson, and a Lancaster (PD328) named *Aries*.

The CNS had been established primarily to hold courses for post-graduate navigators and trained navigator instructors and also to carry out research into navigational techniques. The latter had remained static from 1918 until September 1939 and little attempt had been made to forecast the requirements of a future war. Apart from improvements to compasses and maps, the design and manufacture of specialised navigation equipment had not been considered. This sad omission was to change in 1939 when it became obvious that the RAF could not hope to win the air war without a drastic improvement in the situation.

From 1939 until 1941, attempts were made to improve navigation but only to the extent of issuing the astrograph and the integrating sextant which improved the accuracy of astro-navigation. It did not help the RAF to accurately hit a designated target. It is a fact that in 1941 night photographs revealed that less than 5% of bombs fell within five miles of the target aiming point. While this had very little to do with world navigation, it must be mentioned in the general context of the advances that radar was to bring. Due to the experiments and stirling work being done by the Telecommunications Flying Unit (TFU) at nearby Defford, by 1943 Bomber Command had navigational aids such as Gee, Oboe and H2S (see *Herefordshire and Worcestershire Airfields in the Second World War*, published by Countryside Books). For Bomber Command this was a turning point. Radar was also to help the CNS in their navigation of the far-flung parts of the Empire.

As well as Cranage where No 2 School of Air Navigation had been set up in 1940, No 1 School had been established at Port Albert in Ontario, Canada. Because of the many air raid alerts and enemy action over Britain during 1940, it was felt by the Secretary of State for Air, the Right Honourable Archibald Sinclair, PC, CMG, MP, that Canada offered the opportunity to train navigators without interruption. While Port Albert catered for the specialist courses, Cranage took over most of the other functions. However, by the middle of 1943, Specialist Navigation Training was once again back at Cranage.

It was from here on 14th August 1943 that the first (new series) course ended. It had been a success with an average of 144 flying hours achieved by each pupil during the nine months of the course. At the end of August one of the Wellingtons was flown as far as Iceland, the first of a series of navigational flights to various parts of the world. Several more were to follow including liaison missions to the Middle East and radar reception trials in the North Atlantic and Iceland. Shortly after this No 2 Specialist Navigation Course began with, amongst many interesting lectures, one outlining the future plans of BOAC. Even though the war was far from over, it gave an insight into the plans of how British commercial aviation, with modern navigation, intended to lead the world.

By the time the CNS arrived at Shawbury, the aircraft establishment included 42 Wellington XIIIs and four Stirling IIIs. Under the command of Gp Cpt G.I.L. Saye, OBE, AFC, it was judged that the Stirling was the best aircraft to undertake experimental navigation flights during early 1944. Because this was still a delicate stage of the war and the enemy was still very active, on 21st May LK508 was

The first Aries, *the Lancaster PD328 with its crew. (via M. Jones)*

chosen to fly such a mission to the Republic of Ireland. Having left Shawbury and climbed successfully to its predetermined height, LK508 suddenly developed engine problems. The captain of the aircraft, Sqd Ldr D.C. McKinley, DFC, ordered his crew to bail out. This they all did successfully although the two civilian scientists, Professor Cox, a Senior Scientific Officer at CNS, and Mr Smith, a meteorological officer, suffered injuries on landing. Sqd Ldr McKinley stayed with his aircraft and with difficulty landed it at RAF Long Kesh.

Fitted with all the latest radio aids for long-distance navigation, Stirling LK589 of the CNS left Shawbury on 2nd June for Dorval (Montreal) via Prestwick, Reykjavik and Goose Bay. Its crew were also a lecture and demonstration team which included once again, Sqd Ldr McKinley. From Dorval, where lectures were given, the aircraft flew across Canada to Vancouver Island and back in fourteen days. It arrived at Shawbury on 26th June where it was estimated that over 4,000 personnel had been shown over the aircraft.

No 3 Specialist Navigation Course began in August 1944. Sadly, two officers, Flt Lt Grimshaw and FO Auld were killed when Wellington LZ699 crashed into hills near Llangollen at 02.00 hrs during a night exercise. Despite the tragedy, the Course flew three Stirling aircraft to Canada during September at the same time as the CNS was redesignated the Empire Central Navigation School (ECNS). The

The Lancaster Aries *arrives in New Zealand. (via M. Jones)*

command was taken by Air Commodore P.H. Mackworth, CBE, DFC, and with the success of the earlier flights, a Lancaster BI (PD328) was prepared to undertake a round-the-world navigational flight. This was the beginning of what became known as the *Aries* Project.

Equipped with over a ton of the latest navigational equipment, including fourteen aerials, one of the purposes of the flight, just like its forebears, was to familiarise training establishments and operational squadrons with up-to-date navigational aids. Data would also be collected regarding the performance of a Lancaster in extreme climates and a study made of the American methods of navigation in the Pacific theatre of war.

Having been modified to carry the latest aids, with the world still at war and a second battle of London being fought with the advent of the V2 rocket, PD328 left Shawbury and what was now renamed the Empire Air Navigation School (EANS) on 20th October 1944. This time the crew were: Wg Cdr D.C. McKinley, DFC, AFC (Captain and Pilot); FO A.C. Shipway, DFC (2nd Pilot); Sqd Ldr J.F. Davis, DFC (No 1 Navigator); Flt Lt N.B. Blakey, DFC (No 2 Navigator); Flt Lt R.L. Butt (Radar Navigator); FO J. Stringer (Wireless Op); Mr H.C. Pritchard (Royal Aircraft Establishment); LAC E. Pashley (Rigger); LAC E. Wiggins (Engineer) and LAC H.J. Dean (Electrician).

The official record entry of the epic flight went into the annals of aviation history when *Aries* returned to Shawbury on 14th December. It also hit the world's headlines and was reported in papers such as *The Times* and the *Daily Telegraph*:

The tour was designed to establish a practical liaison between the EANS and training and operational units under RNZAF and

Shawbury – station parade with the Mayor of Shrewsbury to welcome back the first of the Aries *projects. (via M. Jones)*

RAAF control; to collect, collate and disseminate material of navigational interest and to observe the behaviour of automatic instruments and radar installations under very variable conditions. A working schedule which was for the greatest part drawn up at Shawbury some weeks before departure was maintained throughout with the exception of a 48-hour delay in New Zealand due to tyre trouble. There were no other instances of unserviceabililty or weather which delayed or postponed any take-off. The entire flight covered a distance of some 36,000 nautical miles (nm) of which the longest stage was 2,710 nm and six stages were over 2,200 nm and thirteen over 1,000 nm. Total flying time was 202 hrs of which 15 hrs 08 mins was the longest non-stop stage. The tour lasted 53 days during which some 400 lectures were given.

In January 1945 the EANS learned that the twenty Lancasters it was to have received had been changed to eighteen Halifax BIIIs. In addition two Lancaster BIs, a Mosquito XVI and either a Thunderbolt or Mustang fighter would be given to the unit.

In the middle of February, the now famous Lancaster PD328 *Aries* left Shawbury, once again under the command of Gp Cpt McKinley and with Air Commodore Mackworth in charge of the mission. This was to be a month-long liaison flight to navigation training

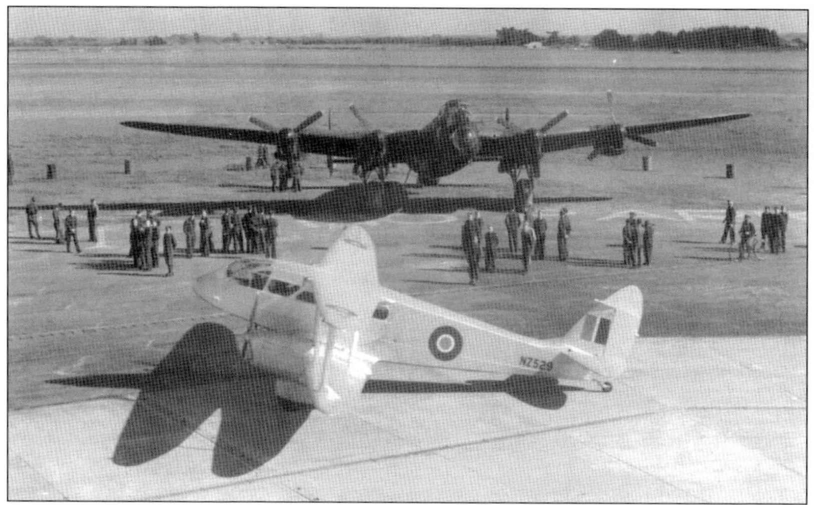

Aries *pictured on the ground in New Zealand. (via M. Jones)*

establishments in Canada and the United States. At the end of March *Aries* was off again, this time to South Africa. Further flights were to follow until April 1945 when *Aries* was flown to RAF Waddington for extensive modifications in preparation for some of the most gruelling flights of the period, a reconnaissance of the North Pole and the polar regions.

Avro's aircraft repair organisation replaced the nose and tail turrets with streamlined fairings, fitted extra fuel tanks and carried out various other modifications. The wartime camouflage livery was removed to leave polished metal with the name *Aries* emblazoned on the nose. Four new Merlin XXIV engines were fitted, as well as extra instrumentation to check magnetic data at the Pole.

On 10th May 1945, two days after VE Day, *Aries* left Shawbury with Wg Cdr McKinley once again the captain. After a short stop at Prestwick, the aircraft flew on to Reykjavik to carry out final checks and preparations. The weather was found to be against them for a few days but take-off for the North Geographical Pole took place on 16th May. Unfortunately, ice caused problems with resultant loss of power and *Aries* was forced to return to Iceland.

A glance at the met forecast revealed that an imminent improvement in the weather was on the cards. *Aries* was hurriedly refuelled in order to make a second attempt. For the first few hours all

The Lancaster Aries *of the Empire Central Navigation School at Shawbury – 2nd October 1944. (via M. Jones)*

went well but an increase in cloud meant that the crew had to fly without observations of the sun or moon for a considerable number of hours. Turbulence was also a problem but luckily in the vicinity of the North Pole the cloud dispersed giving the crew an excellent view of the polar surface. At last they were able to get navigational fixes and a good last stage was completed to the Pole. The minimum temperature

Close-up of Aries *at Shawbury. (via M. Jones)*

Photograph showing a more streamlined Aries *with her crew. (via M. Jones)*

recorded outside was minus 30 degrees Centigrade whilst in contrast the flight deck temperature made it necessary to fly in short sleeves. The mission was deemed a great success and *Aries* returned to Iceland safely. On 18th May it once again departed Iceland with Wg Cdr McKinley as captain, this time bound for the Magnetic North Pole. Problems with the starboard generator forced a landing at Goose Bay but with the problem quickly rectified, *Aries* left the next day.

No problems were encountered on take-off but later in the flight, 'George' the auto pilot decided not to work, thus increasing the crew's workload. Eventually the flight ended at Dorval, a position almost 200 miles north-north-west of the Pole's plotted position. In triumph, *Aries* and her crew received a rapturous welcome, having accomplished the two main aims of the mission: flying over the areas of both the Geographical and Magnetic North Poles.

Preparation now began for the remainder of the pioneering flights, including the final stage from Whitehorse in Canada to Britain on which further studies of navigation and climate phenomena were to be conducted. *Aries* and her crew departed on 23rd May with a request to stop at the RCAF Central Navigation School at Rivers honoured. Here an audience of high-ranking and pupil navigators listened in awe to

The newly streamlined Lancaster PD328 prior to its record-breaking flights to Canada. (via M. Jones)

the crew's accounts of flying over the polar regions. A final stop at Edmonton to check the serviceability of the aircraft and equipment before leaving for Whitehorse, was the crew's last task.

Early next morning *Aries* departed Edmonton and flew to Whitehorse, some 6,000 miles from Britain. After a night's sleep the crew boarded the Lancaster and set off for Shawbury. During the course of the flight, observations and photographs were taken of different phenomena relating to long-distance flight. *Aries* landed back at Shawbury on 26th May 1945 having flown some 20,000 nautical

The first Aries *in flight. (via M. Jones)*

SERIAL No.

ROYAL AIR FORCE.

Air Master Navigator's Certificate.

*T*HIS is to Certify that ..... *Wing Commander D.C. McKinley, R.A.F.* .....

..... *Royal Air Force.* .....

has successfully qualified as an Air Master Navigator.

DATED 1st June, 1945.

Roderic Hill Air Marshal
AIR MEMBER FOR TRAINING,
AIR MINISTRY

Wing Commander D. C. McKinley's Air Master Navigator's Certificate (via Mike McKinley)

miles, half of which were completed within the Arctic Circle. This completed one of the longest series of flights within the polar regions.

The crew had been presented with 'blue nose' certificates awarded for flights within the Arctic circle by the CO of RAF Reykjavik and on their arrival home were honoured with the following awards: Wg Cdr D.C. McKinley, DFC, AFC – Bar to AFC; Wg Cdr K.C. Macheure – AFC; Wg Cdr E.W. Anderson, OBE, DFC – AFC; LAC E. Wiggins – AFM; LAC H.B. Dean – AFM. The Queen's Commendation for Valuable Services in the Air was awarded to Wg Cdr R.M. Winfield, DFC, AFC; Sqd Ldr A.J. Hagger; Flt Lt S.T. Underwood; FO S. Blakeley; WO A.F. Smith; Corporal W.S. Gardner; and LAC E. Pashley.

With the war over, many liaison flights were taking place to various parts of the world. Command of the EANS had now passed to Air Commodore N. H. D'aeth, CBE, who was to see No 3 Specialist Course graduate on 15th June. The new year of 1946 began with *Aries* undertaking a record-breaking flight from RAF Thorney Island in Hampshire to Cape Town in South Africa. It was flown in just 32 hrs 11 mins. *Aries* undertook another notable flight when it left Shawbury for Australia and New Zealand on 20th August. During the flight three records were broken:

(a) London–Karachi, 19 hrs 14 mins. Average speed 205 mph
(b) London–Darwin, 45 hrs 35 mins. Average speed 189 mph
(c) London–Wellington, 59 hrs 50 mins. Average speed 195 mph

Visits to Canada and the USA took place in October and November. Upon return the crew had been away for 32 days and covered 12,300 nautical miles. This was to be the last flight for the Lancaster known as *Aries*. On 24th February 1947, Lady Conningham, wife of the AOC-in-C Fighter Training Command, christened Avro Lincoln BII RE364 *Aries 2*. This was an extensively modified Lincoln which became known as a 'Lincolnian'. Modifications consisted of: all armour and turrets removed; Lancastrian-type nose and tail fitted; three bomb-bay and one nose tank fitted so as to increase the total fuel capacity to 4,612 gallons; six Anson-type seats and a rest bunk fitted in the rear fuselage; rear fuselage lagged; heating extended aft; paint removed and skin polished; oxygen supply supplemented to provide sufficient for twelve crew at 20,000 ft for 24 hours

Aries 2 was to undertake several more epic flights before a new and sinister period began – the 'Cold War'. Once again the authorities' lack of interest in furthering knowledge of navigation was obvious, as this quote from the Air Ministry shows: 'It is unfortunate that, during this period of history, the period of the beginning of the Cold War and the Berlin Air Lift when air power and air navigation in particular, were once again becoming of prime importance to our country that the official records show so very little interest in the functions and progress of the Specialist Navigation Course and the EANS.'

A new commandant, Air Commodore L.K. Barnes took over the EANS on 19th January 1948. In July 1949 the RAF Flying College was established at Manby. Some of the staff were taken over by the new college, and the EANS disbanded at Shawbury at the end of the month. The station once more became the home of the CNS. This heralded the end of the *Aries* Project as such, for the Lincolns were found to be inferior to the Lancaster. However, perhaps we should end this chapter on a lighter note before we come to the final analysis of what was accomplished.

The medical report on the liaison flight to SE Asia during January and February 1945 in Wellington XIII JA625 states: 'Apart from a few head colds (contracted before leaving Shawbury) and a distressing indisposition acquired by all personnel after an interval of between 7-10 days in India and leading to frequent if not prolonged visits to the "thunderbox", the general health of the crew was excellent. There was one severe case of bug bite, contracted from a chair in Colombo and confined to the posterior of the victim. There was also one case of prickly heat which persisted until leaving India. At Bombay a rat of uncertain colour joined the crew and defied capture by retiring into the wings. Attracted by sandwich crumbs in the bilges, it made access via the tail wheel unit and stayed for the rest of the journey to live on bananas brought by the crew for home consumption.'

There is no doubt that the *Aries* series of record-breaking flights from Shawbury contributed to the navigational aids in use today. The discovery of the weakness of the bombing offensive forced the pace in the development of navigating instruments and techniques during this period. Never in such a short space of time has a science been subjected to such a forced growth the results of which were truly astonishing. Which makes it all the sadder that no memorial exists to the endeavours of Gp Cpt McKinley, his crews and those that followed.

14
CIVILIANS AT WAR

On 31st August 1939, Adolf Hitler issued his 'Directive No 1' for the conduct of war. In it he stated that 'the attack on Poland is to be carried out in accordance with the preparations made. The date of attack is 1st September 1939. The time 04.45 hrs.' The directive further stated that 'the responsibility for the opening of hostilities should rest unequivocally with England and France'.

At Chartwell in Kent, Winston Churchill requested his former Scotland Yard detective, Inspector Thompson, to come out of retirement and hurry forthwith to Chartwell, instructing him to bring his pistol with him. He acknowledged to his wife, Clementine, that 'in these hours I knew that if war came – and who could doubt its coming? – a major burden would fall upon me'. As history records, Great Britain and France declared war on Germany three days later, but Churchill was not to become Prime Minister until after the fall of Dunkirk in May 1940.

This war was to be different from the first conflict in that it would be not only a soldier's war but also a civilian's war. It was not unexpected, for between the end of June and the first week in September 1939, around 3,750,000 people moved to what were thought safer areas. Hospitals were also evacuated, not for reasons of safety but in anticipation of the expected casualties resulting from a war. When after 3rd September nothing happened, many people returned to their homes only to leave them again several months later. This, however, was the period known as the 'phoney war' and it is here that the story of the civilians must begin.

At 11 am on Sunday, 3rd September 1939, the BBC stated that they were standing by for an announcement by the Prime Minister, Neville

Chamberlain. Shortly after, Downing Street was filled with people waiting for news. At 11.12 am, after a phone call to Berlin, it was confirmed that no reply had been received to the British ultimatum. In Berlin the head of the Treaty Department of the Foreign Office, Robert Dunbar, made his way across the city to hand over the British Government's declaration of war to Dr Kordt, the German Chargé d'Affaires. At 11.15 am, sitting in the BBC studio, Neville Chamberlain, described as looking 'crumpled, despondent and old', began his speech. After referring to the ultimatum delivered in Berlin some two hours earlier he solemnly declared, 'I have to tell you now that no such undertaking has been received and that consequently, this country is at war with Germany. You can imagine what a bitter blow it is to me that all my long struggle to win peace has failed.' In conclusion the PM said: 'Now may God bless you all. May he defend the right. It is the evil things that we shall be fighting against, brute force, bad faith, injustice, oppression and persecution. And against them all I am certain that right will prevail.'

The Sunday papers were already carrying news of the fighting from Poland and plenty of advice on what to do when war broke out. Radio talks and government notices had prepared the country for air raids, food shortages and disruption to the British way of life. In Shropshire, as in the rest of the country, Salopians wondered just what this war would bring to them.

The county had been making preparations for war for some months with even the children helping by using their seaside spades to fill sandbags. Trenches had been dug in Shrewsbury as a precaution against air raids and as early as 1936, Shropshire had been divided into six Air Raid Precautions (ARP) areas under the command of a Regional Controller for the West Midlands. By the time war broke, there were 1.5 million ARP wardens in Britain, 9,000 of them in Shropshire. Across Britain one in six wardens were women. In Shropshire it was one in 1,700! Their duties were many, including being responsible for organising emergency services, distributing gas masks, enforcing the black-out and sounding the air-raid sirens. Many a Salopian can recall the blustering voice of a red-faced warden shouting, 'Put that b————— light out'!

Fearing a gas attack, by the outbreak of war everyone had been issued with a gas mask and it was the duty of wardens to see that they were carried everywhere as the law demanded. Official instructions were issued on how to put on your gas mask with the advice to 'practise wearing it' and to 'spit on the mica window to stop it

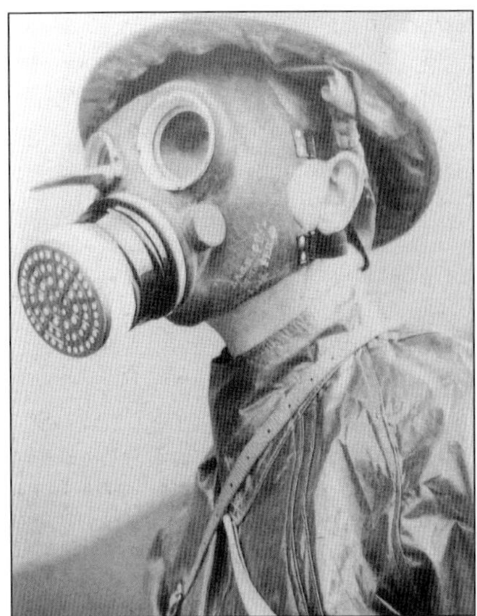

A Shrewsbury ARP warden in full wartime gear. (Fox)

steaming up'. The masks were certainly not popular, with the smell of rubber and disinfectant prevailing. They also emitted strange rude noises when attempts were made to speak with them on, much to the delight of the younger generation.

In Shrewsbury, the county town, all resources were put to the war effort. The Ditherington Flax Mill became an Army training camp with the town constantly full of servicemen from the Army and the RAF. The King's Shropshire Light Infantry came to a war footing as they prepared to see service throughout Europe and North Africa. Moving to France as part of the British Expeditionary Force in 1939, Corporal Thomas Priday of the 1st Battalion was the first recorded British Army casualty when he was killed by a mine near Metz on 9th December. He was just 27 years old and was the first of many to lose their lives fighting in the county battalions. The Shropshire Yeomanry was the county's cavalry regiment, but on mobilisation it became the 75th and 76th Medium Regiments of the Royal Artillery. They too were to lose many young lives.

Another young man from Shrewsbury to lose his life was Fl Lt Eric Lock. Born at Bayston Hill in 1920, a five-shilling trip with Cobham's Flying Circus had given him his first taste of flying. In 1939, he joined the RAFVR and was mobilised on the outbreak of war. Short in stature, his comrades nicknamed him 'Sawn-off', a name he was to carry to his death. He survived the Battle of Britain in continuous fighting with the Luftwaffe and was a highly decorated pilot. Sadly, though, his career ended in 1941 and his name is carved on the Runnymede Memorial in Surrey, along with 20,000 British and Commonwealth airmen who vanished without trace during the war.

For the civilians the message was 'Don't panic', but although the people did not the authorities sometimes did. In considering what

Many in the major cities close to Shropshire suffered devastation. This photograph shows a lucky family in Coventry whose Anderson shelter saved them.

defence the country and civilians in particular had against the bomber, they realised there was very little. In order to rectify the situation, the Home Office urged local authorities to spend more money on civil defence, especially in the form of shelters. Some elected to do so, others did not. For people with gardens the local authorities handed over two million DIY family shelters. Designed by an engineer named Anderson for the Home Secretary John Anderson, the 'Anderson shelters'

One of Shropshire's many platoons of the Home Guard.

consisted of curved steel which was bolted together and had to be dug into the ground and covered with three feet or more of earth. Shropshire being a rural county, it was found that 69% of people had a garden in which to erect a shelter capable of accommodating an average family. The majority of people were able to make them quite comfortable although most were prone to some flooding during the winter.

Another type of shelter also designed to protect civilians was the Morrison shelter. This was intended for use inside the house and whilst it was not bomb-proof, it did protect against flying debris should a house be hit. Looking rather like a cage, the idea was that you slept in it and ate your meals from the top of it. It was both a bedroom and a dining room table. Encouraged by the fact that a pamphlet issued by the Ministry of Home Security stated, 'Almost no shelter is proof against a direct hit from a heavy bomb, but the chances of your own home getting a direct hit are very small indeed', most Salopians had both.

Local councils were very reluctant, however, to spend large amounts of money on ways of protecting the population. In Newport in 1939, just two air-raid sirens were sited, at Ashworth's Timber Yard and at the Audley Engineering Works. The latter also provided two cars adapted to carry a siren each in order to patrol the streets and give warning of an air raid when necessary. Firefighting for Newport received similar

The Home Guard keep watch for souvenir hunters on a crashed Dornier 17 'somewhere in the Midlands'. (Central Press)

treatment, with just £600 being spent on equipment in 1938. This was obviously inadequate but it took until 1941 before the government formed the National Fire Service and began to use central funding to supply cities and towns with proper fire engines.

Defence of the civilian population was also part of the remit for the Local Defence Volunteers (LDV). Established on 15th May 1940, it was the most fantastic and democratic army ever raised in Britain. It was founded on individual initiative and improvisation and was the result of a broadcast by Anthony Eden, then the new War Secretary, who spoke to men who for some reason could not join the regular military forces:

'Since the war began, the government has received countless inquiries from men of all ages who wish to do something for the defence of their country. We want large numbers of men in Great Britain who are British subjects between the ages of 17 and 65, to come forward now and offer their services. The name of the new force which is now to be raised will be the Local Defence Volunteers. This is a part-time job so that there will be no need for any volunteer to abandon his present occupation. When on duty you will form part of the armed forces. You will not be paid but you will receive a uniform and be armed.'

This was not a new idea for in October 1939, Churchill, then First Lord of the Admiralty, had proposed that a Home Guard be formed made up of 500,000 men all over the age of 40. However, within 24 hours of Eden's speech, a quarter of a million men had enrolled in the LDV and between 1940 and 1944, the number of volunteers never fell below one million.

Shropshire was to support eleven battalions made up of 31,000 members, including Belgians and Eastern Europeans who had taken refuge in the county. Like the ARP wardens, these men were to become the butt of many a comedian's jokes, with names like 'Dad's Army' due to the fact that many were First World War veterans and the interpretation of the initials LDV as 'Look, Duck and Vanish'! However, that they took their job seriously was never in doubt as one security-minded person in the Burford district LDV demonstrated. When asked by a private motorist the way to Ludlow he replied, 'This road led to Ludlow in peacetime. But danged if I'm telling yer where it leads now there's a war on!'

At first the only identification that anyone was a member of the LDV was an armband bearing the three letters. Weapons too were in short supply with golf clubs, pickaxe handles and imitation rifles being the main arsenal. The preferred anti-tank weapon was the notorious 'Molotov cocktail', as dangerous to the carrier as to the recipient. Bottles filled with a mixture of tar and petrol or paraffin with a soft rag thrust into the neck ready to be ignited were stockpiled in woodsheds and garages. When in August 1940 the LDV became the Home Guard, the battallions were usually affiliated to county regiments; in the case of Shropshire it was the King's Shropshire Light Infantry. Many units were attached to particular towns such as Company A (Ellesmere) 2nd Battalion, Jackfield Home Guard, Company D (Clun) 7th Battalion and Company B (Craven Arms) which was also a battalion headquarters.

Leslie Frost, in conversation with his son Allan, recalled some of his Home Guard experiences: 'During the war I was in what you'd call a reserved occupation at Sankey's in Hadley. I was responsible for the drawing office end of things; when drawings came from Vickers headquarters at Castle Bromwich, the Spitfire headquarters, management at Sankey's sent the drawings through to me for amendment. It was my job and responsibility to see that Vickers got the latest drawings. When the invasion scare came in 1940, the government decided to form Local Defence Volunteers to help to patrol and watch for any parachutists being dropped over here, as spies I suppose: you never knew whether you were being told the truth or lies during the war. We had no weapons, it was after Dunkirk when the big evacuation came through and the blitz had started. There wasn't enough weaponry to go round the existing forces let alone anybody else so people were wandering around the countryside on bikes with very little protection.

'The idea was to report anything unusual and one big advantage was that you could go anywhere on anybody's land and you couldn't be stopped. There was no question of anybody trespassing or anything like that. Certain areas were mapped out as routes so you patrolled these areas. When munitions began to come in from America and Canada the position improved and the government decided to run us on a more military basis and so formed the Home Guard into proper Army units. We were affiliated to the regular army units of the KSLI and we were the 5th Battalion. We belonged to D Company whose headquarters were up at Wrekin College. Eventually I was made a Lance Corporal and then a Corps Sergeant and ended up as a Second Lieutenant and training officer for the company.'

The Home Guard units began patrolling the day after Eden's radio broadcast. With invasion expected they set up road blocks, removed signposts and patrolled key installations such as armament factories, railway yards and stations and industrial buildings. With no coastline, all of the Shropshire major sites were under the scrutiny of the Home Guard. By late 1941 the standard Army uniform was issued to all men and rifles, albeit of early design, replaced the motley array of wooden hardware. By 1942, women were encouraged to join the Home Guard to undertake clerical work, but many of them chose to work instead in the various armament factories within the county.

With the end of the war in sight, the Home Guard was stood down in November 1944. It was a sad day, for many had forged long-lasting friendships. By keeping an eye on Britain's coastline and factories, they had released younger men to train and join the regular forces. Had the expected invasion come, there is no doubt that the Home Guard would have defended the realm and the civilian population to the last man.

As we have read, industrial plants and manufacturing war equipment factories within Shropshire would have received protection. Although the main production of ordnance in 1939 was at the Woolwich Arsenal in south-east London, with the expected bombing raids on the capital it was felt prudent to move much of the work to a safer area. Thus in the summer of 1939, munitions production was moved from Woolwich to Donnington near Telford. With it came many workers both from London and the Midlands, in addition to the local people recruited. This influx of workers found accommodation hard to find in rural Shropshire. Local people were asked to let spare rooms with refusal considered a crime. It was a difficult time for Shropshire people, as to them the Londoners appeared brash and forceful. However, between 1941 and 1943 a vast building programme for housing began in the county with 844 houses being built for the workers at the Ordance.

It was not only Donnington that became part of the industrial war effort. Ditton Priors Naval Armament Depot was built in 1941 for the storage of 40,000 tons of explosives. A railway spur line was built to transport the goods in whilst local buses were employed to bring in the workers from Madeley and Ironbridge. Nesscliffe was also an ammunition store, much of which was kept hidden in large semi-sunk bunkers. A long-closed branch line of the Shropshire and Montgomeryshire Railway was brought back into use to serve this very important installation. The Sentinel Wagon Works in Shrewsbury built machine tools, Bren gun carriers and landing ramps, many of the latter being constructed for the promised Allied invasion.

Aircraft manufacture was also prominent with Sankey of Hadley producing three or four Spitfire fuselages, including engines, every day. The Audley Engineering Works made valves, some of which were used in tanks. They also made valves for the PLUTO and FIDO installations, together with special tools for Rolls-Royce and the Merlin aero engine. PLUTO, which stands for 'Pipeline Under The Ocean', was a system of cables laid under the Channel from the Kent and Hampshire coasts to carry fuel to the Allied forces on the Continent; whilst FIDO stands for 'Fog Intensive Dispersal Operation', a system of pipes laid alongside a runway carrying gas which was lit to disperse fog and allow aircraft to land. As an indication of how important Shropshire women came to be in armament manufacture, by 1944, 80% of the workforce was female. Donnington survived the post-war reduction in armaments to continue and today, still in use, the Ministry of Defence Depot holds the bronze from enemy guns captured during the Crimean War which is used to make the Victoria Cross.

In various chapters the phrase 'a gift of war' has been used. This relates to aircraft purchased with donations from industry, countries and more importantly in relation to this book, counties. Shropshire was not to be left behind in this respect and a Spitfire Vb, serial number BL863 and named *Shrewsbury* was presented to the RAF with a donation of £6,472 by the Shrewsbury Spitfire Fund. It was taken on charge by No 24 MU at RAF Tern Hill on 8th February 1942. Issued to No 54 Squadron at Castletown on the 12th for convoy patrols, it joined No 167 (Gold Coast) Squadron on 21st May at Scorton before the squadron itself moved to Castletown in June. When No 167 moved

Squadron Leader Denis Secretan in Spitfire Mk Vb BL863, named Shrewsbury. *(Imperial War Museum)*

elsewhere, BL863 was taken over by the incoming No 610 (County of Chester) Squadron on 14th October.

Despatched to Air Service Training for a major inspection, it moved around various units before being allocated on 26th December to No 341 (Alsace) Squadron at Perranporth. It then continued to be engaged on convoy patrols, anti-shipping sorties and the occasional sweep. Passed to the Fighter Leaders School at Milfield on 3rd August 1944, it was relegated to the training role at No 57 OTU at Eshott on 14th September. BL863 sustained damage Category 'B' on 18th November when FO Emmerson suffered an engine failure and had to force-land the aircraft. It was recategorised Category 'E' on 19th December and struck off charge. Although *Shrewsbury* had no victories to its credit, it did nonetheless contribute to many sorties and thus earned its place as a 'gift of war'.

There were also four further Spitfires associated with the civilians of Shropshire. *TASCOS 1* was the first of four Spitfires presented to the RAF by the Ten Acres and Stirchley Co-operative Society. The Mk Vc (tropicalised) LZ819 was taken on charge at No 9 MU Cosford on 5 April 1943. It was then passed to No 82 MU at Lichfield on the 14th to be crated for shipment to Casablanca. From there it was despatched to Malta where it joined No 249 (Gold Coast) Squadron at Qrendi until 16th August 1943, when it overshot the runway and hit a brick wall. It was then beyond repair and struck off charge on 2nd October 1943.

TASCOS II was Spitfire Vb BL530, taken on charge at No 33 MU, Lyneham on 17th December 1941. Allocated to No 123 (East India) Squadron, it passed through Nos 167 (Gold Coast) and 165 (Ceylon) Squadrons before being allocated to the 335th Fighter Squadron, Fourth Fighter Group USAAF. After destroying a Do 217 on 19th August 1942, upon landing at Gravesend the undercarriage collapsed. It was repaired at No 1 Civilian Repair Unit at Cowley and passed to the 336th Fighter Squadron of the same group. It suffered various accidents and upon repair served with further RAF squadrons. Its last duty was with No 1353 Anti-Aircraft Co-operation Flight at West Freugh before finally being struck off charge on 14th September 1945.

TASCOS III (also named *Sir Harry* and *Lady Oakes IV*), Spitfire Vc LZ870, was taken on charge at No 9 MU Cosford on 24th April 1943 and sent overseas to Australia on 18th May. No further details are available. *TASCOS IV*, a Spitfire Vc (either MA652 or MA672) was taken on charge at No 9 MU Cosford on 28th May 1943. It was then sent to India, sustaining Category 'E' damage and being struck off charge on 27th November 1944. All of these aircraft are part of the aviation history of Shropshire.

Shropshire's civilians were also concerned with one of the most important secrets of the war. Built during 1942, the radio masts of Criggion were situated on the Shropshire/Welsh border and were a dominant feature of the landscape. Consisting of three masts and three towers, their purpose was to allow communication between the Admiralty in London and Royal Navy ships. Covering an area of some 300 acres, the aerials that were strung between the towers received and transmitted very low frequency signals capable of reaching any ship in the world.

The site operated under the guise of the 'GPO Telecommunications Centre' and was built as a back-up station to a similar one which was sited at Rugby in Warwickshire. It was felt by the authorities that this, being sited near heavy industrial areas, would be prone to enemy attack and therefore easily put out of action. The Criggion station was far from any potential targets and therefore would hopefully not be attacked and continue operating throughout the war.

The GPO workers and technicians at Criggion never realised just how secret and important the station was until after the war. Its greatest moment came in 1943 when signals between the Admiralty and a large British battle fleet culminated in the destruction of the German battleship *Scharnhorst*, which happened at 19.45 hrs on the evening of 26th December, Boxing Day, 1943. Despite several past

'Spitfires are made of this'. Pots and pans collected for the war effort.

attempts to sink her by the RAF, the *Scharnhorst* had survived, even to the extent of sailing through the English Channel virtually unscathed a year earlier. However, she was to meet her doom when a superior force of naval ships, led by the British Flagship *Duke of York*, found and sank her 60 miles north-west of North Cape.

Criggion had played its part well and continued to monitor and pass naval messages for the duration of the war. Peacetime saw the station continue as a vital relay station for the Royal Navy's nuclear submarines in the Cold War. With about 160 people working there, it became a target for anti-nuclear protestors until the end of the 1990s when the Cold War was deemed to have ended. It continued playing a role for the Royal Navy until 2003 when, with the advent of new technology, Criggion closed down. Arrangements were made to dismantle the steel towers but this eventually took many weeks to achieve. After three weeks the site was finally cleared and today there is no sign of what the locals called 'The Secret Masts of Criggion'.

For the ordinary housewife, the daily struggle with ration cards, queues and shortages of all kinds became the normal way of living. Rationing was first introduced to Britain in January 1940 although ration cards had been stockpiled by the government since 1938. The first items to be rationed were butter, sugar, bacon and ham followed by meat in March. Offal, fish, potatoes and bread were left untouched although white bread vanished in 1942 and was replaced with the very unpopular National Wheatmeal Loaf. So scarce was food that to be seen throwing away even the mouldiest pieces could incur a hefty fine. In November 1940, a points system was introduced to restrict the purchase of canned meat, fish and vegetables. The arrival of the first American Lend/Lease goods in May 1941 not only eased the restrictions but also gave the housewife other types of canned meats, including Spam which became very popular.

In order to supplement the meagre rations, people began to turn their flower gardens into vegetable patches. The slogan 'Dig for Victory' was to be seen on posters and shown on screens in the cinemas. Neat little suburban lawns were turned into ploughed patches filled with as much produce as possible. And when it came to waste, separate containers would be filled with tins to be recycled to make tanks and aircraft, old bones to make glue and glycerine for explosives and scrap food to feed pigs. The wartime housewife wasted nothing and would make every sacrifice necessary to help the country in its hour of need.

It was, however, not only the worry of food shortages that affected the civilian population. Another upheaval, and possibly of greater significance, was the evacuation of school-age children, pre-school children and their mums, pregnant women, and teachers and helpers. Codenamed Operation 'Pied Piper', the first one million evacuees from those cities and towns thought to be most at risk from German bombing were on the move by September 1939. When the expected onslaught did not happen, most returned home by Christmas only to be evacuated again once the bombs began to fall in 1940. Shropshire received over 13,000 evacuees between September 1939 and May 1942, mostly from the Midlands industrial areas. Newport was to take the largest numbers of children overall, while Atcham received 1,550 children in two days in September 1939.

They all arrived with their names written on labels attached to their clothing and clutching either small cases or large paper bags containing a change of clothes. All of them carried their gas masks in cardboard boxes around their neck. Coming from the large inner cities, most found it difficult to adjust to country life. In return the locals found the majority of city children dirty and full of bad habits. In Ludlow and Ironbridge, the inhabitants set up de-lousing stations when they found evidence of lice and fleas on evacuee children. While

A group of child evacuees leave London for Shropshire. (Picture Post)

local papers hailed the evacuation a success with headlines like 'Hearty Shropshire welcome for mothers and children', for many who took in the evacuees it was far from the truth.

It was a very tearful time for some parents and their children; for others it was the start of a big adventure. One evacuee recalling the period said, 'We had never seen fields or trees or cows before. It was very exciting.' Another said, 'We went to Wales, a whole train full of us. We thought we were going to the ends of the earth.' The evacuation has sometimes been called 'the largest mass movement of people the country has ever known'. This, in addition to the 70,000 children who were sent abroad, is a statistic that has yet to be broken.

Another aspect of the 'Dig for Victory' campaign was the introduction of the Women's Land Army. First created during the First World War, it was rigorously reformed in 1939 under the leadership of the Marchioness of Reading. For the girls it was hard work toiling in the fields from dawn to dusk and for very little pay. For a 50-hour week a Land Army girl would receive £1 17s 0d, a sum that was increased in 1944 to £2 17s 0d a week. They often lived with the farmer's family upon whose land they were working and board and food invariably came free. Even so it was back-breaking work. In their familiar uniform of dungarees or brown corduroy breeches they became a regular sight around Shropshire. One of the worst periods of work for them was the annual harvest. Gathering in the wheat or corn or barley in all weathers, it was the driest periods that were bad with the dust getting everywhere. Aching limbs and blisters were normal and with the prospect of only having a bath once a week, life could seem depressing.

The Women's Land Army in Shropshire were tasked with planting all kinds of produce. During the war years the county produced 80,000 tons of home-grown produce, much of which was taken to Liverpool to help feed bombed-out families. An additional 47,000 acres of land had been ploughed and sown with potatoes, barley and wheat. Some of the girls volunteered to join the Forestry division of the WLA known as the 'Timber Corps' and were noted for wearing green berets. When conscription of women into the armed forces was introduced in December 1941, some left the WLA and joined the WRNS, ATS or WAAF. The pay was better and the work not so hard. However, whatever branch women served in, the country could not have done without them.

'Over-sexed, overpaid and over here': by 1942 over 40,000 US servicemen were stationed in Shropshire. Some were infantrymen and some were airmen. Whatever they were, the women of the county had seen nothing like them before and it did not take the Americans long to make their way into British hearts. With the country going through

GI brides depart Britain; many left Shropshire for a better life. (Popperfoto)

Some of the first American black airmen to arrive in Shropshire pictured at the Beacon Hotel, Madeley, Telford, with Malcolm Scott (young boy), his father and grandfather. (Malcolm Scott)

a time of shortages in almost every commodity, the impression that planted itself in the minds of the local populace was one of their extreme generosity. Village dances were held to integrate the servicemen and many locals took them into their homes to make them feel welcome. In response, dances would be held on the American bases for the locals. It was not always as platonic as this, though, for whilst the Americans treated the elderly with respect, when it came to the fair maidens of Shropshire it was a different story! There was also a problem when it came to the black servicemen. Many Shropshire people had never seen a black man before and were therefore cautious of them. Others were not troubled and were not worried if they were seen with a black American. Some GIs, black or white, married local girls who went back to America with them when they returned home. For the people of Shropshire this was a time of mixed emotions.

Thousands of couples met at dances held in glittering ballrooms, as well as village and church halls. Whilst the traditional dances were popular, it was the American dance, the jitterbug, that epitomised the Anglo-American dance halls. One of the favourites of the time was the Glenn Miller Band of the Allied Expeditionary Force. Although the band played at many American bases in Britain before Miller's

The bandleader Glenn Miller broadcasting to British troops and civilians over the American Broadcasting Service in Europe. (Imperial War Museum)

Frank Phillips reads a wartime news bulletin.

mysterious disappearance, the closest they got to Shropshire was a US Army Hospital in Cirencester in Gloucestershire. Many, however, travelled the relatively short distance to hear the greatest band of the period.

If you couldn't go to see them you could always hear their broadcasts over the radio. This media became the life blood of the nation with a varied selection of news, topical tips, advice, comedy and music. Many people will remember the dulcet tones of Alvar Lidell, Frank Phillips, Bruce Belfrage or Wilfred Pickles announcing, 'And here is the news read by …'. Then there were the comedians who demonstrated that the nation still had the ability to laugh in the face of adversity – programmes like *ITMA*, one of the most popular of the time, with Tommy Handley making fun of British wartime life. With phrases such as 'Can I do yer now, sir?' from Mrs Mopp, and Colonel Chinstrap with 'I don't mind if I do', no wonder it became so popular. Nothing, not even bombs, would keep the listening public from their share of comedy on the radio.

Music was also a tonic for the civilian population. Thousands of requests poured in for the programme *Sincerely Yours* hosted by the wartime sweetheart, Vera Lynn. Songs like *We'll Meet Again* and *The White Cliffs of Dover* somehow brought people together with a vision of better times to come. Music such as this was played on many factory floors encouraging the workforce to maintain the wartime spirit. *Music while you work* was listened to by over 90 million workers and was to continue to broadcast until the middle of the 1960s.

It was the wartime policy of the BBC not to broadcast propaganda programmes. German propaganda did find its way onto British radio, however, in the form of 'Lord Haw Haw'. This radio announcer was an American-born supporter of the Nazis, named William Joyce. Adopting a false, high-class British accent, he would announce himself with something akin to 'Jairmany calling, Jairmany calling'. He would then broadcast misleading information to the British public. Many did believe what he was saying and thus it did undermine morale among some people. He continued to broadcast throughout the war until he was arrested, tried in a criminal court and hanged for treason.

This chapter portrays just a fraction of the civilians' war in Shropshire. After six years of rationing and enduring death and destruction, sorrow and sadness, victory came at last. Shropshire suffered lightly with just eight lives being lost due to bombing. Two people were killed on 29th August 1940 in Church Street, Bridgnorth, whilst three more were killed by bombing in Ellesmere Road,

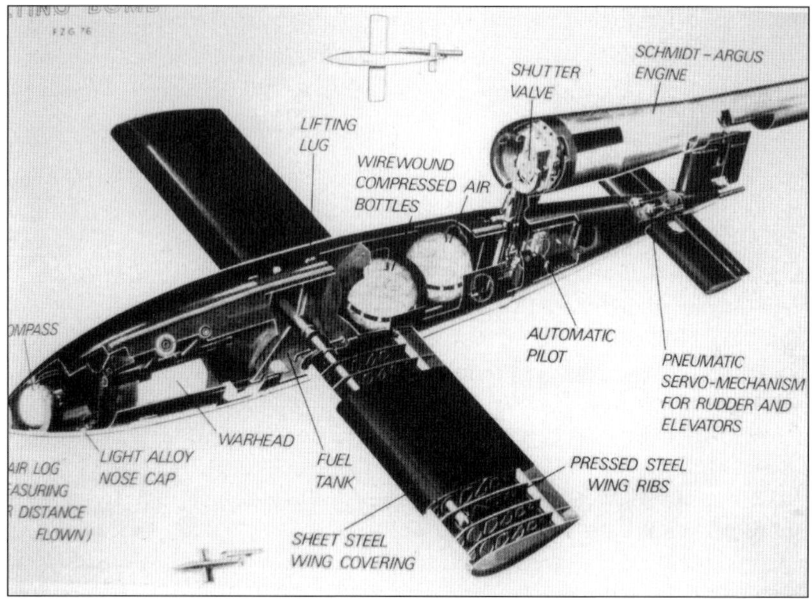

An illustration of a V1 'Doodlebug'. (R.V. Jones)

Shrewsbury. Two further fatalities occurred within the county and it was a miracle that there were not more. Shropshire never received the blitz that so many other counties did yet the threat was always there from bombs jettisoned by raiders returning to France.

Though there is no doubt that D-Day was a success, there was a sting in the tail. It came in the form of the V1, Hitler's revenge weapon, more commonly known as the 'Doodlebug'. The first of these flying bombs crossed the Kent coast at 1.40 am on Tuesday, 13th June 1944, after a period of long-range shelling from enemy guns situated along the Pas-de-Calais. When this stopped, two Royal Observer Corps men perched high on a Martello tower on Romney Marsh, heard and saw 'a black object with fire coming from its tail'. The first of the V1s had arrived.

Whilst the aiming point was the Tower of London, many V1s fell in the sea or into the ground over Kent, Sussex, Surrey and Hampshire. They were brought down by three methods – attack by fighter aircraft over the sea, by heavy anti-aircraft guns installed along the Kent coast, or by a balloon barrage. By the end of August 1944 a lot of the launch sites in France had fallen to the Allies and in a last desperate attempt to bring the civilian population to its knees, later variants of the V1 were carried by aircraft and launched over the North Sea. It was one such V1 launched from a Heinkel He 111 that reached as far inland as Newport.

Essentially a pilotless aeroplane with a simple pulse-jet engine sitting on the tail, the V1 carried a warhead of 3,000 lbs of high explosive. The Newport V1 was launched from an He 111 which had taken off from its base in Belgium or Northern Germany. Crossing the North Sea, the crew fired the V1's sparking plugs before the rocket 'unstuck' from the mother aircraft and continued on its deadly journey.

Christmas Eve 1944 was a time of great expectation for the county. It was to be the first Christmas when victory could be expected to happen sometime in the new year. In Newport people were thinking of the few days' holiday, children were becoming excited and there was a general air of good feeling. Being a Sunday, people were thinking of going to church and to the many carol services. Suddenly, at 6 am the quiet was shattered by a large explosion as the V1 came down just outside the town. A little more flying time and it would have landed in the centre of Newport. However, although it fell in fields, several buildings were shattered in the explosion.

By now the local residents were up and wondering what on earth had happened. The local police and ARP wardens were soon on the scene together with the fire service and ambulance. Luckily the latter was not needed although a few people were suffering from shock. The local Home Guard were soon preparing a cordon around the crater and by 10.30 am, most of the wreckage had been cleared. One thing, however, did bother the local authorities. They knew from news of London of the devastation caused by the V1 yet the Newport crater was relatively small. During the clearance, pieces of paper were found all over the crater and blowing in the wind. These were apparently letters written by British POWs to their families at home. It appeared as though the Germans were using these V1s as a propaganda platform by packing some of the warheads with pamphlets and letters which upon impact flew everywhere. The first had appeared in Kent, with others following in East Sussex. The information contained in the Newport V1 was later found to be a 'special Christmas edition' of propaganda.

The *Newport Advertiser* of 29th December 1944 ran a heavily censored report: 'Recently enemy air activity has been directed towards northern as well as southern England. One bomb fell near a small market town but the only casualties were a rabbit (which eventually found its way to the pot) and a frog. There was considerable damage to glass in business premises and private houses from the blast but in no case was the structure of a building damaged. The bomb it is said contained what purported to be letters from prisoners of war. The letters are in both photostatic and printed form and are marked "POW Post". Printed on top of these leaflets are these words: "The finder is requested to cut out or copy the letter printed here and to transmit them to the addressees so that they receive them as soon as possible. The original letters are being sent through the Red Cross in the usual mail channel".'

Although this particular V1 was apparently aimed at Manchester, it fell short of its target and in doing so gave the people of Newport a fright that has never been forgotten.

Despite these damaging occurrences, the contribution that the county made to the war effort was incalculable. The other claim to fame for Shropshire was that it played host to Charles de Gaulle, the leader of the Free French, when he and his wife rented Gadlas Hall near Ellesmere. Arriving on 13th June 1940, their daughter attended the Convent of Our Lady of Sion at Acton Burnell. They remained until the autumn of 1941 whilst General de Gaulle travelled to Gadlas every few weeks. For Salopians, however, it was only with the death of Hitler on 2nd May 1945 that they realised victory was close.

When it came the county celebrated with street parties, flags flying and partying until the small hours. Large bonfires were lit with effigies of Hitler on top and the church bells rang out. However, it was not entirely over, as war still raged in the Far East. It was the dropping of two atomic bombs that brought a quick end to the conflict and Britain celebrated VJ Day on 15th August 1945.

The war was not won without terrible loss on both sides. In Shropshire alone, 7,000 persons who went to war did not come back. To the throngs of people gathered in Whitehall on 8th May, Winston Churchill said it all when he declared: 'This is your victory.' It was a people's war as well as a military one and the memories will forever remain.

APPENDIX A

THE MAIN SQUADRONS AND UNITS OF THE SHROPSHIRE AIRFIELDS

ATCHAM – 74 (Trinidad), 131 (County of Kent), 232, 350 (Belgian).
HIGH ERCALL – 41, 68, 247 (China-British), 255, 257 (Burma), 535.
SHAWBURY – 90, 131 (County of Kent), 137.
TERN HILL – 19, 78, 87 (United Provinces), 131 (County of Kent),132 (City of Bombay),133 (Eagle),134, 306 (Torun) Polish, 605 (County of Warwick), 611 (West Lancashire).

MAINTENANCE UNITS

COSFORD – 9 MU
HIGH ERCALL – 29 MU
SHAWBURY – 27 MU
TERN HILL – 24 MU

OPERATIONAL TRAINING UNITS

MONTFORD BRIDGE – 61 OTU
PEPLOW – 83 OTU, 23 Heavy Glider Conversion Unit
REDNAL – 61 OTU
SLEAP – 81 OTU
TILSTOCK – 81 OTU

UNITED STATES ARMY AIR FORCE

ATCHAM – 31st Fighter Group consisting of 307th, 308th and 309th Fighter Squadron; 14th Fighter Group consisting of 48th and 49th Fighter Squadron;1st Provisional Gunnery Flight; 6th Fighter Wing, renamed the 2906th Observation Training Group, renamed the 495th Fighter Training Group, consisting of 551st and 552nd Fighter Training Squadron
HIGH ERCALL – 309th Fighter Squadron (Pursuit)

OTHERS

ATCHAM – 5 (Pilot) Advanced Flying Unit, 6 Service Flying Training School
SHAWBURY – 6 Anti-Aircraft Co-operative Unit, 11 Flying Training School, 11 (P) Advanced Flying Unit, 1534 Beam Approach Training Flight
TERN HILL – 5 Service Flying Training School, 5 (P) Advanced Flying Unit.
TILSTOCK – 1665 Heavy Conversion Unit.

APPENDIX B

GLOSSARY OF TERMS

AACU	Anti-Aircraft Co-operation Unit
ADU	Aircraft Delivery Unit
AEF	Air Experience Flight
AFS	Advanced Flying School
AGS	Air Gunnery School
ANS	Air Navigation School
ASU	Aircraft Storage Unit
CFS	Central Flying School
CRO	Civilian Repair Organisation
ECFS	Empire Central Flying School
EFTS	Elementary Flying Training School
E&RFTS	Elementary & Reserve Flying Training School
FTS	Flying Training School
HCU	Heavy Conversion Unit
HGCU	Heavy Glider Conversion Unit
MU	Maintenance Unit
OCU	Operational Conversion Unit
OTU	Operational Training Unit
(P)AFU	(Pilots) Advanced Flying Unit
SFTS	Service Flying Training School
SoTT	School of Technical Training
VGS	Volunteer Gliding School

RAF RANKS

FO	Flying Officer
PO	Pilot Officer
Flt Lt	Flight Lieutenant
Sqd Ldr	Squadron Leader
Wg Cdr	Wing Commander
Gp Cpt	Group Captain

ACKNOWLEDGEMENTS

I acknowledge with grateful thanks all the individuals and organisations who have assisted me in the writing of this book. I list them in no particular order.

Sqd Ldr Martin Locke, RAFR (Shawbury); WO Mick Jones, MBE, FinstLM (RAF Shawbury retired); Reg Howard (Ex 758 Sqdn FAA); Ruth Newby; Michael Davies, LRPS, FRSA; Allan Frost; Toby Neal (*Shropshire Star*); Dave Birrel (Nanton Lancaster Air Museum, Canada); Andy Thomas; Mike McKinley (*Aries* Project); John H. Vaux (Shawbury); Malcolm Scott; Clive Gwilt; Peter Winters; Mrs Diana Harman; Gregory J. Hackenberg (Louisiana); John Millington; Alf 'Jim' Harris (29 MU); Cliff Marsh; Rita Lovett nee Robinson (MT Driver WAAF); LACW Jean 'Blondie' Smith (later Renshaw); the *Shropshire Star* newspaper; Shropshire Archives; Shropshire Library; Dr Chris Samson; Mrs A. R. Edwards; Rob Evans; Neville Smith.

If I have omitted to mention any person or organisation or incorrectly credited any photographs, please accept my apologies. It will be corrected on any reprint. Final thanks go to my wife Barbara for her patience and correcting skills.

INDEX